# IN
# Defense
# OF Faith
# THE

## DAVE HUNT

**HARVEST HOUSE PUBLISHERS**
Eugene, Oregon 97402

Cover by Koechel Peterson & Associates, Minneapolis, Minnesota

---

The author's free monthly newsletter may be received by request. Write to:

Dave Hunt
P.O. Box 7019
Bend, OR 97708

---

**IN DEFENSE OF THE FAITH**

Copyright © 1996 by Dave Hunt
Published by Harvest House Publishers
Eugene, Oregon 97402

Library of Congress Cataloging-in-Publication Data
Hunt, Dave.
    In defense of the faith / Dave Hunt.
        p.    cm.
    ISBN 1-56507-495-5 (alk. paper)
    1. Faith—Miscellanea.   2. Faith—Biblical teaching—Miscellanea.
I. Title.
BT771.2.H86   1996                                         96-11198
230—dc20                                                   CIP

Printed in the United States of America.

97 98 99 00 01 / BC / 10 9 8 7 6 5 4 3 2

# Contents

*It is no sin to doubt some things, but it may be fatal to believe everything.*

—A.W. Tozer

*There is a place for skepticism as well as a place for faith; and in considering an investment or embracing a religion, skepticism should come first.*

—Irwin H. Linton
in *A Lawyer Examines the Bible*

# Why Believe?

Most people, if asked why they hold a certain belief, would have a difficult time giving a solid basis for their opinion. Generally one's personal convictions are a matter of loyalty to a particular heritage or tradition. It is amazing how much belief is based not on fact but on blind allegiance to an institution or a political party or a church or a religious system. What passes for religious faith is often adherence to a particular religion more out of loyalty to parents or to the priest or pastor than from real conviction based upon solid evidence.

### SCIENTISTS—TODAY'S HIGH PRIESTS?

The same holds true in the secular world. Beliefs are held for social reasons—to remain acceptable in one's circle of friends or among one's colleagues. For example, not to believe in evolution would cause one to be ridiculed by his peers and even to lose one's standing in the academic community. Robert Jastrow, one of the world's leading astronomers, was the founder (and for years the director) of the Goddard Space Institute that sent Pioneer and Voyager into space. An agnostic, Jastrow shocked his colleagues by admitting at a national conference of the Association for the Advancement of Science that the evidence seems to demand an intelligent Creator of the universe. He also found the courage to write:

> Astronomers are curiously upset by...proof that the universe had a beginning. Their reactions provide an interesting demonstration of the response of the scientific mind—supposedly a very objective mind— when evidence uncovered by science itself leads to a conflict with the articles of *faith* in their profession... There is a kind of *religion* in science. (emphasis added).[1]

British Museum of Natural History senior paleontologist Colin Patterson confessed: "Evolutionists—like the creationists they periodically do battle with—are nothing more than believers themselves. I had been working on this stuff [evolution] for more than twenty years, and there was not one [factual] thing I knew about it. It's quite a shock to learn that one can be so misled for so long."[2] Speaking before a group of his fellow biologists, D.M.S. Watson, popularizer of evolution on British television (as Carl Sagan has been on American TV), reminded them of the common *religious faith* they all shared:

> Evolution itself is accepted by zoologists not because it has been observed to occur or...can be proved by logically coherent evidence to be true, but because the only alternative, special creation, is clearly incredible [i.e. something many scientists don't want to admit].[3]

Eminent British astronomer Sir Fred Hoyle reminds us of the well-known mathematical fact that "even if the whole universe consisted of organic soup" the chance of producing the basic enzymes of life by random processes without intelligent direction would be approximately one in 10 with 40,000 zeros after it. In other words, it couldn't happen—*ever!* Says Hoyle, "Darwinian evolution is most unlikely to get even one polypeptide [sequence] right, let alone the thousands on which living cells depend for survival." Why then is this completely impossible theory still honored? Hoyle accuses the evolutionists of defending a *religious faith*:

> The situation [mathematical impossibility] is well known to geneticists and yet nobody seems to blow the whistle decisively on the theory....
>
> Most scientists still cling to Darwinism because of its grip on the educational system.... You either have to believe the concepts, or you will be branded a heretic.[4]

## NO ONE LIKES TO BE WRONG

Considering the fact, then, that even supposedly objective scientists cling to beliefs for less than factual reasons, it should be no surprise that the average person does so as well. "I was born a Hindu and will remain a Hindu until I die!" is a typical statement. And for the word "Hindu" one could substitute "Muslim," "Catholic," "Baptist," "Mormon," or many other religious designations. Unfortunately, what seems to be a deeply held "faith" is often reinforced by pride and native stubbornness.

No one likes to be wrong. It would be especially humiliating to admit that one's religious faith of a lifetime had been misplaced and that the religion inherited from one's ancestors (or the "scientific" point of view picked up in university) was in fact false. Science, after all (as even some scientists now admit), and the atheism it sometimes produces are also religious "faiths."

Many people accept what is reported on radio or television or in newspapers and magazines as though the media makes no mistakes and is above prejudice. Of course, both assumptions are foolish. No one and no agency is either infallible or without personal bias. That also goes for schools and educators and textbooks. We know that a false history has been taught in Communist countries but often fail to recognize that similar falsehoods are instilled in the West because of equally dangerous prejudices and dishonesty. It takes both courage and humility to face the facts, especially when they may upset long-standing biases and loyalties.

## A Universal Gullibility

If one did not see a particular incident occur, there would seem to be no other choice than to believe the testimony of an eyewitness. Under such circumstances it would seem reasonable to believe the report if one personally knew and had full confidence in the person relating it. It would be disloyal to doubt what a good friend said. In fact, to doubt would seemingly be the same as accusing the person of lying or at least of not knowing what he or she was talking about and therefore of being unreliable.

But a word of caution is in order. Even when the eyewitness is a close friend in whom one has complete confidence, sincere mistakes could be involved. A prudent person will ask intelligent questions to make certain that what happened was accurately reported and that the witness understood the event as it actually occurred. Only when the facts are clearly established should one believe the report, no matter by whom it was told.

Most of us are much too gullible most of the time. For that reason con artists find enough easy-to-convince targets to defraud millions of victims each year in the United States. We all need a healthy dose of skepticism. The story is told of the man walking down the street who dropped a quarter into the tin cup being held out by a man wearing dark glasses and holding a sign reading, "Help the poor blind man." After taking a few steps, the donor turned around and was shocked to see the "blind man" remove his dark glasses and peer into the cup. The donor hurried back and angrily declared, "You're not blind!" to which the "blind man" replied, "No, sir, I'm not. The blind man's on vacation and I'm just taking his place. I'm usually the deaf-and-dumb man on the next street."

It wouldn't have taken many questions of the "blind" man to discover the truth before the coin went into the tin cup. Nor does it take many questions to discover the truth about a particular religion. Yet few questions are usually asked; and most often, when it comes to religion, questions are not even allowed. In many years of traveling around the world speaking to varied audiences in different countries and cultures, I always value the time when the listeners have an opportunity to challenge me with questions. I am told, however, that most preachers and teachers rarely offer such an opportunity.

### What Is The *Reason* For Your Faith?

All religions at some point demand faith—and often not in God but in the religious system or church itself or in its founder or current leader. As a result of putting one's trust in something or someone less than God, even though it or he or she may claim to represent Him, disillusionment inevitably sets in. One can become cynical and turn away from all religion and from then on reject the very possibility of truth. Or one could become a more earnest and wary seeker, wiser and more determined than ever to know God, but now extremely cautious about the promises and teachings of mere men.

As we shall see in the following pages, any "faith" which is not based upon reason supported by irrefutable evidence is the utmost folly. The Bible presents the record of what it calls *"the* faith," that body of truth which provides the only reliable answers to all of life's ultimate questions. We want to face those questions honestly and openly and at the same time take the greatest care to be certain that the answers we arrive at are valid. We will allow the critics to challenge the Bible from every angle, and we will discover that the evidence in support of *"the* faith" is absolutely overwhelming.

There is nothing wrong with asking questions in the search for truth. Indeed, probing questions are essential in the process of finding the truth. Whatever answers are offered must be questioned further until one is satisfied that the truth has been found. This book, then, is simply a series of questions which sincere seekers (and many critics, skeptics, and atheists) have asked, together with a reasoned response for each.

The questions found in the following pages have been asked of the author by many earnest people around the world who were either honestly seeking the evidence which alone can sustain true faith or were doing their best to destroy the Bible and "*the* faith" it offers to all mankind. The concerns expressed by the questioners cover a variety of topics, from how one can know whether the Bible is true and whether Jesus Christ really exists to whether or not He is the Savior of sinners and how one can have assurance of salvation. The accuracy of biblical prophecy is another of the many topics which will demand our attention. The Bible's historical and scientific validity, as well, will be examined along with the question of the existence of the God of the Bible and other concerns of vital importance.

The format is very simple: A question is asked and the response is offered as the author has come to understand the issues from the Bible, science, history, and experience. The chapters are divided according to the general subject being discussed.

*He who wishes to philosophize must begin by doubting all things.*

—Giordano Bruno[1]

*When the founder of a new religion complained that it made but little headway among the people, Talleyrand replied: "It is no easy matter to introduce a new religion. But there is one thing I would advise you to do.... Go and be crucified, then be buried, and then rise again on the third day; and then work miracles, raise the dead, heal all manner of disease and cast out devils, and then it is possible you may accomplish your end." This was Talleyrand's shrewd way of saying that religion was a humbug; that it must be founded on a lie.*

—Samuel P. Putnam[2]

*How was it that a carpenter ... born of a people whose great teachers were narrow, sour, intolerant, pedantic legalists, was the supreme religious Teacher the world has known ... the most important figure in the world's history?*

—W.S. Peake[3]

*No revolution that has ever taken place in society can be compared to that which has been produced by the words of Jesus Christ.*

—Mark Hopkins[4]

*For the theoretical mind [Christianity] can accommodate all that science can discover and still challenge science to dig deeper and deeper.*

—Gordon Allport[5]

# 1

# Evidence, Reason, and Faith

## A Leap In The Dark

*Question:* I have always understood that there is a difference between belief and faith—that belief is based upon fact and that faith, since it is related to religion, must be divorced from evidence and reason. That seems reasonable, but lately I've been wondering whether, and why, this should be true. Can you help me?

*Response:* You are struggling with a serious misunderstanding that has brought multitudes throughout history into religious bondage. The Bible puts belief and faith on an equal footing, with no difference between them. Common sense itself and a little reflection will tell you that *faith* must have as sure a factual foundation as *belief*. Faith is not a leap in the dark. Furthermore, faith in God and His Word, because it involves eternal matters, is far more important than belief about things of this life.

Faith, therefore, ought to have an even more solid basis than mere belief. One may be willing to allow some uncertainty in earthly matters, but only a fool would be comfortable with even the smallest degree of doubt in things which affect him eternally. No wonder the great apostle Paul wrote, *"Prove* all things; hold fast to that which is good" (1 Thessalonians 5:21).

Luke tells us that during the 40 days Jesus spent with His disciples after His resurrection, He "showed himself alive . . . by many *infallible proofs"* (Acts 1:3). Clearly, Christ did not consider it enough merely to show Himself to His disciples without providing irrefutable evidence of His resurrection. He considered it both legitimate and essential to *prove* that He was the very same One who had been crucified and that He had risen from the dead in the same body (but now in a new and glorious form) that had been placed lifeless in the grave.

"Behold my hands and my feet, that it is I myself," Christ told the shocked disciples the first time He came to them after His resurrection. "Handle me and see, for a spirit [ghost] hath not flesh and bones, as ye see me have" (Luke 24:39). They had thought they were seeing a ghost, but He proved otherwise to them. To doubting Thomas, who had not been present on this first occasion, Christ declared later: "Reach hither thy finger and behold my hands; and reach hither thy hand and thrust it into my side . . ." (John 20:27). Here was irrefutable, tangible evidence.

It is only common sense that strict proof should be demanded before making a commitment or an investment in this life. How much more important, then, to be absolutely certain based upon solid proof before accepting by faith those things which affect one's eternal destiny. True "faith," as we shall see, can only be founded upon fact—not upon feelings, intuition, or emotion. Much less does faith arise out of blind submission to some religious authority.

## Is Seeing Really Believing?

---

*Question:* A famous adage says, "Seeing is believing." Yet the Bible says, "We walk by faith, not by sight" (2 Corinthians 5:7). These two ideas seem to be in direct conflict with each other. Which one is right?

*Response:* The first saying, while partially true, can be very misleading; the second is totally true. While it helps to "see" something with one's own eyes or to witness an occurrence, one doesn't always "see" accurately. Thus "seeing" is not always a sufficient reason for believing. Nor is "seeing" *essential* for believing because we obviously believe in much that we have never seen.

---

For example, most Americans have never been to China and have thus never seen that country with their own eyes, yet they believe that such a place exists because of the abundance of testimony by those who have been there and because of much other evidence as well. No one has ever seen gravity, though we have observed what we believe to be its effects. Nor has any scientist seen energy, yet we now believe it to be the stuff out of which the entire universe is made.

Moreover, appearances can be deceptive, as everyone knows by experience. A mirage can make it seem that the burning sand of a dry desert is water. A stage magician can deceive his audience into "seeing" the impossible. In fact, in *no instance* do we really "see" what we are looking at. The reader doesn't actually see the page and print of this book. What he "sees" is the impression made upon his brain cells of a reflection carried by light waves into his eyes and then along nerve connections to the brain. Whether that impression is precisely what the page and ink really "look" like or really "are" can never be known by mortals. So "seeing" isn't what one thinks it is and is surely not the best basis for believing. British astronomer Sir James Jeans declared:

> The outstanding achievement of twentieth-century physics is not the theory of relativity . . . or the theory of quanta . . . or the dissection of the atom . . . [but] it is the general recognition that we are not yet in contact with ultimate reality. . . .[6]

## We Walk By Faith, Not By Sight

The words of Jesus when He showed Himself to doubting Thomas are very instructive: "Thomas, because thou hast seen me thou hast believed; blessed are they that have not seen and yet have believed" (John 20:29). Of the risen Christ now at the Father's right hand in heaven, Peter wrote: "Whom having not seen, ye love; in whom, though now ye see him not, yet believing, ye rejoice with joy unspeakable and full of glory" (1 Peter 1:8). If "seeing is believing," then those alive today who, unlike Thomas, have never seen and handled Christ physically, could not believe in Him.

Indeed, if "seeing is believing" were true, no one could ever believe in God because He dwells "in the light which no man can approach unto; whom no man hath seen, *nor can see . . .*" (1 Timothy 6:16). The apostle John declares that "no man hath seen God at any time" (John 1:18; 1 John 4:12). Yet we are to believe in God, and multitudes of intelligent people do so without ever having seen Him with their physical eyes. Obviously, then, faith does not involve seeing with one's eyes, but faith makes contact with that which is invisible. The great faith chapter of the Bible begins with "Faith is . . . the evidence of things *not seen*" (Hebrews 11:1).

These statements from Scripture reveal the great deception in the teaching of visualization. For example, the pastor of the largest church in the world insists that it is impossible to have faith and to receive an answer to prayer without visualizing clearly the object or result for which one is praying.[7] On the contrary, to attempt to visualize and thus to "see" is destructive of faith, which can only involve that which is *"not seen"!* Remember, "we walk by *faith, not by sight,"* and the two are incompatible.

The most important elements in this physical life (love, joy, peace, purpose, contentment, truth, justice, etc.) can neither be seen not explained. Not long ago it was widely believed in the world of academia that physical science would one day explain everything, even consciousness. That vain hope is no longer embraced by most scientists. Nobelist Sir

John Eccles pointed out that the recent recognition that minds are non-physical entities has caused the collapse of scientific materialism.[8] Nobel laureate Erwin Schroedinger who played a vital role in giving the world today's new physics, put it very bluntly:

> The scientific picture of the real world around me...is ghastly silent about all...that is really near to our heart, that really matters to us.... [I]t knows nothing of...good or bad, God and eternity....
>
> Whence came I and whither go I? That is the great unfathomable question, the same for every one of us. Science has no answer to it.[9]

"Seeing" has serious limitations and therefore has little to do with "believing" and *nothing* to do with "faith." If we are to know those most important things in life which science cannot reveal and concerning which it has nothing to say (love, joy, peace, truth, purpose, etc.), we must have faith. Yet that statement immediately raises the serious question of how one can possibly believe in what or whom one has never seen and indeed cannot see. *Faith must stand on the basis of evidence which is independent of physical sight and scientific verification, but which is irrefutable.* The remainder of this book will have a great deal to say about that.

## IS IT WRONG TO WANT EVIDENCE FOR WHAT ONE BELIEVES?

---

*Question:* I was raised from childhood in a particular church and believed everything the priest and my parents taught me when I was young. As I grew older, however, I began to have many doubts; but when I asked the priest, he told me that I must accept what the Holy Father and the bishops declared. I want to believe, but the questions keep nagging at me. Is it wrong to want some evidence and even proof for what a church teaches?

*Response:* It is amazing how many people who regularly attend a church have accepted the illogical and dangerous idea that when it comes to religion one should never raise any questions, because to do so shows a "lack of faith." On the contrary, questions *must* be asked, and one must not be satisfied until one is certain of the answer. Skepticism is in fact *essential* as the first step toward faith so long as it doesn't harden into pride or become a cloak for prejudice. Gullibility is no help to true faith but is actually its enemy.

---

Faith is absolute and total trust. Clearly no one nor anything other than God is worthy of our absolute and total trust and thus of our faith. Jesus said, "Have faith in God" (Mark 11:22). Therefore, whenever faith is associated with someone (pastor, priest, guru) or something (church, religion, institution) other than God, it is misplaced. Only God is omnipotent, omniscient, and omnipresent and therefore cannot fail us when we trust in Him. Only He is worthy of our total trust; and He holds each of us accountable to know Him personally and on that basis to put our total trust in Him *alone*.

Know Him *personally*? Yes. Both the Bible and common sense tell us that. Any priest, pastor, guru, or church which claims to act as a mediator between man and God and says "Trust *me*" is by that claim demanding the total trust that we are to place in God alone. Obviously, if any person is to act as the mediator between God and the rest of mankind, He must also be God, for no one else is worthy of our unquestioning confidence. Jesus Christ is God who became man through the virgin birth. That is why the Bible says, "There is one God, and one [and *only one*] mediator between God and men, the man [who is also God] Christ Jesus . . ." (1 Timothy 2:5).

Any religious system which demands faith in its teachings on the basis of its alleged *authority* rather than on the basis of hard evidence, and which is unwilling to allow its doctrines and claims to be examined freely by sincere, inquiring minds, should not be trusted. The idea that only an elite priesthood or clergy is qualified to determine truth in the area of religion, morals, or faith, and that their dogmas must be accepted unquestioningly, is a lie that has cost multitudes their freedom and peace of mind on earth and damned them for eternity. God Himself has said to mankind, "Come now and let us *reason* together . . ." (Isaiah 1:18). We hope to follow that advice throughout this book.

## WHAT ROLE DO EVIDENCE AND REASON PLAY?

---

*Question:* I can see that it makes no sense and would be very dangerous to believe something simply because some church or religious leader says I must do so. Clearly there must be some basis for believing. But I'm confused because it wouldn't seem to be "faith" if reason and evidence support my belief.

*Response:* Your confusion comes from imagining that if reason and evidence were involved *at all* in faith, that would cause faith to become *completely* rational—which, I agree, would make no sense. Clearly no faith is required to believe anything that is self-evident or that can be proved completely, such as the fact that the sun is in the sky and sending its warmth to earth.

---

On the other hand, reason and evidence may legitimately point the direction for faith to go—and *must* do so. Indeed, faith must not violate evidence and reason or it would be irrational. Faith takes a step *beyond* reason, but only in the direction which reason and evidence have pointed.

The idea of a "leap of faith" (that faith must be irrational) has been promoted by some schools of philosophy and religion. If that were true, however, there would be no basis other than feelings or intuition for what one believes. As a consequence, one could believe or have faith in anything. As the saying goes, "If it works for you, it's okay"— a senseless idea that denies the absoluteness of truth.

By this theory, it is *faith* that is important rather than the *object* of one's faith. Never mind *what* one believes.

One has to believe in *something*, so take the leap. It is the *believing* that causes the effect one seeks—a theory that has some temporary and limited truth. Yes, believing in the Star Wars Force or that God is some kind of magic genie who exists to do one's bidding may indeed bring a superficial sense of well-being for a time. Eventually, however, that belief will prove to be a delusion and the bubble of euphoria will burst, leaving the person worse off than before.

## Faith Is A Response To Proven Truth

On the surface it may seem legitimate to reject reason and evidence because God is far beyond our ability to fully comprehend and thus beyond any proof we could understand. How could evidence, much less *proof*, have any part to play in one's faith in God? As we have noted, however, if reason doesn't have *some* role to play, then one could believe in any kind of "god"—an idea which is clearly false. One must have *some* evidence even to believe there is a God. Otherwise, how could the idea of God be sustained?

Thankfully, the evidence is all around us: "The heavens declare the glory of God. . . . For the invisible things of him [God] from the creation of the world are clearly seen, being understood by the things that are made, even his eternal power and Godhead, so that they [all mankind] are without excuse" (Psalm 19:1; Romans 1:20). One cannot learn very much of the incredible nature of the universe, from the beautiful simplicity of the atomic structure of the elements to the incomprehensible complexity of a living cell with ten thousand chemical reactions going on at once in perfect balance with one another, without realizing that it couldn't have happened by chance.

The design of a leaf (and how much more so of the human brain) demands an intelligent Designer who Himself is beyond our highest thought or He wouldn't be capable of creating and governing the universe. It is certainly appropriate to observe the incredible order in the universe and from such evidence to draw the conclusion that the universe and we ourselves couldn't have happened by chance but must have been designed and created by an intelligent Being capable of doing so. *Evidence and reason point to God.* This is not only legitimate but an essential first step in knowing Him.

This God, however, in order to be the Creator and Sustainer of the universe must have capabilities that are infinitely beyond our capacity to comprehend. Reason can follow the evidence only so far and then finds itself beyond its ability to go any further. It is at this point that faith takes the next step, a step which is beyond the capacity of reason to accompany it but which is (and must be) in the *direction* which reason and the evidence have pointed.

The atheist sees the same evidence, and he too takes a step of "faith" beyond reason. Sadly, however, in trying to escape the consequences of admitting God's existence and thus his accountability to his Creator, the atheist takes a "leap of faith" in the opposite direction from which reason and the evidence so clearly point. He chooses to deny the evidence, and thus his "faith" is totally irrational and therefore not genuine faith at all.

There is much other specific evidence for believing both in God and in the Bible as His Word, but we will deal with that evidence later.

### BEWARE OF TRYING TO "FORCE" YOURSELF TO BELIEVE

---

*Question:* I have struggled with this thing called "faith" all of my life. I want to "believe" in God and the Bible, but can't make myself do it. I keep having these nagging doubts. What am I supposed to do?

*Response:* By all means don't "make" yourself believe in God or the Bible. Let me suggest that you begin by facing the logical necessity of God's existence. Without God, neither the universe nor we ourselves would exist and there would be no purpose or meaning for anything. The Bible begins like this: "In the beginning God created the heaven and the earth" (Genesis 1:1). It doesn't argue God's existence because that fact is self-evident from the universe we see around us and has been implanted by God in every person's conscience.

---

The Bible unapologetically declares, "The fool hath said in his heart, there is no God" (Psalm 14:1; 53:1). Any thinking human being must agree with this pronouncement. Only a fool could believe that the universe came into existence by chance. Just one living cell in the human body is, according to Nobel Prize winner Linus Pauling, "more complex than New York City." To imagine that life itself (which is a mystery beyond the capability of science to fathom) and the incredible complexity of matter that sustains life could happen by chance is absurd.

## All The Evidence Points To God

Suppose two survivors of a ship that sank have drifted for days in a life raft across the South Pacific and at last are washed ashore on an island. Their great hope, of course, is that the island is inhabited so they can find food, medical attention, and a means of returning to their distant homes. Pushing their way into the jungle, they suddenly come upon an automated factory operating full tilt. Though no person is visible, products are being manufactured, packaged, and labeled for shipping.

One of the parties exclaims, "Praise God! The island is inhabited! Someone must have made and oversees this factory!"

"You're crazy," replies his companion. "You've been out in the sun too long. There's absolutely no reason to believe that this thing was designed and put together by some intelligent being. It just happened by chance over who knows how many billions of years."

The first man looks down at his feet and sees a watch with a broken wristband lying in the dirt. Again he exclaims, "Look! A watch! This proves the island's inhabited!"

"You've got to be kidding," retorts his companion. "That thing is just a conglomeration of atoms that happened to come together in that form by chance plus billions of years of random selection."

No person in his right mind could imagine that a factory or a watch could just happen by chance. Then how could any rational person insist that the universe came into existence by chance, much less that the complex life forms on earth did so! A single cell in a leaf or in an animal's body is thousands of times more complex than the factory and the watch put together. The human body consists of trillions of cells, thousands of different kinds, all working together in perfect balance. Our top scientists can't produce a human brain even with all of the computers and technology that exist today. Only God could do so. Certainly chance could not!

Nor does it make sense that God would create man without having a definite purpose for him. Nothing is so frustrating to an intelligent person as having no purpose in life. Yet the very idea of purpose could not arise by chance, for purpose and chance are opposites. There can't be design without a designer. We know, therefore, that God had a purpose for creating us. And if so, He must have a way to communicate that purpose.

The Bible claims to be the Word of God to mankind and explains God's purpose and plan. We are not expected to believe that claim without sufficient evidence, but in fact that claim is supported by a vast body of evidence, much of it held in museums around the world and so irrefutable that no one capable of reading the Bible has any excuse for doubting its claims. We will present many such proofs throughout this book.

The major proof of God's existence which the Bible offers is the fulfillment of hundreds of specific prophecies. In Isaiah 46:9,10, God says that He will prove His existence by telling what will happen before it happens. In Isaiah 43:10 God tells Israel that she is His witness, both to herself and to the world, that He is God. How is that so? Because of the many prophecies God made concerning Israel that have come to pass: that the Jews would be scattered to every nation on earth; that they would be hated and persecuted and killed as no other people (anti-Semitism); that they would be preserved in spite of a thousand Hitlers trying to exterminate them; that they would be brought back to their land in the last days . . . and many other prophecies which have clearly been fulfilled and are in the process of being fulfilled before our very eyes.

We won't go into these details here because we have dealt thoroughly with prophecy in other books. The point, however, is that no one should believe anything without a solid reason for doing so, and that the evidence compelling mankind to believe in God and the Bible is absolutely overwhelming.

## GIVEN EVIDENCE AND REASON, WHY FAITH?

---

*Question:* If evidence and reason are essential parts of faith, I don't see why God should demand faith at all. Why not give us the proof of everything? To have to take that step of faith seems unreasonable to me.

*Response:* The answer to your question is dictated by our own limitations, not because of some unreasonable demand that God makes. In order for everything to be proved and reasoned out for us we would have to be equal to God. Obviously we are not: We are finite and God is infinite. We simply don't have the capacity to *understand* everything about God and His universe. Therefore we need to trust Him when He tells us about things which we cannot fully comprehend. That's where faith comes in.

---

What we can understand of the universe and of our accountability to God from reason and our conscience is sufficient to point us in the right direction. Knowing on the basis of the evidence that God exists, we ask Him to reveal Himself to us and to show us His will for our lives. We are willing to trust Him in whatever He tells us even though we cannot understand it all. We discover (as we shall see) that He has spoken to us in the Bible, and very clearly and comprehensively.

## FAITH REVEALS A UNIVERSE
## BEYOND HUMAN COMPREHENSION

True faith opens to us a knowledge of God and His truth which we could not otherwise discover. Such is the value of faith in God. Once we know Him and have confidence that we are indeed hearing from Him, then we understand His truth by believing what He says. As a result, we can know and understand what would otherwise be impossible for us to grasp. For example, the Bible declares: "Through faith we understand that the worlds were framed by the word of God, so that things which are seen were not made of things which do appear" (Hebrews 11:3).

These words, penned nearly two thousand years ago, clearly tell us that the universe was made out of an invisible substance. No one at that time nor during the many centuries that followed had the scientific knowledge to provide the evidence to support this statement. The *proof* had to wait until modern science had caught up with what the Bible had said 1800 years earlier. Today we know that the entire universe is composed of an invisible substance called energy. In spite of the brilliant advancements of science, however, though we know much *about* energy, we still don't know exactly what it is. Yet by faith the believer knew all he needed to know: that God spoke the universe into existence by His infinite power and that He made it out of something which is invisible.

That these words are found in the Bible is one of many reasons to believe it rather than any of the other scriptures which are sacred to the world's many religions. By contrast, those scriptures, far from containing statements which science can only confirm and never refute (as is the case with the Bible), contain numerous ridiculous ideas which reflect the level of understanding of mankind at the time and of the culture when and where they were written.

It was once believed that the earth was flat and was supported on the back of a tortoise floating in a sea. The Greeks thought that Atlas, a giant, held the universe in his arms. The Egyptian account of creation involved gods (such as the sun god, which was born on a flower), some of whom were part animal and part human. Plato thought the world was a living being and that earthquakes were caused when it shook itself. The Bible, though written in the same time period and by men who lived in these same cultures, is completely free of such myths. Even the Koran, of far more recent origin, contains Arabian myths. As it has often been pointed out:

> The Bible is the only ancient book that is accurate in all scientific details. Other ancient holy books from the East include legends and errors too childish for consideration. Even comparatively modern books like the Koran abound in historical and chronological blunders.[10]

There are many other reasons for believing that the Bible is, as it claims to be, God's infallible Word. We will consider them in the following pages in response to numerous other questions.

## Is Faith A Power Of The Mind?

*Question:* One of my favorite books has been *The Power of Positive Thinking.* In it the author says that "positive thinking" is just another word for "faith." I notice that his chief disciple says much the same thing: that "faith" is what he calls "possibility thinking." He has called Jesus Christ "the greatest possiblity thinker of all time." Something about that bothers me, but I don't know why. Can you explain?

*Response:* We have already noted that Jesus said, "Have faith in God" (Mark 11:22), and that faith can only be in God because He alone is worthy of complete trust. Yet an atheist can teach "Positive Thinking" seminars, and many atheists do so. Obviously, then, positive thinking has nothing to do with faith. It is, in fact, the exact opposite of faith.

The theory of positive thinking is that one's thoughts, whether "positive" or "negative," influence one's own body and personality and thus health. Moreover, one's thoughts are believed even to influence other people and the world around. Thus success or failure is allegedly created by the power of one's mind. This is actually an ancient occult belief which its modern proponents claim works through some mysterious psychic power which we all possess but have to learn to use.

Faith, on the other hand, is placed in God and His omnipotence, not in the alleged power of one's own mind, whether conscious or unconscious. What a difference! For positive thinking, it doesn't matter whether God is real or not; what matters is one's *belief.* Thus "God" is turned into a placebo that activates belief. One could believe in some cosmic energy source or anything else. All that matters is simply that one *believes.* It is the power of *belief* that supposedly causes the desired effect. What triggers this belief is unimportant. Clearly, then, whoever confuses positive/possibility thinking with faith has turned from God and His truth and power and has been badly deceived in both temporal and eternal issues.

## AN INESCAPABLE AND VITAL CHOICE

Here is the choice we face: Either we trust in the power of a firmly held belief activating some mysterious psychic power of the mind, or else we trust in God and His infinite power, which is obviously demonstrated everywhere in the universe. Only a fool would choose the power of the mind over the power of God. True faith looks to God to do that which neither one's mind (conscious or unconscious) nor talents nor efforts could accomplish.

An important element of faith, therefore, is *submission to God's will.* Faith could hardly be expected to believe that God would do what is contrary to His will, nor would faith desire Him to do so. Faith trusts God to fulfill His Word and to effect His will in one's life.

Here is another error: Many religious people try to use "faith" to cause God to put *their* will into effect. Many people think of prayer as a religious technique for getting their own way. They set their sights on what they want and then use prayer as a means of trying to talk God into making it work out for them. And if someone comes along offering a seminar on techniques for getting prayers "answered" (such as visualizing what one is praying for, or speaking forth with confidence that one has already obtained what one is praying for, etc.), people will sign up by the millions to learn how to get their own way.

By His example, Jesus made it clear that no one has even begun to pray until he can first say from his heart to God, "Not my will but thine be done" (Luke 22:42). Paul exemplified the same truth. He had an affliction which he referred to as his "thorn in the flesh" and from which he asked Christ to deliver him:

> For this thing I besought the Lord thrice that it might depart from me. And he said unto me, My grace is sufficient for thee, for my strength is made perfect in weakness. Most gladly therefore will I rather glory in my infirmities [weaknesses], that the power of Christ may rest upon me (2 Corinthians 12:8,9).

No one can have faith in God—that is, absolute and total trust in Him—without knowing Him. And if one truly knows God, then one sincerely wants God's will rather than one's own will. Obviously, God is wiser than any mere human. Furthermore, He has proved that He loves us. Then doesn't it make sense, rather than trying to get one's own finite and fallible will to be done, to trust God's infinite wisdom and love to effect what is best in one's life? That is true "faith in God." Nothing else makes sense.

## CONFRONTING LENIN'S DILEMMA

---

*Question:* Obviously, the whole idea of faith in God was invented by religious leaders in order to deceive and enslave their followers. That's one thing all religions have in common: an elite class of clergy who get the people to believe in some mythical God and then pretend to be the go-betweens to this God to hold the people in their power—and charge them plenty for it!

*Response:* That was Lenin's theory. He was also a materialist. Nothing existed for Lenin except the physical world, and the only way to know about that world was to come in contact with it. In agreement with Freud, Lenin believed that man was a stimulus-response mechanism without spirit or soul, just a lump of protein molecules wired with nerves. Man's behavior was learned from experience and could therefore be reprogrammed through "behavior modification," a polite word for "brainwashing," which the Communists developed to a fine art—except that it only worked by destroying the person.

---

Of course, there was no room for God in such a theory, and that was precisely what created problems for Lenin when he dared to think about it. Man can only know about that which exists in the physical realm. Animals don't have gods, so why should man in the evolutionary process have ever developed such a fantasy?

Since man is a stimulus-response mechanism, according to this theory, he can only know of that which stimulates him. He touches something hot or cold and learns of "hot" and "cold." He touches something hard or he is hit by something hard and he learns about "hard." All he can know of anything is what he has experienced: the stimulus from the physical world and his instinctive response inherited through millions of years of evolution and then modified and reprogrammed by his own experience. Even science has no other source of knowledge.

Man can't even *think* or *fantasize* about something that doesn't exist in the physical world, according to this theory. Of course, with the help of a little alcohol he can have visions of pink elephants, but pink exists and so do elephants. He could dream of "paradise" or "heaven," but it would always conform to his experience: a "happy hunting ground" of the American Indian or a land of luxury for Pharaohs, evidenced by the bows and arrows or robes and jewelry buried with the dead.

## What "Stimulus" Caused The Response, "God," In Human Minds?

The theory seemed consistent and could be demonstrated by challenging doubters to visualize a new prime color for the rainbow. No one could. Obviously, then, nothing exists but the material world and no one can even conceive of anything that doesn't exist and which he hasn't experienced. There was only one flaw: Foolish people have this fantasy about God. Where did that come from?

Those despicable clergy must have invented "God" and have ever since been filling the minds of the common people with this delusion in order to keep them in bondage. Communism would set them free from this opiate of the people! Yes, but where did the clergy get this idea if no one can think of anything that doesn't exist? What was the "stimulus" that caused this "God-response"? There's the rub. By Lenin's own theory God had to exist or no one would have ever dreamed up the idea.

Isn't it interesting that in contrast to the philosophers who have been trying to develop proofs for the existence of God for centuries, the Bible doesn't waste its time in that manner? The Bible is the one Book where one would certainly expect to see many complex arguments presented for God's existence, yet not one is given!

Surely that very fact says something important about the Bible and about God: *He has already made contact with every person in his or her conscience.* Everyone knows that God exists, and that includes you. So the Bible doesn't even argue about the issue, because the very fact that all of mankind has this concept says that He exists.

If we must worship a power greater than ourselves, does it not make sense to revere the Sun and stars?

—Carl Sagan[1]

The only difference between Pantheism and Atheism is in the use of the word God. The Atheist affirms that all existence is one; he affirms the universality of law; he affirms natural morality equally with the Pantheist.

—Samuel P. Putuam,
nineteenth-century atheist leader[2]

# 2
# Who Is God?

## "A HIGHER POWER BY WHATEVER NAME"?

---

*Question:* Why are Christians so adamantly opposed to the many other concepts of God that are honored in other religions? I agree with what Vice President Al Gore said at the 1993 Presidential Prayer Breakfast in Washington D.C.: "Faith in God, reliance upon a Higher Power, *by whatever name,* is in my view essential." Think of the unity there could be if religions would stop quarreling and honor all concepts of God in an open-minded and brotherly fashion!

*Response:* Yes, think of the unity there could be if we would all agree that two plus two equals five—but that wouldn't make it so. A "Higher Power"? How *high? Higher* than what? And what does this mean?

---

With all due respect to you and the Vice President, what you both propose is completely irrational. Furthermore, you aren't being "open-minded and brotherly," as you think you are. By insisting upon the acceptance of *any* "Higher Power" and thus *any* god, you thereby refuse to honor the one true God or even to admit His existence.

This very fallacy was exposed in Alan Bloom's book *The Closing of the American Mind*. Bloom pointed out that "openness" had become the new fad in America, especially in education. Every idea must be respected, nothing could be wrong, and no one should be "put down" by suggesting that someone might be in error. He explained that Americans had in fact become so open to everything that they had become closed to the idea that something might be right and something else wrong. The *closing* of the American mind...by *openness*! In much the same way, you and the Vice President have become so open to every god that you are closed to the possibility that there just might be one true God and all the others false.

## SOME PRACTICAL CONSIDERATIONS

Let's put your proposal on a practical level. How would you like it if everyone denied your unique individuality and specific personal identity and looked upon you as simply a representative of the general concept of humanness? Would you like being confused with a murderer, rapist, cheat, thief, or some other criminal simply because each one of them also represents humanness? And what would you think if, to justify this travesty, it was said that "any human" will do? Why not, if "any Higher Power" will do?

There could hardly be any greater insult than such a denial of the truth about you as a unique person! You have definite qualities and traits that distinguish you from all other persons who have ever existed or will ever exist on this earth. You are an individual and not to be confused with anyone else. To deny your individuality would be to deny your very existence.

Suppose that your wife or husband and your children and friends felt no personal relationship with you but simply looked upon you as some kind of generic representation of humanness. Suppose your husband or wife cared not whether it was you or some other form of humanness sharing their home and intimacies of the husband-wife relationship! After all, such a relationship need not be with a *particular* person but merely with *any* person—just as *any* "Higher Power, by whatever name" is good enough. Let's not be narrow-minded!

Is it not an even greater farce to suggest that God's personal qualities and attributes, which separate Him by an impassable gulf from His creation and all beings in it, are meaningless? What a travesty to say that "any Higher Power," "any god," will do! How dare you say that God's love for you means nothing, but you would be just as happy worshiping and trusting and loving some cosmic energy source or an idol or even the devil!

## TO CREATE THE UNIVERSE REQUIRES DEFINITE QUALITIES

The fact is that no thinking person can embrace just "any god" as the Creator of this universe—and there must be a Creator. The logic of our own existence and the incredible design and structure of the universe around us force us to certain conclusions about God. Based upon such conclusions we must reject any concept of God that violates these requirements. It isn't true that "any god" will do. And no "power," no matter how "high," could create the universe and mankind in it. Only a personal God of infinite power, wisdom, and love could do so.

Certainly no one could reasonably attribute the creation of this universe to some idol made by human hands out of clay or wood or stone! Much less could an *idol* create mankind. Nor could any *idol* love us or be worthy of our love. Nor could any *idol* set the standards of good and evil that we each recognize have been placed in our consciences. Who could possibly believe that an idol which itself was made by human hands and has to be carried about had any power at all to do either good or evil?

Yet the majority of mankind down through history has trusted in idols. Even in today's supposedly modern world with radio and television widely publicizing the amazing advancements of science, several billion people still worship idols. Nor is this true only in Africa, Asia, and South America. Multitudes in the modern cities of North America and Europe as well trust in and worship actual physical idols. Such misplaced trust leads to spiritual darkness and bondage.

Mankind will be judged for such folly, and justly so. The very conscience and intelligence that God has given us contradict such superstitious madness. The Bible points out the folly of trusting in idols:

> Their idols are silver and gold, the work of men's hands. They have mouths, but they speak not; eyes have they, but they see not; they have ears, but they hear not; noses they have, but they smell not; they have hands, but they handle not; feet they have, but they walk not; neither speak they through their throat. They that make them are like unto them; so is everyone that trusteth in them (Psalm 115:4-8).

Yet one must include idols and every other concept of "god" as equally valid if "any Higher Power" will do. If not, then where does one draw the line? When he gathered snake worshipers, fire worshipers, spiritists, animists, and witch doctors along with Hindus, Buddhists, and Muslims at Assisi, Italy, to pray for peace, Pope John Paul II made the astonishing statement that they were all praying to the same God![3] Obviously there are innumerable false gods and false religions, and the Bible denounces every one of these because they seduce mankind from knowing and obeying the one true God.

## Who Is "Allah"?

---

*Question:* "Allah," contrary to what you have written in *A Cup of Trembling* and elsewhere, is the one true God of the Bible. This is proved by the fact that the Hausa translation of the Bible in northern Nigeria, where there are many Muslims, uses Allah as a designation for the true God of Abraham, Isaac, and Israel, Jehovah of the Old Testament, and the God and Father of our Lord Jesus Christ. What better way could we encourage Muslims to believe the Bible?

*Response:* Unfortunately, this is a common error that is found in Arabic translations of the Bible as well, which are used in some Muslim countries. It is a serious mistake. Far from helping Muslims, it leaves them trusting their false god, Allah. Identifying Allah as Jehovah has caused a great deal of confusion and harm.

---

One of the major promoters of this delusion is the Roman Catholic Church. The Vatican imagines that the difference between the God of Christianity and the Muslim's Allah can be swept under an ecumenical rug. For example, *The Canons and Decrees of Vatican II* declare that Allah is the "Creator...the one, merciful God, mankind's judge"—in other words, the one true God of the Bible.[4] Yet nothing could be further from the truth.

### THE MOON GOD OF MOHAMMED'S TRIBE

Allah is *not* the generic Arabic word for God, but the *name* of a particular god among many deities traditionally honored in ancient times by the nomadic tribes in Arabia. Allah was the chief god among the approximately 360 idols in the Kaaba in Mecca. In that pagan idol temple, still standing in Mecca today but now the focus of Muslim worship, there was a deity to suit each of the thousands of travelers passing through in the trade caravans.

Allah is a contraction of *al-Ilah*, the name of the moon god of the local Quraish, Mohammed's tribe, which they had worshiped with animal and human sacrifices for centuries before Islam was invented. Ibn Ishaq, Mohammed's earliest biographer, tells how Mohammed's grandfather was about to sacrifice one of his sons, Abdullah (who would later become the prophet Mohammed's father), when a sorceress persuaded him to sacrifice a camel instead.

The name of Mohammed's father, Abdullah, is a contraction of *Abd ul Allah*, which means "servant of Allah." It is a historic fact that Allah was worshiped long before Mohammed was born. When Mohammed rejected polytheism, he took the name of his own tribe's traditional deity, the moon god, as the designation for the one God of Islam, his allegedly new religion.

## PAGAN PRACTICES CONTINUE IN ISLAM TODAY

In fact, much of Islam is a carryover of primitive tribal laws and customs already in existence in Mohammed's day. Even the holy month of Ramadan had long been established.[5] Nor can Muslims deny that for centuries before Mohammed, Allah had been one of the many pagan deities (such as Baal or Molech) whom the God of the Bible, Jehovah, had forbidden His people, the Israelites, to worship. Surely Allah and Jehovah are not the same!

Allah's symbol was the crescent moon, which Mohammed also carried over into Islam. This symbol is still seen on mosques, minarets, shrines, and Arab flags. When he conquered Mecca after breaking on a pretext the peace treaty he had made with the leaders of that city, Mohammed smashed the idols in the Kaaba, including Allah, and began preaching against idolatry. Nevertheless, the new self-proclaimed prophet kept the idol temple and retained the pagan ritual (long an integral part of the worship of the idols) of kissing the black stone which had for centuries been embedded in the southeast corner of the Kaaba, "five feet from the ground, just right for kissing," as historian Will Durant points out.[6]

That stone, actually of "dark red material, oval in shape, some seven inches in diameter,"[7] remains in its centuries-old position to this day and must still be kissed by Muslims on their required pilgrimage to Mecca as part of the allegedly new religion of Islam. It would seem that Mohammed kept the black stone as well as the god Allah (without its image) as a partial concession in order to preserve something of familiarity to the Arabs.

## DECEPTIVE AND GRIEVOUS CONFUSION

Bible translators, by using Allah for God, far from being helpful, have succeeded instead in creating confusion. Allah is no mere linguistic designation for God, as

*Dios* in Spanish or *Dieu* in French. Allah is the *name* of an ancient pagan idol adopted as the god of Islam. If Allah were merely the generic Arabic word for God, then Muslims would not hesitate to use the word for God in each language into which the Koran has been translated. Instead, they insist that *Allah* must be used in every language. It would be blasphemy to call the Muslim's god anything else. And blasphemy against Allah carries the death penalty in Pakistan and elsewhere.

The God of Israel, too, has a *name*, YHWH, now pronounced Jehovah but anciently as Jahweh or Yahweh. Most Christians are unaware of God's *name* because the Old Testament substitutes LORD for YHWH. God told Moses, "By my name YHWH was I not known to them" (Exodus 6:3); and at the burning bush God explained the meaning of His name: "I AM THAT I AM" (Exodus 3:13,14). YHWH means not just one who *is*, but the self-existent One who *is in and of Himself*.

## CONTRASTING "ALLAH" AND "YAHWEH"

That Allah is *not* the God of the Bible is very clear for a number of other reasons. His very character and characteristics are the opposite of the biblical God's. The Koran says that Allah is not a father, has no son (though he had three daughters, Al-Uzza, al-Lat, and Manah, represented among the idols in the Kaaba), and is not a triune being but a single and unknowable entity. Allah destroys rather than saves sinners, has compassion on only the righteous, does not deal in grace but only rewards good deeds, and has no just and righteous way to redeem the lost, as does the God of the Bible. That Allah should become a man to die for the sins of the world would be heresy to a Muslim. It is very clear from what the Koran and the Hadith (Islamic tradition) teach about him that Allah is *not* the God of the Bible.

In contrast, the God of the Bible *is love*, an impossibility for Allah. As a single entity, Allah is incomplete: He was lonely and could not love or fellowship until other entities came into existence. Not so with YHWH or Jehovah.

YHWH is three Persons in One: Father, Son, and Holy Spirit, complete in perfection and in need of no others to love and fellowship with ("the Father loves the Son," there is communion within the Godhead, etc.). Only of this God could it be said that He *is love* in Himself.

Allah could never say, "Let *us* make man in *our* image" (Genesis 1:26). The Muslim scholar has no explanation for this expression, which is even found in the Koran's paraphrase of this Bible verse. We could point out other reasons, but this should be enough to show that to use the *name* Allah for the God of the Bible in the Hausa translation or in any other translation is a grave error!

## CONTRADICTORY CONCEPTS OF GOD— WHICH IS CORRECT?

*Question:* The oldest and most popular concepts of God are either pantheism, the belief that everything [i.e. the universe] is God, or polytheism, the belief that there are many gods. Why couldn't either or both of these be true? Why is the Bible so adamant against these beliefs and why does it so severely condemn what it calls the pagans who have sincerely held these beliefs for thousands of years, certainly long before Jesus Christ came along?

*Response:* Pantheism is really the same as atheism. Obviously, if everything is God, then nothing is God because the very term has lost any meaning. Pantheism leads to numerous contradictions: God would be the emptiness of a vacuum as well as the substance of matter; He would be sickness as well as health, death as well as life, evil as well as good. Furthermore, if the universe itself is God, then there is no outside reference point from which the universe can be evaluated and given purpose and significance. Nor is there any hope of changing its downward course or that of mankind.

Nothing has meaning or value in and of itself, but only as some personal being has use for it and values it. This is a universal truth which holds equally for *everything*. A car has no meaning in itself, no purpose unless there is someone to drive it. The most costly diamond ring has no value unless there is someone who wants to buy and own and wear it . . . and so on. Obviously, what is true of every part of the universe is equally true of the whole.

According to the second law of thermodynamics (the law of entropy), this universe is running down like a clock. Left to itself and without some outside Intelligence of infinite power rescuing the universe from its certain doom, all of man's personal and corporate dreams and schemes will one day be like sand castles washed out into a cosmic ocean of nothingness. The entire universe will be approaching absolute zero and all will be as though it had never been. What kind of god is this? Without a Creator who had an eternal purpose for His creation and who is able to reach in from outside (not with reincarnation or evolution but with *resurrection* and new creation), neither the universe nor man in it could have any ultimate meaning. Pantheism can offer only meaninglessness, hopelessness, and ultimate despair.

There is a neopantheism in the world of academia today called *ecotheology*. It is the old pantheism, but now held by some highly educated people. One of its advocates, Georgetown University professor Victor Ferkiss, says it "starts with the premise that the Universe is God." Like many other ecologists today, Ferkiss seems to think that the pantheistic worship of nature will "prevent the environmental exploitation of the Universe."[8]

## Neo-Paganism And The Return To Nature

One can't worship both the creation and the Creator; and the Bible says there are serious consequences that come from worshiping the creation instead of the Creator (Romans 1:18-32). One's conscience becomes dull and mankind falls prey to all kinds of evil and cruel behavior because there are no morals in nature. Try to find a compassionate lion or an honest eagle—or a sympathetic hurricane.

Historian/philosopher Herbert Schlossberg reminds us, "Animals do not act morally or immorally; they only act naturally. A system of ethics that says human beings ought to base their behavior on nature therefore justifies any behavior, because nature knows no ethic."[9] Nobelist Sir John Eccles agrees:

> The concepts of injustice, unfairness... the obligations to honor, to respect... are intelligible only within a *moral* context and to moral beings.
> In the mindless universe of mere nature...there is neither justice nor mercy, neither liberty nor fairness. There are only facts.... [10]

The temptation to worship the universe seems to be virtually an occupational hazard for atheistic scientists. Their arguments against God often betray an almost-subconscious adoption of pantheism both as an excuse for denying the infinite Creator (to whom man would otherwise be accountable) and an attempt to find some other basis for purpose and meaning. Consider these words in the frontispiece of a huge (more than 800 pages) compendium of atheism titled *400 Years of Freethought* and published in 1894: "Yet I doubt not thro' the ages one increasing purpose runs, and the thoughts of men are widened with the powers of the suns."[11]

The cornerstone of Freethought is explained in the book as the rejection of "all authority" and "the conquest of nature."[12] Whence then this "purpose," what are the purposeful "powers of the suns," and what part could they play in widening the thoughts of men? The contradiction is almost humorous, but what option does the atheist have in attempting to repress his innate recognition that purpose and meaning exist? He is forced to attribute something of the sort to nature itself.

Carl Sagan, a modern atheist, becomes very reverent and worshipful in the presence of the Cosmos, which he credits with having spawned us and all life. As quoted at the beginning of this chapter, he says it makes sense to reverence the sun and moon. *Reverence the sun and moon?*

On what basis? And how is that different from bowing down to a piece of wood or stone as one's god? What could the sun or moon have to do with morals, with purpose and meaning, with love and beauty?

## THE FOLLY OF POLYTHEISM

As for polytheism, if there is more than one god, then who is in charge? The many gods of polytheism fight wars and steal one another's wives, with no one to set the standard and call the universe to account. There is no basis for morals, truth, or peace in heaven, nor therefore could there be on earth.

If one God is stronger or has more authority than the others, then none of the rest of the gods can really be God, so we are back to monotheism. As the Bible says:

> Among the gods there is none like unto thee, O Lord; neither are there any works like unto thy works. . . . For thou art great, and doest wondrous things: thou art God alone (Psalm 86:8,10).

If there are many gods, to which god should one pray? To one's favorite god? On what basis has a particular god become one's favorite? Is it because it was once prayed to and seemed to provide an answer? How can there be any assurance that a particular god can do what is asked? It is like praying to the various saints. Yet Saint Christopher, the patron saint of the travelers to whom millions looked for protection, has lately been removed from the Catholic pantheon. It is now admitted by the Church hierarchy that Christopher was a myth and that any power he seemed to have wielded on behalf of his devotees was obviously a delusion.

So it is with all the gods of the world's many religions. In fact, they are worse than myths; they are representatives of Satan and his minions. Behind each idol is a demon using it to draw people away from the true God, as Paul states: "The things which the Gentiles [pagans] sacrifice [to their gods] they sacrifice to devils and not to

God; and I would not that ye should have fellowship with devils. Ye cannot drink the cup of the Lord and the cup of devils; ye cannot be partakers of the Lord's table and of the table of devils" (1 Corinthians 10:20,21).

There is no compromise with God because at stake is the eternal destiny of every person who has ever lived or will ever live. Suppose a certain man convinces a large group of people to give him their possessions and to follow him to what he promises will be a veritable paradise on earth—and instead he leads them into a swamp where they are all swallowed up in quicksand. Should he not be prosecuted as a liar and murderer? How much more serious is it to promote false gods and to sell tickets to heaven which actually take people to hell!

## KNOWING GOD

---

*Question:* I would like to know God and I have asked Him to reveal Himself to me, but nothing happens. No lights have gone on, no messages in the sky, no sudden revelation. It seems to me that if God really existed He would want us to believe in Him and He would therefore do something tangible to let us know He exists. Is it wrong to ask for *some unmistakable evidence* of God's existence?

*Response:* No, and the evidence is all around you—more than you need. The kind of evidence you seem to be hoping for, however, wouldn't help at all. Suppose some message with your name in it suddenly appeared in the sky. How would you know that God put it there? Suppose right now you heard an audible voice saying loudly, "I am God! Worship me!" What would that tell you about God—and how would you know He had actually spoken?

---

In fact, God *has* spoken to you. The design of the universe is a message from God telling you of His existence as Creator and of His infinite wisdom and power. Those things that you value most highly and which you know in your heart make life worthwhile—love, joy, peace, moral purity, goodness, truthfulness, justice, kindness—tell you of God's character. Your conscience tells you that you are morally accountable to God, that you have violated His laws and have fallen short of His perfect standard. Your conscience also tells you that there is no way you can make up for having broken God's laws. You can't buy Him off with sacrifice, prayers, good deeds, or ritual.

Suppose you got a speeding ticket. Would you waste your time telling the judge that you've driven that stretch of highway *within* the speed limit more often than *above* it? Would he let you off under the theory that your "good deeds outweigh the bad"? You know that won't work with an earthly judge, and it certainly won't work with God.

Would you tell him that if he lets you off this time you will never break the law again? You know what the judge would say: "If you never break the law again, you're only doing what the law requires. You get no *extra* credit for that. It doesn't make up for having broken the law in the past. The penalty will have to be paid as the law prescribes it." You know it's the same way with God.

## The Witness Of Conscience

Your conscience tells you that the only way you could possibly escape the severe penalty which God's infinite justice must demand for having broken His laws would be if He forgives you. And you know He can't just wipe the slate clean for no reason. For one thing, that would hardly encourage you to improve your behavior. Furthermore, it would violate His own law. He must have some way of paying the penalty Himself—a penalty you can't pay—so that you can be forgiven by His grace.

You don't know what that method may be, but you know that a God of perfect love and perfect justice would somehow provide it. If there is an explanation of this good news, it would surely be in the Bible. In fact, God has explained it all in those pages. Have you seriously studied the Bible and checked out the evidence which shows that it is God's infallible Word?

There is more than sufficient historic, archaeological, and scientific evidence to prove that the Bible is God's infallible Word. In fact, in this volume alone we provide overwhelming evidence of that fact. But you don't really need it. That kind of proof is like icing on the cake. If you just read the Bible with an open heart and mind, you will know that God is speaking to your heart as only He can speak.

I recommend that you begin with the Gospel of John and continue through Acts and Romans, then read those three books again. God has promised in His Word: "Ye shall seek me and find me when ye shall search for me with all your heart" (Jeremiah 29:13). That is a promise you can count on! Seek God with all your heart and put Him to the test by looking in the Bible for the revelation of Himself!

## Must I Believe God Exists Before I Seek Him?

---

*Question:* In my daily Bible reading I came across a verse that really puzzles me: "Without faith it is impossible to please him [God]; for he that cometh to God must believe that he is, and that he is a rewarder of them that diligently seek him" (Hebrews 11:6). Rather than God revealing Himself to a seeking heart, it sounds as though one must already believe in God before seeking Him. How can that be the case?

*Response:* Would someone seek God if he didn't already believe He existed? It would be a waste of time. In fact, everyone, including you, knows that God exists.

---

The true story is told of a London street preacher who announced to his audience that every atheist was a fool because the Bible said so. A well-known atheist in the crowd shouted back at him that it was a slanderous insult, which he took personally, and that he would sue the preacher for damages. The preacher responded, "It's not slander to tell the truth."

The atheist countered, "And it's not truth unless you can prove it! You'll have to prove in court that I'm a fool or I'll take every pound you've got!"

"I don't have to go to court to prove it," said the preacher calmly. "You say you're an atheist?"

"Yes, and not just a casual one. I've spent my life proving God doesn't exist. It's a pernicious myth!"

"Spent your life proving God doesn't exist, have you?" replied the preacher. "Tell me this: if a man who spends his life fighting against something that doesn't exist isn't a fool, who is?"

Likewise, one would have to be a fool to spend any time at all seeking to know a God without being convinced that He exists. God expects every person, as the first step in knowing Him, to admit the obvious fact that He exists. Furthermore, God expects each person coming to Him to have a proper concept of who He is. He won't honor prayers to an idol or to some "force" or "higher power." Each person is accountable on the basis of the evidence to come to a proper understanding of God and not to be seeking some false god. God also requires that those who come to Him truly believe that He is not a God of caprice or trickery but a God who "rewards those who diligently seek Him."

## WHAT "GOD" DO YOU SEEK?

What is it that any sincere seeker should already have concluded about the God he wants to know? Reason and evidence dictate the following: To create the universe, God must be all-powerful (omnipotent) and all-knowing (omniscient) and in touch with every part of the universe at once (omnipresent). He would have to be at least as personal a Being as we are in order to create us. He would need to perfectly embody all that we recognize as the highest qualities to which mankind could aspire—love, truth, justice, patience, kindness, compassion, etc.—or there would be no explanation for our admiration of such attributes. Furthermore, He would have to know the future consequences of every action in His universe. Otherwise He could make some terrible blunders. And of course He must have existed eternally as God. He certainly couldn't have evolved or developed out of something or someone that was less than God.

The true God must also be able to create everything out of *nothing* and not just build or manufacture His universe out of materials already available. Not energy, not matter, not gravity or electricity, but *God alone* must be self-existent in order to be the cause of all. Finally, He must be perfectly good and just or there would be no explanation for the common recognition of right and wrong written in the conscience of all mankind all over this earth. These are the minimum qualifications of the true God, without which we couldn't trust and worship and love Him.

Although we can understand the necessity of the above abilities, it is also completely beyond our capacity to comprehend such a Being: a God who has *always* existed and thus is without beginning or end; who not only created everything out of nothing but in order not to lose control of His creation must know where every subatomic particle in every atom ever was or ever will be; who must also know what every person who ever lived or ever will live has ever thought or ever will think or say or do, etc. Obviously, such a God is beyond our ability to fully comprehend.

At the same time that God is beyond our comprehension, however, we have seen that both reason and evidence demand such a God as the only explanation for our own existence and that of the universe around us. To deny this God, though He is incomprehensible, would fly in the face of reason and common sense. It is both impossible and unreasonable for there to have been a time when nothing existed and to have everything, including God, somehow arise out of that void of nothingness. It is totally unreasonable to suggest that life and intelligence sprang unaided from dead, empty space and thereafter evolved by chance.

Having come to these conclusions about God on the basis of the evidence all around him and in his own conscience, the seeker is now in a position to cry out to this true God to reveal Himself. The precise steps and circumstances and inner convictions through which God will reveal Himself vary with each individual. It is through His Word, however, that the fullest and clearest revelation of God comes. And in this Word God has revealed Himself in Jesus Christ, who declared, "He that hath seen me hath seen the Father" (John 14:9).

Jesus also said, "No man cometh unto the Father but by me" (John 14:6). Whoever wants to know God must get to know Jesus. He is revealed in God's Word, and He reveals Himself to those who open their hearts to Him. As He said, "Behold, I stand at the door [of every human heart] and knock; if any man hear my voice and open the door, I will come in to him..." (Revelation 3:20).

## WAS JESUS CHRIST REALLY GOD?

*Question:* Our adult Bible class teacher says Jesus was half God and half man. He insists that God can only act in response to our prayers and that when the one prayed for isn't healed it's because there hasn't been enough prayer and fasting. Are these ideas biblical?

*Response:* No. Until evidence to the contrary arises, however, let's give the teacher the benefit of the doubt and assume that he *believes* what is right but is having difficulty *expressing* it. Yes, God is Jesus' Father and Mary is His mother, but that doesn't make Him half God and half man. That error is similar to the Roman Catholic teaching that Mary is "the mother of God." Jesus existed as God from all eternity and thus eons before Mary was born. Obviously, then, she is not the mother of Jesus *as God* but only of the *human body* by which He was born into this world.

Mary was a virgin when Jesus was born. Consequently, as the Bible tells us, the baby she gave birth to was conceived by no man but by the Holy Spirit. It is impossible for us to understand fully what that means, but we know what it doesn't mean. The virgin birth is not like having an Irish father and French mother and thus being half Irish and half French.

Jesus is fully God and fully man: "God manifest in the flesh" (1 Timothy 3:16), not half God manifest in half flesh. The same verse calls this a "great... mystery." Isaiah called the virgin-born child "Emmanuel," which means "God [not half God] with us" (Isaiah 7:14; cf. Matthew 1:23) and "the mighty God [not half-God], the everlasting Father" (Isaiah 9:6). If this were not the case, Jesus could not be our Savior.

Throughout the Old Testament God says that He is the *only* Savior (Isaiah 43:11; 45:15,21; Hosea 13:4). Obviously this must be true because salvation is an infinite work, including as it must the full payment of the infinite penalty for sin required by God's infinite justice—something which only *God* could accomplish. Consequently, for Jesus to be our Savior He must be *God*. Paul called Him "God our Savior" (1 Timothy 1:1; 2:3; Titus 1:3,4; 2:10,13; 3:4), as did Peter (2 Peter 1:1) and Jude (verse 25).

Yet the Savior must be *man* as well because it is man who is the sinner, not God. The penalty for sin is pronounced against *man*, not against God; therefore it must be paid by a *man*. But no finite man could pay that penalty. Thus God in His infinite love and grace became a man through the virgin birth so that He, as a man, could take the judgment we deserved and make it possible for us to be forgiven.

To be our Savior, Jesus had to be *fully God* (Isaiah 43:11) and *fully man* (Romans 5:12-21), not a hybrid composed of half of each. Ask your teacher if this is what he means.

## OUR PRAYERS

That God doesn't need our prayers to act is obvious. He managed to exist for an eternity and to create the universe and angels and mankind without our prayers. Certainly our prayers didn't cause Christ to be born into the world and to die for our sins. Nor is it our prayers that will usher in a new universe, though God gives us the privilege to pray, "Thy kingdom come."

If God could act *only* in response to our prayers He would be at our mercy, His hands tied most of the time, unable to do what He in His infinite wisdom and knowledge knows ought to be done but which we in our limited understanding were ignorant of or hadn't thought about. Moreover, He couldn't meet emergencies that we didn't know would occur and thus hadn't prayed about. The idea that God "can only act in response to our prayers" is unbiblical and illogical.

To say that failure to be healed results from too little prayer and fasting is equally false. That teaching implies that we can cause God to do whatever we pray for if we pray and fast long and hard enough—in other words, that we can impose our will upon Him. What about God's will? It also suggests that God's will is to heal everyone every time. On the contrary, He has something better for us than perpetuating our lives endlessly in these bodies of sin. There is a detailed discussion on prayer and faith in *Beyond Seduction* that I recommend you read.

## "NOTHING EXISTS EXCEPT GOD"?

---

*Question:* I saw an interview with Sir John Marks Templeton in Robert Schuller's *Possibilities* magazine. He is the man who awards the annual Templeton Prize for promoting an appreciation of the benefits of all the world's religions. I was shocked to read in the interview that Templeton believes that "nothing exists except God." I'm confused. I thought this was pantheism, yet there it was promoted in the magazine of a man who is looked up to as an evangelical leader. How can this be?

*Response:* It *is* pantheism. It is also a basic tenet of cults such as Science of Mind, Religious Science, and Christian Science. What they teach is basically the same as Peale's positive thinking and Schuller's possibility thinking, which explains why the latter would promote it in his magazine. Here is how "nothing exists except God" works in the mind science and positive/possibility thinking arena: God is good and God is all. Therefore all is good. Thus, anything that isn't good—sin, sickness, suffering, death, etc.—is not real but is a delusion of one's negative thinking. The way to be delivered from these negative delusions is to become a positive or a possibility thinker.

---

The Bible, however, teaches that sin, suffering, sickness, and death are real indeed. "The soul that sinneth, it shall die" (Ezekiel 18:4) is the pronouncement of God's just judgment and certainly treats both sin and death as real. Jesus healed the sick and raised the dead. He didn't teach them to deny the reality of these things through positive thinking or possibility thinking. Such concepts are completely alien to the Bible.

Our deliverance from sin and death comes not by denying the reality of these evils through the power of the mind, but by faith in Christ, who suffered the agony of the cross and paid the penalty which His own justice had pronounced upon sin. He died for our sins and "was raised again for our justification" (Romans 4:25). If sin and death don't exist, then the death of Christ for our sins and His resurrection are merely allegories and not real events—contrary to the historical facts.

If "nothing exists except God," then the universe is God and we ourselves are all part of God and thus divine and perfect beings. Indeed, if "nothing exists except God," then Satan, who is certainly presented in the Bible as real, is God. One could not imagine a greater delusion.

The God of the Bible is separate and distinct from His creation, which He made out of nothing. That creation is running down like a clock because it is separated from Him by the rebellion of His creatures (Satan and his minions joined by mankind), a rebellion which caused God to pronounce His judgment upon this entire creation. If God were the universe, then He too would be running down like a clock. That is *not* the God of the Bible!

## WHAT ABOUT THE TRINITY?

---

*Question:* Christians generally believe in the Trinity, a "God" who is three Persons and yet one Supreme Being. Yet the word "Trinity" doesn't appear even *once* in the Bible, which plainly declares that there is only *one* God, not *three*. How can you possibly justify a belief in the "Trinity" from the Bible?

*Response:* There are only two basic concepts of God: 1) pantheism/naturalism—that the universe itself is God; and 2) supernaturalism—that God or gods exist distinct and apart from the universe. We have already shown the folly of the first concept, which leaves us only with the latter. Within supernaturalism are two opposing views: 1) polytheism—that there are many gods (Mormons as well as Hindus are polytheists); and 2) monotheism—that there is only one God. We have shown that polytheism, too, has fatal flaws. Its basic problem is diversity without unity.

---

There are also two opposing views within monotheism: 1) the belief that God is a single personage, as in Islam and Judaism, which insist that Allah or Jehovah is "one," meaning a single being. The same belief is also held by pseudo-Christian cults such as the Jehovah's Witnesses and the Oneness Pentecostals, who deny the Trinity and claim that Father, Son, and Holy Ghost are God's three "titles" or "offices." Here the fatal flaw is *unity without diversity.*

### THE NECESSITY FOR BOTH UNITY AND DIVERSITY

That God must have *both unity and diversity* is clear. The Allah of Islam, or the Jehovah of Jehovah's Witnesses and Jews, or the God of unitarian "Christian" groups would be incomplete in Himself. He would be unable to love, commune, or fellowship before creating other beings capable of interacting with Him in these ways. The quality of love and the capacities for fellowship and communion, by their very nature, require another personal being with which to share them. And God could not fully share Himself except with another Being equal to Him. Yet the Bible says that "God *is* love" in Himself alone. This could only be true if God Himself consisted of a plurality of Beings who were separate and distinct, yet one.

Although the actual word "Trinity" does not occur in the Bible, the concept is clearly expressed there. The Bible presents a God who did not need to create any beings to experience love, communion, and fellowship. This God is complete in Himself, existing eternally in three Persons: Father, Son, and Holy Spirit, individually distinct from each other yet at the same time eternally one. These three loved, communed, fellowshiped, and took counsel together before the universe, angels, or man were brought into existence.

In contrast, the god of Islam and contemporary Judaism could not *be* love in and of himself, for whom could he love in the solitude predating his creation of other personal beings? Such a deficiency in God would affect man, who is made in His image, at every level of his being.

## Plurality And Singularity: Both Apply

The very first verse in the Bible presents God as a *plural* being: "In the beginning God created the heaven and the earth." If God were a single personage, then the singular word for God, *Eloah*, would be used. Instead of the singular form, however, the plural, *Elohim*, which literally means *Gods*, is used. Yet a singular *verb*, *bara*, is used with *Elohim*. This *plural noun* (*Elohim*) is used for God more than 2500 times in the Old Testament and almost always with a singular verb, thus indicating both unity and diversity and both singularity and plurality in the God of the Bible. It was Elohim (Gods) who later in this first chapter of Genesis said, "Let *us* make man in *our* image, after *our* likeness" (verse 26).

At the burning bush God (*Elohim*—literally *Gods*) said unto Moses, "I am that I am . . ." (Exodus 3:14). Here *Gods* speak but do not say, "We are that we are" but "*I am that I am."* Nor is the word *Elohim* the only way in which God's plurality is presented.

Consider, for example, Psalm 149:2 NKJV: "Let Israel rejoice in their Maker" (in the Hebrew, "makers"); Ecclesiastes 12:1: "Remember now thy Creator" (Hebrew, "creators"); and Isaiah 54:5: "For thy Maker is thine husband" (Hebrew, "makers" and "husbands"). Unitarianism has no explanation for this consistent presentation of both God's unity and plurality throughout the Old Testament.

At the very center of Israel's confession in Deuteronomy 6:4 of God's oneness (known as the *shema*) is the plural form for God (*elohenu*): "Hear, O Israel: The Lord our God is one Lord" (*Shema yisroel adonai elohenu adonai echad*). The word used for one, *echad*, often means a unity of more than one. Were that not the intention, then *yachid*, which means a single and *absolute one*, would have been used. The word *echad* is used, for example, in Genesis 2:24, where man and woman become *"one* flesh"; in Exodus 36:13, when the various parts "became *one* tabernacle"; in 2 Samuel 2:25, when many soldiers "became *one* troop"; and elsewhere similarly.

The great Hebrew prophet Isaiah declared of the birth of the Messiah: "For unto us a child is born, unto us a son is given; and the government shall be upon his shoulder; and his name shall be called Wonderful, Counselor, *the mighty God, the everlasting Father . . ."* ( Isaiah 9:6). Such a concept is found nowhere else in the world's religious literature but is unique to the Bible: A Son would be born into this world who, though a man, would be the Mighty God. And though a Son, He would at the same time be the Everlasting Father.

Isaiah clearly presents the *deity* of Christ, the Fatherhood of God, and the oneness of the Father and the Son. All three Persons in the Godhead (Father, Son, and Holy Spirit) are clearly seen in the following: " . . .from the beginning . . . there am I; and now the Lord God and his Spirit hath sent me" (Isaiah 48:16). It could only be God who is speaking, this One who has been in existence from the beginning; yet He says that He has been sent forth by God and His Spirit. In the Trinity, two Persons are invisible (God the Father and the Spirit of God) while one is visible, the Son of God who became man.

## Some Helpful Analogies

How can we fully understand this concept of three Persons, each separate and distinct (the Father is not the Son and the Son is not the Holy Spirit) yet comprising one God? We can't. Critics argue that because the Trinity can't be fully explained by human reasoning it therefore cannot be true. Yet who can fully explain God even if He is only a single entity? No one. We can't even explain the *human* soul and spirit, much less the Spirit of God, yet these terms are used repeatedly in the Bible.

We can, however, see analogies to the Trinity everywhere. The universe is comprised of three elements: space, time, and matter. The first two are invisible, but matter is visible. Each of these is itself divided into three: length, breadth, and height; past, present, and future; energy, motion, and phenomena. Length, breadth, and height are each separate and distinct from each other, yet they are one because each is the whole. The length takes in all of space, as do the width and height. So it is with time: past, present, and future are each distinct from one another, and yet each is the whole. And here again, two (past and future) are invisible while the present is visible.

Man himself, who is made "in the image of God" (Genesis 1:27; 9:6; etc.) is composed of three elements: body, soul, and spirit, of which again two (soul and spirit) are invisible and one, the body, is visible. The way man functions as a being also reflects the same analogy to the Trinity. We conceive something in our minds (invisible), perhaps a poem or a symphony; we express it in speech or writing or in music and it enters the present, visible world; it is then appreciated in the emotions, once again invisible.

We could offer more analogies, but these should be enough. There is no doubt that the Bible clearly presents three Persons who are distinct, yet each is God. At the same time, we repeatedly have the clear statement that there is only one true God. Christ prays to the Father. Is He praying to Himself? We are told, "The Father sent the Son to be the Savior of the world" (1 John 4:14). Did He send Himself? Or did one "office" pray to and send a "title," as the United Penecostal Church would have us believe?

Christ said, "The words that I speak unto you I speak not of myself [on my own initiative], but the Father that dwelleth in me, he doeth the works" (John 14:10); "I will pray the Father, and he shall give you another Comforter ...even the Spirit of truth" (John 14:16,17). Throughout the New Testament, Father, Son, and Holy Spirit are each separately honored and act as God, yet only in concert with one another.

*With perhaps a dozen exceptions, the text of every verse in the New Testament may be said to be so far settled by general consent of scholars that any dispute as to its readings must relate rather to the interpretation of the words than to any doubts respecting the words themselves.*

*But in every one of Shakespeare's thirty-seven plays [written only 400 years ago] there are probably a hundred readings still in dispute, a large portion of which materially affects the meaning of the passages in which they occur.*

—John Lea[1]

# 3

# Is the Bible
# Reliable?

## DO THE DEAD SEA SCROLLS REFLECT
## BADLY ON THE BIBLE?

*Question:* It is my understanding that the discovery of
the Dead Sea Scrolls was a blow to the Bible. The oldest copies
of some Old Testament texts ever found were included in this
find and turned out to be far different from the later copies already in our possession. If the copyists had made such errors
in those few centuries, how far must the Bible of today be
from the original Old Testament manuscripts!

*Response:* I don't know where you got your informa-
tion, but it is false. It was *anticipated by Bible critics* that great
differences would be found, but that turned out not to be the
case. Consider, for example, the manuscript of Isaiah now
housed in its own museum in Jerusalem. The earliest copy
we had of Isaiah prior to the Dead Sea discoveries was dated
about A.D. 900 and the one discovered in the Dead Sea collection was dated about 100 B.C. So here was an opportunity
to see what changes might have occurred through copyists'
inadvertent errors over the span of 1000 years.

A comparison revealed a few spelling variations,
some stylistic changes, and a rare word here and there

that had either been left out or added but which did not change the meaning of the text. So in 1000 years of copying the text had been preserved without any real or significant change. The fact is that the discovery of the Isaiah scroll in the Qumran cave provided hard evidence that we have in our hands today the Old Testament as it was in the original documents.

## What About Divine Inspiration?

*Question:* The Judeo-Christian Bible is not the only book which claims to be inspired of God. There are the Koran, the Hindu Vedas, the Book of Mormon, and others which claim to have come from God. Doesn't the very fact that Christianity teaches that the other books are not true cast serious doubt upon the Bible as well? If so many others could be wrong, why not one more? After all, an atheist only doubts one more book than the Christian doubts.

*Response:* Whether the scriptures of other religions are true or false has no bearing upon the Bible's validity or lack thereof. The fact that 10 of 11 contestants failed to win a race could hardly be taken as a plausible argument that therefore no one could have won. That there is counterfeit money in abundance does not suggest for even a moment that real money doesn't exist. In fact, it argues for its existence, because otherwise counterfeiting would have no purpose. That billions of people are willing to accept the sacred writings of various religions as having been inspired by God shows a deep hunger within mankind for divine revelation that has always existed in all ages, in all races and cultures, and in all places.

Such a universal and powerful hunger could not have been developed by evolution. The human body does not hunger or thirst for some nonexistent food or drink but only for that which exists and would sustain its life. The only exception would be if one had tasted something which was harmful but delicious or which produced deceptive feelings of well-being or power and then craved it unnaturally. A craving for that drug or intoxicating beverage would never have arisen, however, had it not actually been tasted or experienced. Thus one could not claim that belief in God was "the opiate of the masses" without admitting God's existence. Someone must have "tasted" something real, as the Bible challenges us: "O taste and see that the LORD is good..." (Psalm 34:8).

Logically, then, the universal hunger for God argues persuasively for His existence; and the hunger for revelation from Him argues that such revelation exists as well. Whether what claims to come from God actually does so, however, can only be determined on the basis of the facts—and only the Bible passes that test, as we shall see.

The fact that the world is filled with false prophecies claiming to come from God is exactly what one would expect, given this innate thirst for God and the willingness of the human heart to deceive itself and others. Nor can it be inferred from the fact that many false prophecies have been proclaimed that therefore no true prophecy has ever been uttered. That mankind has universally in all places, at all times, and under all religions been susceptible to false predictions is evidence of an intuitive belief that true prophecy must be possible and important.

The Bible must be examined on its own merits. It will be shown to be either true or false on the basis of the internal and external evidence taken together—not by comparing it with the sacred writings of other religions. Furthermore, the Bible's very claim to be the *only* revelation from God to mankind requires that all other sacred writings be false. So their falseness, far from proving that the Bible can't be true, is an argument in its favor.

## How Reliable Are The Biblical Documents?

*Question:* I was taught in seminary and have read the same charge in a number of scholarly books that the New Testament is not reliable because it was written centuries after the time of Christ by men who weren't even alive in Christ's day. The "Jesus Seminar," a group of scholars with impressive credentials, makes this claim today. Is there any evidence to the contrary?

*Response:* That accusation is disproved not only by the manuscripts themselves but by the quotations which we have of the entire New Testament in other writings from the late first to early second century. There is proof even from the writings of Christianity's enemies. For example, Celsus, a bitter opponent of Christianity who was born early in the second century, referred to the four Gospels as part of the sacred books of Christians and already well-known in his day. Just that one piece of evidence disproves the claim that the New Testament wasn't written until centuries later! In addition, there is more than sufficient proof from within the New Testament itself that it was, as its writers claim, written by contemporaries of Jesus.

---

The authors of the epistles of Peter and John testify to having known Christ personally and to having been eyewitnesses of all He said and did during His ministry. Peter writes: "For we have not followed cunningly devised fables when we made known unto you the power and coming of our Lord Jesus Christ, but were eyewitnesses of his majesty" (2 Peter 1:16). Speaking for himself and the other apostles, John testifies to an intimate relationship with Christ: "That which...we have heard, which we have seen with our eyes, which we have looked upon, and our hands have handled..." (1 John 1:1).

If the New Testament, which includes such sworn testimonies, was not written by the apostles themselves but was concocted centuries (or even only decades) later by other parties, the whole thing is a fraud! Whoever wrote such tales was lying and was doing so with the deliberate intent of deceiving untold multitudes throughout the coming centuries. And tragically, if this is the case, the deceit has been swallowed by hundreds of millions ever since. That very scenario, however, contains numerous insurmountable problems.

## IRREFUTABLE INTERNAL EVIDENCE

First of all, there is an internal consistency within the Bible's 66 books, even though they were written over a period of about 1500 years by more than 40 persons, most of whom had never met one another. Living in different historical eras and widely differing regions and cultures, the only thing these writers of Scripture had in common was the claim that what they wrote was inspired by the one true God. The intricate pattern of truth woven without contradiction throughout the Bible from Genesis to Revelation bears powerful witness to the validity of that claim, which can be explained in no other manner. As for seeming contradictions, we will deal with them.

This continuity and agreement throughout the Bible is one of the most powerful arguments that it is the Word of God. To show how remarkable this argument is, Josh McDowell tells this true story:

> A representative of the *Great Books of the Western World* came to my house recruiting salesmen for their series. . . . I challenged him to take just 10 of the authors, all from one walk of life, one generation, one place, one time, one mood, one continent, one language and just one controversial subject (the Bible speaks on hundreds with harmony and agreement).
>
> Then I asked him: "Would they (the authors) agree?"
>
> He paused and then replied, "No."[2]

Obviously, any fraudulent writer (for example, of the life and works of Christ) would have to know the entire Bible intimately and be able to maintain its supernatural internal consistency. It is highly unlikely that any deliberate liar would have either the motivation or the ability to do so.

There is a further problem. Careful study of the New Testament reveals a sincerity and truthfulness that would be virtually impossible to fake. Moreover, the Bible has demonstrated a supernatural power to rescue human beings from sin and degradation and to bring liberty, joy, love, and a transformation of life to all who believe its message. That a deliberate fraud could effect so much good is preposterous. It would require more faith to believe *that* scenario than to accept the Bible's claim to divine inspiration!

## CONTEMPORARY CORROBORATION

Additional proof abounds of a different nature. We know from archaeological discoveries of quotations in other writings that the New Testament in its entirety was in circulation at least by the end of the first century. Many people were still alive at that time who had known the apostles and to whom their writings rang true to fact. There would have been an enraged outcry had the epistles not told the truth—yet we have no such evidence. The Jewish rabbis unquestionably would have jumped on the slightest lie or exaggeration and used it to discredit this "new religion," as they considered it, which was undermining their leadership and resulting in conversions by the thousands from Judaism. There is no record of any attack on those grounds from that quarter.

Furthermore, there is abundant and indisputable evidence within the New Testament itself that it was written by eyewitnesses. Luke, for example, referred to the other Gospel writers as having been eyewitnesses "from the beginning" and affirmed that what they had recorded was "most surely believed among us." He was not some gullible idiot who was willing to believe any tale that came along, but claimed himself to have had "perfect understanding of all things from the very first" (Luke 1:1-3). He declared that he had undertaken to write down the story of Jesus for his friend Theophilus so that he could "know the certainty of those things . . ." (Luke 1:4).

Modern archaeological discoveries have confirmed the veracity of Luke's testimony and the fact that he was indeed a contemporary of the apostles and thus in a position to know and report the facts. In chapter 2 Luke refers to "a decree from Caesar Augustus that all the world should be taxed" and asserts that this occurred "when Cyrenius was governor of Syria" (verses 1,2). Some critics continue to dogmatically state that Cyrenius (known also as Quirinius) didn't become governor over Syria until A.D. 6, too late a date for the birth of Christ. They ignore more recent findings which show that Quirinius was governor over Syria *twice*, the first time from perhaps as early as 7 B.C. to about A.D. 1. Luke was obviously referring to his *first* governorship, not the second.

## WATERTIGHT HISTORICAL VERIFICATION

In chapter 3 Luke provides a whole list of detailed information of names, places, offices, and dates which surely would not have been known by someone writing even decades (much less centuries) later:

> In the fifteenth year of the reign of Tiberias Caesar, Pontius Pilate being governor of Judea, and Herod being tetrarch of Galilee, and his brother Philip tetrarch of Iturea and of the region of Trachonitis, and Lysanias the tetrarch of Abilene, Annas and Caiaphas being the high priests . . . (Luke 3:1,2).

Note that Luke's reference is not to just any Caesar, but to *Tiberias*. Even the time of the decree is given: in the "fifteenth year" of his reign. These facts have been verified by modern historians and could not have been known by someone writing centuries later, as the skeptics claim was the case. The technical titles of the offices held by the other parties named—governor, tetrarch, high priest—are given, together with the locations of each. Each fact presented has been verified in recent years after laborious digging and research. It would have been impossible to have made such precise statements even 50 years after the fact. We therefore have every reason to believe that Luke, as he claims, was present when these reported events occurred.

Yes, but what about Pilate, whom Luke says was governor of Judea at this time? The skeptics denied his very existence for many years because no trace of him could be found. Josephus mentioned Pilate in his *Antiquities of the Jews*, but that was suspected to be a later addition by someone tampering with the text. And then one day proof positive was uncovered in an archaeological dig: a large quarried stone about 5 inches thick in the jumbled ruins of an ancient Roman theater in Caesarea.

It turned out that Caesar, having been offended by Pilate, decreed that all evidence of his existence be obliterated. This particular stone, however, because of its precise size, had been saved and used as a seat in a theater. Of course, the side containing the inscription regarding Pilate had been turned downward so it couldn't be seen—until its discovery in the ruins. The stone stands today in Caesaria in modern Israel as one more testimony (among many others) to the reliability of the biblical record.

Today the accumulated evidence authenticating the Bible in every respect is overwhelming. Any critic who continues to parrot the specious charges formerly leveled against the Bible is doing so *in spite of* and not *because of* the facts. Even Bishop Robinson of "God Is Dead" fame, a foremost proponent a few years ago of a centuries-later date for the biblical writings, now acknowledges the historicity of the New Testament documents and that they were written early in the first century by eyewitnesses.

## MUST WE BECOME EXPERTS ON ALL RELIGIONS?

*Question:* Since there are so many sacred books of various religions, all of which claim to be true, how can anyone be sure that the Bible is the true Word of God without first examining all the others? Even though another sacred writing might be mostly false, couldn't it still have enough truth in it to make it worth the time and effort to examine all religious writings?

*Response:* That philosophy leads to liberalism's conclusion that there is no definitive truth and no conclusive answer to any question whatsoever. For example, how could one be certain that two plus two was *only* four without first examining whether it might not also be 3 or 5 or 6 or 7 or every other number? Since numbers are infinite, one would never come to the end of the search. So it is with religion: No one could live long enough to examine every claim of every religion that has ever existed. Nor is such an effort necessary.

Thankfully, truth is not arrived at by a process of elimination. The fact that two plus two equals four *and only four* can be proved without looking at every other number. And so it is with the Bible: Its validity can be determined from examining it alone.

### THE EXCLUSIVITY OF THE BIBLE'S CLAIMS

Whether the Bible is true or not depends upon the facts relating to that particular book. It is not to be arrived at by examining all other sacred books, concluding that none of the others is true, and then because the Bible is the only religious book left, accepting it. Every sacred book, including the Bible itself, could be and would be false if there were no God and/or if God had not chosen to reveal Himself and His will to mankind in written form. Whether He has done so or not is a question which cannot be answered by a process of elimination but must be determined factually.

Furthermore, if the Bible is the Word of God, as it claims (such terms as "Thus saith the Lord," "The word of the Lord came unto me," etc. are found about 3800 times in the Bible), then all other sacred books must be false just as all other gods must be false. The God of the Bible says He is the only true God: "I am the first, and I am the last; and beside me there is no God....Is there a God beside me? Yea, there is no God; I know not any....There is no God else beside me...for I am God, and there is none else..." (Isaiah 44:6,8; 45:21,22). If He is God alone, then the Bible through which He speaks must be His Word alone also.

Once one has come to know the true God, there is no need to check out all other possible gods just in case one of them might have some legitimacy. That possibility has been eliminated by knowing that the God of the Bible is the *only* true God. And once one has verified the Bible's claim to be the *only* Word of God by internal and external proofs, by archaeological and historical evidence, and most of all by meeting the Christ and God of the Bible, then there is no need to examine any other sacred books to see whether one of them might not have some truth in it as well.

The only reason for becoming familiar with other religions and other religious writings would be in order to show those who follow these false systems wherein the error lies and thereby to rescue them.

## WHAT DOES ARCHAEOLOGY SAY ABOUT THE BIBLE?

---

*Question:* I have been told that there is a great deal of archaeological evidence proving that the Bible is not reliable. I don't remember the details and perhaps none were given, but the impression I've gotten from several professors at the university is that the archaeological evidence against the Bible is pretty solid.

*Response:* There have been many claims that the Bible is not true, but none of them has been able to stand up under careful scrutiny. The Bible claims to be the Word of God, which He inspired prophets and apostles to put in writing for the benefit of all mankind. As such it must be infallible and without any error. Therefore, it would not take "a great deal" of archaeological or any other kind of evidence to disprove the Bible. One piece of evidence would be enough.

---

Paul wrote, "All scripture is given by inspiration of God" (2 Timothy 3:16) and Peter declared that "holy men of God spoke [or wrote] as they were moved [inspired] by the Holy Ghost [Spirit of God]" (2 Peter 1:21). Even one error in the *substance* of the Bible (not a copyist's or printer's error) would prove it was not what it claims to be, the Holy Word of God. You have given me no specific examples, so I can only reply in general.

The Bible is without doubt the most remarkable as well as the most controversial book in the world. Its claim to be inspired of God has caused those who don't believe in God and those who follow rival religions to attack its credibility. In fact, it has been attacked by determined skeptics and professional critics for centuries as no other book in history. In every instance, however, when the facts have been established through archaeological findings, the Bible has been proven correct and its critics wrong. This has been the case 100 percent of the time—as it would have to be if the Bible is indeed God's Word.

As just one example, the early chapters of the Bible have a great deal to say about the Hittites. According to the biblical account, they were a numerous and powerful people in the days of Abraham and continuing at least into the time of King David. We are told that one of David's army captains was a Hittite named Uriah. David arranged for Uriah's murder in order to cover the sin of having made his wife pregnant. Yet decades of digging had failed to uncover any archaeological evidence for the Hittites. Consequently the skeptics claimed that the Bible was a book of myths because it presented fictitious details concerning a people who had never existed.

Then the discoveries began to pour in. Today we have abundant archaeological evidence that what the Bible said concerning the Hittites is absolutely true. One entire museum in Ankara, Turkey, is devoted to Hittite relics.

A more recent development comes through the finding in 1993 at Tel Dan of the "now-famous Aramaic [stone] inscription fragment referring to the House of David. Some scholars...[had] denied that David was a historical figure or that a united kingdom preceded Judah and Israel.[3]" Once again the Bible was vindicated. In 1994 two more fragments of the same stone inscription were discovered, again mentioning the House of David.[4] Many other similar examples could be given.

Today no one doubts the existence of King David and the history of his reign as recorded in the Bible. In September 1995, all of Israel began a 15-month-long celebration of the three-thousandth anniversary of the founding of Jerusalem by David.

As a result of its continual verification by archaeological findings, the Bible is used by many of today's archaeologists as a guide in locating ancient cities. In fact, Israeli public schools teach students the history of their land and ancestors from the Old Testament, knowing that it is unfailingly accurate.

The truth is that rather than archaeological evidence pointing *against* the Bible, the archaeological evidence is all in its *favor*. Anyone who says the contrary is either ignorant of the current evidence or is heavily biased and unwilling to face it.

## WHAT ABOUT THE MANUSCRIPTS?

---

*Question:* It is my understanding that the Bible we have comes from a handful of ancient manuscripts which are copies of copies of copies of the originals that have long been lost. These originals, especially for the Old Testament, could have been several thousand years older than the oldest manuscripts. How do we know that what we have today is even close to the originals?

*Response:* Bernard Ramm reminds us: "Jews preserved it [the Old Testament text] as no other manuscript has ever been preserved...they kept tabs on every letter. They had special classes of men within their culture whose sole duty was to preserve and transmit these documents with practically perfect fidelity—scribes, lawyers, massoretes. Who ever counted the letters and syllables and words of Plato or Aristotle, Cicero or Seneca [as the Jews did for the Old Testament]?"[5] No wonder, then, that the Isaiah scroll found among the Dead Sea Scrolls showed no significant variation in 1000 years of copying. In contrast, as already noted, there are many questions concerning the text of Shakespeare, which is only about 400 years old.

---

Biblical scholar F.F. Bruce writes: "There is no body of ancient literature in the world which enjoys such a wealth of good textual attestation as the New Testament."[6] J. Harold Greenlee explains: "[T]he number of available manuscripts of the New Testament is overwhelmingly greater than those of any work of ancient literature . . . [and] the earliest extant manuscripts of the New Testament were written much closer to the date of the original writing...."[7] For the sake of comparison, here are some well-accepted, ancient secular works showing the author, the date written, the number of manuscripts surviving, and the number of years after the date written for the earliest manuscript:

| | | | |
|---|---|---|---|
| Sophocles | 496-406 B.C. | 100 | 1400 |
| Herodotus | 480-425 B.C. | 8 | 1300 |
| Euripedes | 480-406 B.C. | 9 | 1500 |
| Thucydides | 460-400 B.C. | 8 | 1300 |
| Plato | 427-327 B.C. | 7 | 1200 |
| Aristotle | 384-322 B.C. | 5 | 1400 |
| Demosthenes | 383-322 B.C. | 200 | 1300 |
| Caesar | 100- 44 B.C. | 10 | 1000 |
| Lucretius | 60 B.C. | 2 | 1600 |
| Tacitus | 100 A.D. | 20 | 1000 |

In contrast, there are about 24,600 copies of New Testament manuscripts, some of which date back within a century of the originals and many others within about 300 to 400 years. Then why does one continually hear the false claim that the biblical manuscripts are not reliable? The fact that this lie persists in academic circles demonstrates the extreme prejudice against the Bible *because of what it says.* God's Word convicts the conscience. How interesting that questions about the accuracy of the manuscripts are never raised for other ancient writings— unless they offer proof of the Bible's validity. *The Antiquities of the Jews,* by Josephus, offers considerable verification of the New Testament and the life and death of Jesus, so it too comes under vicious attack.

The Bible is the most quoted book in the world, thousands of times more so than any secular work. That is not only true today but has always been the case. Consequently one can reproduce the entire New Testament and much of the Old Testament by quotations contained in personal letters and epistles written within a century after Christ commissioned His disciples to preach the gospel.

## INCOMPARABLE RELIABILITY

As for the validity of the Old Testament manuscripts and their reliability, consider the following from Princeton's Robert D. Wilson in his book *Scientific Investigation of the Old Testament*. Fluent in over 40 Semitic languages, he was one of the greatest language experts and scholars of all time. Professor Wilson writes:

> For forty-five years continuously ... I have devoted myself to the one great study of the Old Testament, in all its languages, in all its archaeology, in all its translations. ...
>
> [T]he critics of the Bible who go to it in order to find fault ... claim to themselves all knowledge and all virtue and all love of truth. One of their favorite phrases is, "All scholars agree." When a man [says that] ... I wish to know who the scholars are and why they agree. Where do they get their evidence ...? I defy any man to make an attack upon the Old Testament on the ground of evidence that I cannot investigate. ...
>
> After I learned the necessary languages I set about the investigation of every consonant in the Hebrew Old Testament. There are about a million and a quarter of these; and it took me many years to achieve my task. I had to observe the variations of the text ... in the manuscripts, or in the notes of the Massoretes ... or in the various versions, or in the parallel passages, or in the conjectural emendations of critics; and then I had to classify the results ... to reduce the Old Testament criticism to an absolutely

objective science; something which is based on evidence, and not on opinion....

The result of those 45 years' study which I have given to the text has been this: I can affirm that there is not a page of the Old Testament concerning which we need have any doubt....

[For example, to illustrate its accuracy]: There are 29 ancient kings whose names are mentioned not only in the Bible but also on monuments of their own time....There are 195 consonants in these 29 proper names. Yet we find that in the documents of the Hebrew Old Testament there are only two or three out of the entire 195 about which there can be any question of their being written in exactly the same way as they were inscribed on their own monuments [which archaeologists have to date discovered]. Some of these go back 4,000 years and are so written that every letter is clear and correct....

Compare this accuracy with...the greatest scholar of his age, the librarian at Alexandria in 200 B.C. He compiled a catalogue of the kings of Egypt, 38 in all. Of the entire number only 3 or 4 are recognizable. He also made a list of the kings of Assyria; in only one case can we tell who is meant; and that one is not spelt correctly. Or take Ptolemy, who drew up a register of 18 kings of Babylon. Not one of them is properly spelt; you could not make them out at all if you did not know from other sources to what he is referring.

If anyone talks about the Bible, ask him about the kings mentioned in it. There are 29 kings referred to, and ten different countries among these 29; all of which are included in the Bible and on monuments. Every one of these is given his right name in the Bible, his right country, and placed in correct chronological order. Think what that means...!

While the study of the religious systems of the ancient peoples has shown that there was amongst them a groping after God, *nowhere* is it to be seen that they reached any clear apprehension of the One True God, the Creator, Preserver, Judge, Saviour and Sanctifier of His people. Their religions were of an outward kind; the Old Testament religion is essentially one of the mind and heart; a religion of love, joy, faith, hope, and salvation through the grace of God. How can we account for this?

The prophets of Israel declared that their teaching came from God. The modern critical school is antagonistic to this claim. They say that the prophets gave utterance to the ideas of their own time, and that they were limited by their environment. But if this is so how does it come about that neither from the oracles of Thebes and Memphis, nor from Delphi and Rome, nor from Babylon, nor from the deserts of Media, but from the sheep-folds and humble homes of Israel, yea, from the captive by the river of an alien land, came forth those great messages of hope and salvation?

## Where Does Prophecy Fit In And Why?

---

*Question:* I have heard it said that the prophecies in the Bible are worded in such a way that their alleged "fulfillment" could fit almost anything. Is this true? And if not, what is the purpose of prophecy? It seems to me that for the Bible even to be involved in prophecy puts it in the realm of speculation and detracts from its credibility and reliability and its excellent teaching on morals.

*Response:* The Bible is about 30 percent prophecy, and for this reason alone it is absolutely unique. There are no prophecies in the Koran, in the Hindu Vedas or the Bhagavad-Gita, in the sayings of Buddha and Confucius, in the Book of Mormon, or anywhere except in the Bible. Nor are there any prophecies concerning the coming of Buddha, Krishna, Mohammed, Zoroaster, Confucius, or the founder or leader of any other of the world's religions. The Jewish Messiah is absolutely unique in this respect. His coming was foretold in dozens of specific prophecies which were fulfilled in minutest detail in the life, death, and resurrection of Jesus Christ.

---

There are a number of reasons for biblical prophecy: to prove God's existence by telling us what will happen in advance; to identify the Messiah by specifying numerous details concerning His coming, including even when and where; and to warn the faithful of conditions and dangers in the last days. (We deal with these elements of prophecy in other books.) As for being "worded in such a way that its alleged 'fulfillment' could fit almost anything," that simply is not true, as any examination of biblical prophecy proves.

### AN IMPECCABLE PROPHETIC RECORD

Inasmuch as fulfilled prophecy proves conclusively both the existence of God and that the Bible is His Word, the Bible's prophecies have been critically examined in many strenuous attempts to disprove them. For example, so many factual details are given in the book of Daniel concerning the Medo-Persian, Grecian, and Roman empires that the skeptics tried hard to prove that these prophecies had actually been written after the events had occurred. Otherwise they would have to admit that the Bible had indeed foretold the future. The date of Daniel was therefore attacked from every imaginable angle over the past two centuries. Every assault failed, however, and the book of Daniel stands impregnable today.

It was, of course, a complete waste of time to attempt to prove that Daniel had been written after the rise and fall of the four world empires which it foretold. Even the most critical skeptics had to admit that this book had been part of the canon of the Old Testament at least before the coming of Christ and that events subsequent to Christ's birth were presented accurately. The book of Daniel, for example (as we shall see later), foretold the very day (April 6, 32 A.D.) that Jesus would ride into Jerusalem on a donkey (as Zechariah 9:9 had prophesied) and be hailed as the Messiah—the day which is now celebrated as Palm Sunday. Daniel foretold the splitting of the Roman Empire into two parts (East and West) centuries before it occurred. Politically and militarily that split between East and West came in

A.D. 330, when Constantine moved his capital to Constantinople. Religiously it came in A.D. 1054, when Pope Leo IX excommunicated Michael Cerularius, Patriarch of Constantinople.

We will go into specific prophecies later. Before moving on, however, let us consider one brief quote concerning prophecy from the fascinating book *A Lawyer Examines the Bible*:

> The prophecies about the Jews—as about the coming Messiah ... [are] specific (in contrast with the Delphic and other Pagan oracles who ... hedge[d] against mistake[s]) ... [and are] so numerous as to make accidental fulfillment almost infinitely improbable ... [and] of such nature that the events predicted seemed beforehand mutually destructive and were and are unparalleled in human history....
>
> [Consider] the fact that the Jewish Passover has been celebrated continuously ... [for] 3,500 years (although the sacred fires of Persia and those tended by the Vestal Virgins of Rome which were to be kept burning forever have been out for centuries) ... in the light of the words we find in this same old Book:
>
> And ... ye shall keep it [the passover] a feast to the Lord throughout your generations ... forever (Exodus 12:14).[8]

## An Overworked Lie

*Question:* My psychology professor at the university claims that anyone can get any idea he wants out of the Bible. It can be made to say anything the person reading it wants to believe. And he says that's the reason why there are so many differences among those who claim to follow the Bible: for example, between Catholics and Protestants and between the hundreds of Protestant denominations. How then can anyone rely upon the Bible for anything?

*Response:* A moment's thought would show the absurdity of the basic premise in this argument. Language has meaning. A statement may be so constructed that its meaning is uncertain, or it is ambiguous and thus seems to support two contradictory ideas. In such cases, the uncertainty or ambiguity is readily recognized by anyone reading or hearing such a statement. No one would be deceived by nor pay any attention to that which has no clear meaning.

---

The professor's amazing claim, however, goes far beyond saying that the Bible is contradictory or ambiguous. He is saying that *any* idea can be derived from it and apparently justified logically. If that were actually true, then for that reason alone the Bible would be the most remarkable book in the world, for no other piece of writing can be taken logically to mean anything one chooses.

As for the numerous differences in doctrinal opinion and interpretation between Protestants and Roman Catholics and even within the many Protestant denominations and within the Catholic Church as well, that is only to be expected. It is inevitable that human opinions and interpretations will differ simply because we are finite beings. Tragically, stubbornness and pride also enter the equation. These are normal differences, given human frailties, and certainly require no such explanation as the ridiculous idea that the Bible is capable of any interpretation one wishes to find there.

I challenge your professor or you or anyone else to construct even one sentence which can logically be taken to mean anything one wants it to mean. No word has an infinite variety of meanings, much less could a sentence or paragraph of many words put together in meaningful sequence be so constructed as to support numerous contradictory ideas. I too have heard this accusation made against the Bible many times. It shows how badly people want to be able to dismiss the Bible and what foolish ideas they will embrace in the process of doing so.

## Is Divine Inspiration Essential?

---

*Question:* There is no doubt that the Bible contains some of the most sublime teachings on morals to be found in the world's literature. Whether these words were borrowed from other religions or came from the pen of Solomon or the lips of Christ or were written centuries later and wrongly attributed to them seems to me to be beside the point. It is the teachings that count. Nor does the fact that the Bible obviously has many errors and contradictions in it detract from its moral teachings. I don't see why the Bible has to be defended as infallible.

*Response:* There are several problems with your thesis. The Bible doesn't just present some sublime moral teachings but it makes many inescapable claims which have a bearing upon its teachings. It claims repeatedly to be the inerrant Word of God and that its teachings are inspired from God, not invented by men or borrowed from some religion. If it lies about its very foundation, then why should I accept anything else it offers? Furthermore, such a mixture of lies and sublime moral precepts would present a contradiction difficult to explain.

---

The Bible also claims to tell the true history of the Jews and of other ancient nations; the true account of the life, death, and resurrection of Christ; the true account of the early church, its persecution by the rabbis and Roman authorities, the conversion of Paul and his missionary travels, and Paul's teachings, which he claimed to have received not from the other apostles but directly from the resurrected Christ in heaven. If these and many other claims are not true, then the Bible is literally filled with lies. Would you not admit that if the Bible is filled with lies, that fact would reflect badly upon its moral teachings?

Furthermore, these other elements presented in the Bible in addition to its moral teachings are so interwoven with the whole as to constitute an integral part of the Christian faith. The Bible must either be accepted or rejected in its entirety. If it is not true in even one area, then

Christianity becomes untenable. Each part of the Bible is intimately tied to every other, so that if one falls the whole falls with it. The Bible does not contain errors and contradictions, as you suggest; and if it did, it would not be worthy of our trust.

Attorney Irwin H. Linton carefully examined the Bible just as he would a case in court. He based his faith in the Bible upon the evidence. Linton explained the vital importance of whether or not the Bible in its entirety is actually God's Word:

> The accuracy of the record of a case on appeal is a thing that must be settled beyond dispute before an appellate court will undertake or form an opinion about the trial below; and the infallibility of the record upon which rest the eternal essentials of our faith—the deity of Christ, His voluntary, atoning death, bodily resurrection and impending return in power and glory—are all rendered uncertain in a mind in which the accuracy of the Bible record is in doubt.
>
> If we do not give full faith and credit to the Written Word which we have seen, experience proves that we are in great danger sooner or later of diminishing the love and honor we give the Living Word [Christ] whom we have not seen; for our conviction that...God became flesh and dwelt among us...is based upon the facts on which such conclusion rests; and if the record of the facts be impugned, who can retain the conclusion based upon them?
>
> The deadly effect upon my faith and the insuperable difficulties in which I found myself involved when I made a tentative trial of the view... that the Bible may be wrong, and is only human in all but its religious teachings, made this matter clear to me for all time.... [9]

## WHO COULD BELIEVE THE BIBLE'S MIRACLES?

*Question:* It seems to me that the strongest case against the Bible is the miracles it describes. These are so fantastic as to render whatever else the Bible says unreliable. As Reinhold Seeberg said, "Miracle was once the foundation of all apologetics, then it became an apologetic crutch, and today it is... a cross for apologetics to bear." Obviously the Bible was written by very gullible and superstitious men for whom fantasy was normal and who were therefore not embarrassed by telling about alleged miracles. How can you possibly trust a book that presents such obviously fictitious tales, especially when modern science has proven that miracles don't happen?

*Response:* On the contrary, not only has science never "proven that miracles don't happen," but such proof would be categorically impossible, since science deals only with natural phenomena. Of course miracles don't happen *naturally* or in *nature*. A miracle, by very definition, is *supernatural*. It defies all physical laws or it wouldn't be a miracle in the first place. *A miracle must be beyond the ability of science to explain,* and thus it is also beyond the ability of science to disprove.

---

Consequently there is no valid scientific or logical basis for saying that miracles can't occur precisely as the Bible describes them. To insist upon such a position betrays a prejudice which in itself prevents one from facing the abundant evidence in favor of miracles. When Albert Einstein was asked what effect his theory of relativity would have upon religion he bluntly replied, "None. Relativity is a purely scientific theory and has nothing to do with religion."[10]

Miracles are impossible only if the universe is a closed system and all there is. In that case, of course, whatever happens must be a natural occurrence functioning according to the laws that govern the universe. The famous evolutionist and atheist Thomas H. Huxley "proved" that miracles couldn't happen by defining "nature" as "that which is; the sum of the phenomena presented to our experience; the totality of events, past, present, and to come."[11] For all his claim to honor evidence and logic, however, Huxley gives not one piece of evidence or reason to support this assertion. He simply does away with miracles by setting rules that make them impossible, which is like proving atheism by declaring that God by very definition doesn't exist. Miracles would be impossible in pantheism as well because in that belief system nature is everything.

However, if God, the infinite and transcendent Creator of the universe, exists as separate and distinct from His creation, then miracles are possible. Indeed, they are *inevitable* if God is to intervene at all in the downward course of human affairs and of nature. Whenever God reaches in from outside to effect anything that is not according to the normal course of events (such as salvation or raising the dead), it is a miracle. So if you believe in God, you believe in miracles.

### CHRISTIANITY ALONE REQUIRES MIRACLES

Christianity isn't embarrassed by the recital of miracles in the Bible. On the contrary, Christianity is based upon the greatest miracle of all, the resurrection of Christ. Unlike Mohammed, Buddha, Confucius, or any other religious leader, none of whom even dared to make such a claim, Jesus said He would rise from the dead. If He didn't, He is a liar and Christianity is a fraud. Listen to Paul's testimony:

> Moreover, brethren, I declare unto you the gospel...how that Christ died for our sins...that he was buried, and that he rose again the third day ...and that he was seen of Cephas [Peter], then of the twelve....
> And if Christ be not risen, then is our preaching vain, and your faith is also vain. Yea, and we are found false witnesses of God, because we have testified of God that he raised up Christ...(1 Corinthians 15:1, 3-5, 14, 15).

Christianity doesn't apologize for miracles or back away and shrug its shoulders as though it isn't really important whether miracles happen or not. Christianity *requires* miracles. This is not the case with Buddhism or

Hinduism or Islam or any other of the world's religions, which get along quite well without miracles. Their leaders left a philosophy of life and certain rules to follow which have no bearing upon whether Buddha, Krishna, Mohammed, et al are alive or dead or even lived at all. Not so with Christianity.

The Christian faith stands or falls upon the sinless life, the sacrificial death, and the miraculous resurrection of Jesus Christ—and all other miracles are minor occurrences in comparison to that one. If the resurrection actually happened, then for God to open blind eyes or heal any illness or make the lame walk or even to open the Red Sea is obviously within the realm of possibility.

## TESTIMONY THAT STANDS THE SEVEREST TESTS

As for the specious claim that those who recorded the miracles were so simple and ignorant that they thought such things were normal, the evidence is all to the contrary. The disciples were frightened when they saw Christ walking on water (Matthew 14:26). They were fearful of Him, wondering what kind of person He was, when He calmed the storm with a word (Mark 4:41). Thinking they had seen a ghost, they were terrified when He stood in their midst alive after His resurrection (Luke 24:37). In fact, they were so skeptical that He had to prove to them that it was really He!

This was not the behavior of gullible persons who lived in a fantasy world. On the contrary, the disciples had a very clear grasp of what was normal and were frightened by Christ's miracles, which suddenly shattered their world. We hear the ring of truth in their accounts of these events as they confess their fear and unbelief.

We will consider the specific evidence for the resurrection in a later chapter. At this point, however, let us quote some of the world's foremost experts on evidence, experts who were convinced of the resurrection of Jesus Christ precisely on the basis of the evidence. Lord Lyndhurst, recognized as one of the greatest legal minds in British history, declared: "I know pretty well what evidence is; and I tell you, such evidence as that for the Resurrection has never broken down yet."[12] Simon Greenleaf, America's foremost authority on legal evidence during his lifetime, came to the same conclusion, as did Sir Robert Anderson, head of the Criminal Investigation Division of Scotland Yard, plus scores of others whom we have insufficient space to name. Professor Thomas Arnold, who held the chair of Modern History at Oxford, wrote:

> I have been used for many years to study the histories of other times, and to examine and weigh the evidence of those who have written about them, and I know of no one fact in the history of mankind which is proved by better and fuller evidence of every sort, to the understanding of a fair inquirer, than the great sign which God hath given us that Christ died and rose again from the dead.[13]

Many a youthful seeker has been swept into unbelief by the contemptuous declarations of liberal clergy or university professors, delivered with the finality of superior wisdom, that "no intelligent person believes in the miracles in the Bible, much less in the resurrection!" But in fact nothing could be further from the truth. The few statements above should be enough to counter such misinformation. Indeed, many of the most humble and earnest Christians have been the most brilliant, the most knowledgeable, and the best qualified to examine and evaluate the evidence that we will be considering carefully.

*The Bible is not such a book a man would write if he could, or could write if he would.*

—Lewis S. Chafer

*Infidels for eighteen hundred years have been refuting and overthrowing this book, and yet it stands today as solid as a rock. Its circulation increases, and it is more loved and cherished and read today than ever before....*

*When the French monarch proposed the persecution of the Christians... an old statesman and warrior said to him, "Sire, the Church of God is an anvil that has worn out many hammers." So the hammers of infidels have been pecking away at this book for ages, but the hammers are worn out, and the anvil still endures.*

*If this book had not been the book of God, men would have destroyed it long ago.*

—H.L. Hastings[1]

# 4
# Contradictions in the Bible?

## WHAT YEAR WAS JESUS BORN?

*Question:* Matthew says Christ's birth was during the reign of Herod [the Great] (Matthew 2:1). Herod died, by all accounts, in 4 B.C., so Christ could not have been born any later than that. Yet Luke says that Jesus had just turned 30 years old in the fifteenth year of Tiberius Caesar (Luke 3:1,23), who began to reign in A.D. 14. So that would mean Jesus was 30 in A.D. 29? and thus was born in 1 B.C., three years after Herod's death, thoroughly destroying Matthew's timing! In a further contradiction, Luke puts Christ's birth when Cyrenius was governor of Syria, but he didn't take that office until A.D. 6. Episcopalian Bishop John S. Spong of Newark, New Jersey, says that such contradictions prove the Bible isn't reliable.[2] I believe the Bible is true. Can you help me?

*Response:* The seeming contradictions you mention (as well as many others) have been eagerly (in fact, too eagerly) raised by a number of skeptics as "proof" that the Bible contains errors and thus cannot be God's Word. One needs to remember that the Bible has been "proven" wrong many times on the basis of then-available knowledge either of science or history. However, in every case, when all the facts were at last uncovered, the Bible was vindicated and the critics were red-faced. It is the same here.

---

## QUIRINIUS—CYRENIUS WAS GOVENOR OF SYRIA TWICE

First of all, the dates that Bishop Spong and other critics use in this presumed refutation were never by any means certain. Historians did not accept them. It would be foolish to throw away one's confidence in the Bible on the basis of dates which are questionable at best. For example, Will Durant in *The Story of Civilization*, Volume III, indicated that he did not know when Quirinius (another spelling for Luke's Cyrenius) began his governorship over Syria. If Durant, one of the most highly respected of all historians, said the exact date was unknown, I would be suspicious of a critic who, in order to "prove" the Bible wrong, states dogmatically that Quirinius began his reign in A.D. 6!

Furthermore, on the basis of new evidence since Durant wrote his history, as aready noted, other historians such as A. W. Zumpt are convinced that Quirinius was governor over Syria *twice*, the first time from at least as early as 4 B.C. That governorship ended in A.D. 1. John Elder believes Quirinius' first time as governor began as early as 7 B.C.[3] Christ's birth, of course, had to be no later than 4 B.C., which would have been when Quirinius was governor the *first* time, exactly as Luke states.

## AS FOR TIBERIUS CAESAR—MOST INTERESTING!

As for the alleged problem with the date of the reign of Tiberius Caesar, the historical evidence for its resolution has been well-known for many years. Yes, Augustus Caesar died in A.D. 14 and that date is therefore generally listed as the official beginning of the reign of his successor, Tiberius Caesar. However, the skeptics are so eager to find a flaw in the Bible that they fail to dig deeply enough to discover the perfectly sound reason for an earlier date.

In actual fact, Tiberius, though technically not yet the Caesar, had already begun to rule the empire some years before Augustus' death because the latter was elderly and in poor health. Rebellions had cost the lives of those possible successors closest to Augustus. Left without either aide or successor, Augustus had in A.D. 2 adopted Tiberius as his son and coregent. Subsequently Tiberius had been sent out by Augustus to put down the rebellions and had done a masterful job. Will Durant writes:

> When he [Tiberius] returned in A.D. 9, after five years of arduous and successful campaigning, all Rome, which hated him for his stern puritanism, resigned itself to the fact that though Augustus was still prince, Tiberius had begun to rule.[4]

Counting his rule as having actually begun in A.D. 9, "the fifteenth year of the reign of Tiberius Caesar" (Luke 3:1) would be A.D. 24-25. If Jesus was born 4 or 5 B.C., just before Herod's death and during the *first* governorship of Cyrenius over Syria, that would make him 29 years of age in A.D. 24-25, at the beginning of His ministry. Notice that Luke says that He *"began* to be *about* thirty years of age."￼Of course, if He was born in 6 B.C., He would have been 30 sometime during A.D. 24. We don't have precise dates, but what we know certainly confirms the accuracy of Luke's testimony.

The above demonstrates once again how mistaken and deceitfully *biased* are the wishful criticisms of the supposed scholars such as those of the Jesus Seminar (and apostate religious leaders such as Bishop Spong) who claim that the New Testament cannot be relied upon because it was not written until centuries after the time of Jesus. In fact, the dating Luke gives, which archaeological discoveries took years to verify, could not possibly have been known and recorded with such precision even decades, much less centuries, later, as the critics insist. It could only have been known to eye-witnesses on the scene at the time, which the Bible writers claim to have been.

## Why Did God Allow Seeming Contradictions?

---

*Question:* You Christians seem to have a way of somehow coming up with a "reconciliation" of whatever contradictions and inconsistencies "unbelievers" are able to discover in the Bible. However, no matter how convincing the "reconciliation" may seem to be, I am left with a question: Why should there be so many problems that you have to work so hard to solve? It seems to me that the very fact that there are so many inconsistencies (even if you supposedly solved every one) is in itself evidence that the Bible is badly flawed and therefore could not possibly be God's Word.

*Response:* On the contrary, the many *seeming* contradictions and inconsistencies constitute a very convincing proof of the reliability of the Bible. If three witnesses who claimed to have seen an accident each described it in exactly the same language, word for word, one would have good reason to suspect collusion and to throw out their testimony. However, if each described it in his own words and from his own perspective, one would tend to believe them. Moreover, if there seemed to be some conflict in their testimonies, but if that conflict were resolved by probing deeper into the incident, that would add significantly to the trustworthiness of their testimony. So it is with the seeming contradictions in the Bible.

---

Irwin Linton, in *A Lawyer Examines the Bible,* puts it well: "The frank and artless narratives of the Bible are so obviously indifferent to the *appearance* of consistency, and show so clearly that irregularity which is the sure mark of honest handwork in the Oriental rug and of spontaneity in human testimony, that they have often lured opponents into attempts at destructive cross-examination which have only brought the Bible's truth and consistency into clearer light."[5]

One of the Bible's great strengths, then, is the reinforcing power of *apparent* inconsistencies which, in the reconciling, prove the truthfulness of the narrative.

William Paley draws attention to this fact in his writings:

> Now, in historical researches, a reconciled inconsistency becomes a positive argument. First, because an impostor generally guards against the appearance of inconsistency; and secondly, because when apparent inconsistencies are found, it is seldom that anything but truth renders them capable of reconciliation.
>
> The existence of the difficulty proves the absence of that caution which usually accompanies the consciousness of fraud; and the solution proves that it is not the collusion of fortuitous propositions which we have to deal with, but that a thread of truth winds through the whole, which preserves every circumstance in its place.[6]

## TWO GENEALOGIES FOR JESUS

---

*Question:* There are two contradictory genealogies given for Christ, tracing his ancestry back through Joseph. Matthew says Joseph's father was Jacob, but Luke says his father was Heli. Since both can't be true, at least one is wrong, but we couldn't know which. Probably both are wrong. Nor can I see how Christians could defend either genealogy, since they both say Joseph was Jesus' father and thus deny the virgin birth.

*Response:* If one is determined to prove the Bible false in order to justify an unwillingness to believe in God, then I suppose this argument might look like a good possibility, though it would take considerable mental gymnastics to maintain it. On the other hand, a little thought—and fairness—resolve the seeming problem.

---

First of all, neither Matthew nor Luke says or even implies that Joseph was the father of Jesus. On the contrary, both give a clear account of the fact that Mary was a virgin when Jesus was born. One is entitled to reject the virgin birth of Christ, but it is absurd to justify that rejection by claiming that, in spite of clear statements that Joseph was *not* the father, Matthew and Luke nevertheless then turn right around and offer a genealogy saying that Joseph *was* the father.

Let's look at the genealogies. Matthew's carefully calls Joseph "the husband of Mary," *not* the father. He explains this apparent anomaly: when "Mary was espoused [engaged] to Joseph, before they came together, she was found with child of the Holy Ghost." He explains that Joseph "knew her not [had no sex with her] till* she had brought forth her firstborn son" (Matthew 1:25; cf. 1:16, 18). In addition, Matthew declares that the birth of Jesus fulfilled the Old Testament prophecy: "Behold, a virgin shall be with child, and shall bring forth a son, and they shall call his name Emmanuel, which being interpreted is, God with us" (1:23).

Matthew's genealogy is definitely that of Joseph. This is clear because of the use of the word "begat" for each generation, ending with "Jacob begat Joseph, the *husband* of Mary" (1:16). Though not the father of Jesus, Joseph was the head of the household and functioned as the "adoptive father." Because the kingly line ran through the males, Joseph had to be of the house of David.

Luke's genealogy is just as clearly through Mary. The word "begat" is not used. Luke says that Jesus "was supposed [i.e., imagined]" to be the son of Joseph, who was "of Heli" (Luke 3:23). The word "son" is not in the original. Obviously Joseph was the *son-in-law* of Heli, Mary's father.

---

* Matthew is quite clearly indicating that Mary and Joseph had a normal marriage relationship *after* the birth of Jesus, thus denying the dogma of Mary's *perpetual virginity* which was invented some centuries later. This is consistent with both Matthew's and Luke's description of Jesus as Mary's *first*born (Matthew 1:25; Luke 2:7), implying the subsequent birth of other children, who often accompanied their mother, Mary (Matthew 12:46; Mark 3:32; Luke 8:20), some of whose names were even recorded for us (Matthew 13:55,56).

## THE LOGICAL CONSISTENCY

Luke gives the full account of the angel Gabriel's appearance to tell Mary that she would give birth to the Messiah. Her astonished response is recorded: "How shall this be, seeing I know not [have not had sex with] a man?" (1:34) Far from suggesting that Joseph was the father of Jesus, Luke makes it clear that he was not: that she was a virgin and that the Messiah was conceived in her by "the Holy Ghost" (1:35). Immediately thereafter Luke isn't going to offer a genealogy telling us that Joseph, after all, was the father of Jesus! Let's give both Matthew and Luke credit for at least reasonable intelligence.

Nor would Luke contradict Matthew and come up with an entirely different genealogy for Joseph. Matthew tells us that Jacob was the name of Joseph's father and traces his full genealogy. The records were available in the temple and were also kept by each family. Even without consulting any records, Luke would at least know the name of Joseph's father and grandfather merely by talking to friends and neighbors. And he wouldn't give an entire genealogy without knowing that it was accurate. Luke certainly knew the facts, "having had perfect understanding of all things from the very first..." (Luke 1:3) and having taken great care to investigate so that he could apprise his friend Theophilus of "the certainty of those things..." (1:4). One can only conclude that he gives the genealogy through Mary, the mother of Jesus, and there is good reason why he should have done so.

That Jesus was born of a virgin meant that He had none of King David's blood, through male descent, in His veins. Therefore, to have a physical relationship to David, it was essential that His mother be descended from David. Consequently, Luke, whose focus has been almost entirely on Mary up to this point, supplies the missing information by giving us Mary's genealogy. To assert otherwise is to charge both Matthew and Luke with a stupidity that is clearly contrary to the intelligence and honesty to which their full testimonies bear such clear and convincing witness.

## A Confusion About Roosters Crowing?.

*Question:* In Matthew, Luke, and John, Jesus tells Peter that before the cock crows *once* the next morning he will deny Him three times. Yet in Mark 14, Jesus just as clearly tells Peter that his denial will come before the cock crows *twice*. This apparent contradiction troubles me. Can you help?

*Response:* This is one more of a number of *seeming* contradictions which skeptics and critics have exploited in attempting to discredit the Bible. However, a little investigation and clear thinking shows that they are not contradictions at all. Indeed, the fact that different language is used in the four Gospels proves that the authors weren't all copying from "Q" or some such document theorized by critics. It also shows that the inspiration of the Holy Spirit did not destroy the freedom of different witnesses to express themselves. And that very freedom of expression explains many of the apparent contradictions.

Let's carefully compare the story as told in all four Gospels. Matthew 26:34 says "before the cock crow," while Luke 22:34 and John 13:38 use the negative form, "the cock shall not crow." Obviously Christ is not referring to a particular rooster crowing nor to some rooster crowing *once* but to that time in the morning known as "the *cockcrowing*." Such is the expression used in Mark 13:35, for example, when referring to the time ("at even, or at midnight, or at the *cockcrowing*, or in the morning") when Christ might return. So Jesus warns Peter that before the usual *cockcrowing* the next morning he will have denied his Lord three times. In fact, all four Gospels agree that this is what happened.

Far from contradicting the other Gospels, Mark simply gives a further detail in Christ's warning to Peter and thereby provides additional insight. He lets us know that Christ also told Peter: "Before the cock crow *twice*, thou shalt deny me thrice" (14:30). This in itself was an unusual statement. When roosters start crowing, the first is followed rather quickly by a second, third, fourth, and many subsequent crowings building to a chorus if there are many roosters in the vicinity.

Mark then reveals (14:66-72) that although Peter's first denial was long before the time of "cockcrowing" that morning, yet a rooster (or perhaps several) crowed immediately after the words were out of Peter's mouth. How do we know this first crowing was long before the time of "cockcrowing"? Though we are not told how much time elapsed between the first and second denials, Luke does inform us that "about the space of one hour" (22:59) elapsed between the second and third denials.

## A GRACIOUS FIRST WARNING UNHEEDED

The unusual crowing of a rooster an hour or more before the normal time and immediately after Peter's first denial should have brought him to repentance—which was no doubt why the Lord provided that special warning and unusual circumstance. Instead, though Peter had sworn he would die for Christ, he continued in denying his Lord two more times, at the end with extreme profanity (Mark 14:71). Immediately after the third denial, the morning's chorus of roosters (the "*cockcrowing*") sounded, and at last, repentant, Peter went outside to be alone and to weep bitterly (Matthew 26:75; Luke 22:62).

The honesty of the accounts is revealed in the fact that neither repeats the other but that each provides a piece of information which is necessary to the whole. And the inspiration of God guiding what each says, though from independent points of view, is seen in that the remarkable blending together of all four testimonies is necessary to provide us with the whole picture.

In probing deeply enough to reconcile what at first seemed like a contradiction, we have learned a valuable lesson. We see God's grace to Peter, causing a premature crowing of one or more roosters immediately after his first denial to prevent him from going any further. And has God not given similar warning at times to each of us to call us back from the brink of shame and disaster? Sometimes we have heeded, while at other times, like Peter, we have gone headlong until, overwhelmed by remorse, we have wept in repentance.

## More Contradictions Involving Peter's Denial?

*Question:* I read something about Peter's denial of the Lord that stumped me in a paper published by a group of atheists. It pointed out that according to Mark's account, Peter's second denial was the result of questioning by the *same* maid who precipitated his first denial (Mark 14:69). But Matthew 26:71 says it was *another* girl, and Luke 22:58 says it was a *man*. After Peter's first denial, Mark 14:66-69 and Matthew 26:58,71 have Peter leaving the fire in the courtyard and going to the gateway, where he was questioned by whoever it was. But John 18:25 has Peter warming himself at the fire in the courtyard when he was queried. How do we reconcile all of this?

*Response:* I am always impressed at the great deal of time and effort expended by critics in attempting to find some flaw in the Bible. Someone had to work very hard to assemble this series of apparent contradictions. Here is one more instance where it would seem that the desire to find discrepancies zealously manufactures nonexistent problems.

Mark 14:69 clearly says "*a* maid," not the *same* maid, consistent with Matthew's "*another*" maid." Luke 22:58 doesn't say it was a man who queried him. Peter's reply, "*Man*, I am not," could be an expression he used habitually; and if not, then Peter would likely have used it because of the men surrounding him who heard the maid's question. She wasn't whispering in Peter's ear in an attempt to save him embarrassment! Peter's main concern would obviously be to defend himself in the eyes of the men standing around the fire with him, who had heard this damning accusation.

In fact, precipitating the second denial, the maid, as one would expect, is indeed speaking not only to Peter but to the men warming themselves at the fire with him. This is clear from both Matthew 26:71 ("said unto them that were there") and Mark 14:69 ("began to say to them that stood by"). John 18:25 shows more clearly that the men around him got involved in Peter's questioning, exactly as one would expect. No wonder he said, "*Man....*" There is absolutely nothing contradictory in these accounts, though they are being told from slightly different perspectives. To insist upon contradiction betrays the wish as father to the thought.

As for Peter "going to the gateway," there is no such statement or implication in any of the accounts. John tells us that Peter stood outside for a short time when he first arrived until he was brought inside. Matthew, Mark and Luke are consistent in having Peter in the palace, then going onto a porch but still within the palace during his three denials.

## WHO SAW THE RESURRECTED JESUS— WHEN AND WHERE?

---

*Question:* Some of the most blatant contradictions in the Bible involve the account of the supposed resurrection of Christ upon which Christianity is founded. For example, Mark 16:1,2 says Mary Magdalene came to the tomb when the sun had risen. John 20:1 says she came to the tomb while it was still dark. Which was it?

*Response:* I checked more than 20 translations of Mark 16:1,2, and not one says "when the sun had risen." Is your bias causing you to stretch the facts a bit to make your point? I found *one paraphrase* (NEB) which says "just after sunrise"; all *translations* say "at the rising [*anatello*] of the sun."

---

The Greek *anatello* is not an exact statement of time and really means the start of the action. Anyone without an axe to grind would allow "sunrise" to include a period just before the sun peeped over the horizon as well as just after. Furthermore, the expression "cometh Mary" in John 20 would include her entire journey toward the tomb from her home. Some distance being involved, she would have set out that morning "when it was yet dark" (John 20:1) to arrive at the tomb just as the sun was coming above the horizon.

Mary sees, obviously from a distance as soon as she has a clear view of the tomb's entrance, that the stone has been rolled away. John doesn't record her being *at* the tomb until much later. Moreover, the Greek word *skotia*, translated "dark," includes the meaning of dimness, not necessarily pitch-black darkness. To be perfectly honest, if you took these two statements into a court and tried to prove them contradictory, the judge would quickly dismiss the case.

## When And Where Was The Sermon On The Mount?

*Question:* Concerning the famous Sermon on the Mount, Luke 6:12,17 says Jesus *came down* from a mountain and *stood in a plain* to address his audience. But Matthew 5:1 says Jesus *went up on a mountain* and *sat down* to address his audience. How many contradictions such as this does it take before Christians admit that the Bible is not God's infallible Word?

*Response:* Is it possible that in your eagerness to prove the Bible fallible you have overlooked the obvious? Surely you must know that the Gospels do not tell every event in time sequence. In Luke 6:12-19, Jesus goes into a mountain and prays all night, then the next day chooses His 12 disciples. This same incident is told in Matthew 10. It is not connected with the Sermon on the Mount—much less immediately followed by it, as you imply—an event which Matthew presents long before in chapter 5.

There is a break in Luke chapter 6 between verses 19 and 20. Beginning at verse 20 an earlier incident, the Sermon on the Mount, is recited, *out of sequence*. There is no connection between that part of the Gospel which is recounted in verses 12-19 and the Sermon on the Mount, which begins at verse 20. There is no contradiction between Matthew and Luke.

## ANOTHER DETERMINED TRY TO
## PROVE A CONTRADICTION

---

*Question:* The stories of the so-called "transfiguration" of Jesus on the mount seem to contain a serious contradiction. Matthew 17:1 and Mark 9:2 say that it happened *six days* later than the incident just presented. But Luke 9:28 says it was *eight days* later. I'm stumped. Can you help me?

*Response:* Actually, both Matthew and Mark say, "**After** (Greek *meta*) six days," which would be at least the *seventh day; and Luke says* "**about** *an eight days....*" "An eight days" is an idiomatic expression (like "fortnight") for a week later, and the word "about" indicates that the timing is not precise. This criticism of the Gospel account splits meaningless hairs and once again the skeptic accusing the Bible of contradiction would be laughed out of court.

---

## LET'S GET THE ANGELS STRAIGHT

---

*Question:* The resurrection of Jesus is the very foundation of Christianity, yet those who wrote the Gospels seem to be in conflict even on this most important subject! Matthew says an angel came down from heaven, rolled away the stone, and sat upon it. Mary Magdalene and the other Mary approached and were frightened. The angel told them not to be afraid, and invited them into the tomb to see where Jesus had lain (Matthew 28:1-6).

In contrast, Mark says that Mary Magdalene, Mary the mother of James, and Salome did not see the angel until they entered the tomb. The angel then pointed to where Jesus had lain (16:1-6).

In further contradiction, Luke says the women entered the tomb and as they looked for the body of Jesus, suddenly *two* angels appeared to them (Luke 24:1-4). Note also that Mark says his angel was sitting when he addressed the women, whereas Luke states that his two angels were standing (Mark 16:5; Luke 24:4).

One account says the women saw Jesus and then went to tell his disciples; another says Jesus met them on their way to tell the disciples (Matthew 28:9); and yet a third version says they "fled from the sepulchre" and didn't tell anyone or see Jesus (Mark 16:8). The disciples were told that Jesus would meet them in Galilee (Matthew 28:7; Mark 16:7), yet Luke and John say He came to them in Jerusalem. What can you make of this hopeless tangle of contradictions?

*Response:* Let's go over the accounts more carefully, remembering that each of the Gospel writers presents a condensed version of what happened. Not every movement and word of angels, the women, and disciples is recited in each Gospel. Moreover, each account is told from a different perspective.

---

First of all, Matthew does *not* say that the women saw the angel outside and he invited them in. That is nowhere stated in any of the four Gospels.

Matthew begins the story from the point of view of the Roman soldiers. He tells us that the military guard, seeing the angel roll the stone away and sit upon it, were terrified: They "did shake, and became as dead men" (28:4). They then fled to the city (28:11).

Obviously the soldiers had already gone and the angel who rolled the stone away must have been inside by the time the women arrived to find the stone already rolled away from the sepulchre (Mark 16:4; Luke 24:2). We know that the soldiers could not have still been there and the angel still outside of the sepulchre and sitting on the stone, his "countenance...like lightning" (Matthew 28:3). Could anyone imagine such circumstances and these women having the courage to walk through a platoon of terrified soldiers and right up to the awesome angel to ask him where Jesus was?

The invitation by Matthew's angel, "Come see the place where the Lord lay," is similar to Mark's, "Behold the place where they laid him." Both are compatible with directions from inside the tomb given to women who were cautiously peering in, then hesitantly entering. That one Gospel refers specifically to one angel in a certain position (and is silent about the other angel in a different position) while the other mentions *both* angels is no contradiction at all but is simply the normal variation one would expect from two true accounts of the same event given from two different perspectives.

### DIFFERENT WOMEN DO DIFFERENT THINGS

As for the action taken by the women, no Gospel says they saw Jesus before they went to call the disciples. Nor is there any contradiction in the fact that some women fled to their homes and others went to tell the disciples of the empty tomb. There were a number of women ("and certain others with them"—Luke 24:1; "and other women that were with them"—verse 10), not just the three named; and Mary Magdalene acted on her own and not as part of any group of women. She did not enter the tomb but immediately hurried to tell the disciples. The other women went into the tomb and saw the angels, who instructed them to tell the disciples He had risen. Some of the women fled in terror while others went to tell the disciples, and on their way into the city Jesus met them. There is no "tangle of confusion" here at all.

Mary had already alerted the disciples and returned with Peter and John to the grave (John 20:1-11). After they had seen that the grave was empty and went away wondering, she lingered there, confused and heartbroken, and that was when Jesus came to her.

Some of the women returned to their homes, frightened and bewildered, and said nothing. Others of them went to tell the disciples. There is no conflict here at all, but simply the normal differences in action which one would expect among a number of women.

Nor is there any conflict between the instructions to go to Galilee and the fact that the disciples didn't immediately pack up and go, but were in an inner room in Jerusalem that evening when Christ appeared to them. Their reluctance to obey further commands from the One they had *thought* was the Messiah, but no longer appeared to be in spite of rumors of a resurrection, was understandable. There is no conflict whatsoever in the accounts.

One fact is indisputable: The grave where the body of Jesus had been was empty the morning of the third day. All of the accounts make that clear, and all of the evidence supports that fact. Nor were either the Roman authorities or the rabbis able to produce the body of Jesus, though both would have done so had they been able in order to stop this revolution that was creating an uproar everywhere and which later became known as "Christianity."

## Forget "Good Friday"!

---

*Question:* The Bible says Christ was crucified the day before the Sabbath, which would mean on Friday. That the church accepts this is indicated by the worldwide "Good Friday" celebrations. Yet the Bible also says He had to be "three days and three nights" in the grave, which is clearly impossible if He was crucified on Friday afternoon and resurrected early Sunday morning, as the Bible says and Christians believe. Wouldn't this contradiction cast doubt upon all the rest of the Bible, certainly upon the very heart of Christianity, the crucifixion, and the resurrection of Christ?

*Response:* In this case the critics are correct: Christ could not have been crucified on Friday afternoon, nor does the Bible say that He was. Those who defend this position do it something like this: "The Jewish day began and ended with sunset. A partial day counts as a whole, so the day that began at Thursday sunset and ended Friday sunset was the first day; from Friday sunset to Saturday sunset was the second day; and from Saturday sunset until early Sunday morning was the third day."

---

That calculation accounts for three *days* but for only two *nights* (Friday and Saturday). But Christ specifically declared: " . . . so shall the Son of man be three days and *three nights* in the heart of the earth" (Matthew 12:40). That Christ rose on Sunday morning is clear in all four Gospels. Therefore He had to have been dead and in the grave Thursday night as well as Friday and Saturday nights.

## CHRIST WAS CRUCIFIED ON THURSDAY

In fact, it is quite clear from the Gospels that Christ *was* crucified on Thursday and died several hours before sundown (when Friday began). Thus He spent part of Thursday and all of Friday, and Saturday (*three days*) in the grave. He also spent Thursday, Friday, and Saturday nights (*three nights*) in the grave and rose first thing Sunday morning. The confusion arises because His crucifixion was "the day before the sabbath" (Mark 15:42). Luke and John agree: "And the sabbath drew on" (Luke 23:54); "that the bodies should not remain upon the cross on the sabbath day" (John 19:31).

It is a mistake, however, to conclude that because the day after His crucifixion was a Sabbath, He *must* have been crucified on Friday. *Saturday was not the only Sabbath.* There were other special Sabbaths which could fall on any day of the week, depending upon the calendar. In fact, John tells us that the day after the crucifixion was not the ordinary Saturday Sabbath but a *special* one: "That sabbath day was an high [special] day" (John 19:31). Nor are we left in doubt what that special Sabbath was: It was the Passover.

When the rabbis brought Jesus before Pilate the morning of His crucifixion, "they themselves went not into the judgment hall, lest they should be defiled, but that they might eat the passover" (John 18:28). This was the morning after the Last Supper, but the rabbis hadn't yet eaten the Passover—so neither had Jesus and His disciples. The Last Supper was *not* the Passover, as is commonly taught. That was to be celebrated the next night, which, to the disciples' shock and dismay, turned out to be the night of Christ's crucifixion. (We will deal with this in more detail later.)

## On The Cross When The Passover Lambs Were Being Slain

In remarkable fulfillment of prophecy of Exodus 12:6, Christ, whom John Baptist called "the Lamb of God" (John 1:29,36) and Paul called "our passover... sacrificed for us" (1 Corinthians 5:7), was crucified at the very time that the Passover lambs were being slain all over Israel: "It was the preparation of the passover" (John 19:14). The lambs were then roasted and eaten that night with unleavened bread as first commanded in Exodus 12. The Passover marked the beginning of the seven-day Feast of Unleavened Bread, the first day of which was a Sabbath, in which no work could be done: "Seven days shall ye eat unleavened bread...and in the first day [of the feast] . . . and in the seventh day...no manner of work shall be done" (Exodus 12:15,16).

So Thursday at sunset (in this particular year, 32 A.D., when Christ was crucified) marked the beginning of the Feast of Unleavened Bread with the eating of the Passover lamb that night. That first day lasted until Friday sunset and was a special Sabbath, a "high day," the first day of the Feast. It was immediately followed by the normal Saturday Sabbath, from Friday sunset until Saturday sunset. The women, therefore, could not get to the grave until Sunday morning. Christ was in the grave three days and three nights. He was crucified on Thursday, the very day the prophets had foretold (as we shall see). There is no contradiction at all when the facts are known.

## Couldn't Paul Count?

---

*Question:* There seems to be a major flaw in the testimony of Paul concerning the resurrection of Christ. He says that after Christ appeared to Peter he then appeared to "the twelve" (1 Corinthians 15:5). Yet the Gospels clearly state that Judas, one of the original twelve, had committed suicide before the resurrection and that there were only *eleven* disciples alive for Christ to appear to. Is there a way to escape this contradiction? Otherwise it puts all of the rest of the resurrection story in doubt.

*Response:* Of course, Christ "appeared unto the eleven as they sat at meat, and upbraided them with their unbelief" (Mark 16:14); "the eleven gathered together... [and] Jesus himself stood in the midst of them" (Luke 24:33,36). But He also "was seen of above five hundred brethren at once" (1 Corinthians 15:6). Among them was undoubtedly Matthias, who was chosen to take the place of Judas, rounding out the number of the disciples to twelve once again. No doubt, from what Peter said (quoted below) when Matthias was chosen, this man had also seen Christ on other occasions as well.

---

In Acts 1:15-26 we find "about an hundred and twenty" (verse 15) disciples gathered together. Peter reminds them that the prophets had foretold Judas' betrayal of Jesus and his death and had also foretold that "another [would] take" his place (verse 20). To be an apostle, as Paul reminds us, one must have "seen Jesus Christ our Lord" (1 Corinthians 9:1). Therefore, as the eleven disciples were about to choose Judas' successor, Peter declared that the replacement could only be from among "these men which have companied with us all the time that the Lord Jesus went in and out among us, beginning from the baptism of John unto that same day that he was taken up from us" (Acts 1:21,22). It is quite clear, then, that although the focus of the four Gospels is upon the special inner circle of twelve disciples, there were others who were also with Christ at all times, and among them was Matthias.

Meeting these qualifications, Matthias was chosen to take Judas' place and became one of the twelve apostles, having been a witness of all that the other eleven had witnessed, including the resurrection. In fact, he was probably present when Christ first appeared to the eleven. We aren't told how many other disciples were present at that time. Whether he was present that night or not, Christ had appeared to Matthias and he became one of the twelve.

Paul became a Christian some years after the replacement of Judas by Matthias. It would only be reasonable, then, that when Paul declared that Christ "was seen ... of the twelve" (1 Corinthians 15:5), he would mean the twelve (including Matthias) in existence in his day, not the twelve when Judas was one of them.

## COPYISTS' ERRORS, EVEN IN THE KING JAMES VERSION?

*Question:* I came across a list of numerous contradictions in the Bible. Here are just a few: 2 Samuel 8:4 says David took from Hadadezer "seven *hundred* horsemen," but 1 Chronicles 18:4 says David took "seven *thousand* horsemen." A similar discrepancy occurs between 2 Samuel 10:18 ("seven *hundred* chariots [and] forty thousand *horse*men") and 1 Chronicles 19:18 ("seven *thousand* chariots [and] forty thousand *foot*men"). These are just a few of the errors—and they're in the King James Bible, which I have always believed was perfect in every word. Help!

*Response:* The Bible is inerrant in its original manuscripts, not in every copy that someone has produced since then. Not every copyist and every *translator* worked so flawlessly that every copy of the Bible in every language is perfect in every word. These errors you point out were made by someone in centuries past when the documents were copied by hand.

One would have to go to the available manuscripts themselves to determine when these particular errors arose. And no doubt by comparing the many manuscripts we still have with one another it would be possible to determine what the original actually said—whether 700 or 7000, whether footmen or horsemen, etc. However, it wouldn't be worth the time and effort to determine this because these errors do not affect any doctrinal teaching.

Certain kinds of copying or translating errors which affect doctrine could also theoretically have crept into a particular manuscript, but we have so many copies of manuscripts dating back so many centuries that by comparing these with one another such mistakes can be discovered and corrected. In fact, none of the major Bible translations on the market today contains doctrinal errors. While there are certain significant translational differences between the King James Bible and the modern translations (including many deficiencies in the latter), any discrepancies in most translations are corrected by other verses in that same version.

## WAS STEPHEN CONFUSED?

---

*Question:* In his speech before the rabbinical council in Acts 7:15,16 Stephen said that Jacob was buried in Shechem "in the sepulchre that Abraham bought...of the sons of Emmor." In clear contradiction, Genesis 50:13 says Jacob was buried in Hebron in the Cave of "Machpelah, which Abraham bought...of Ephron the Hittite." Was Stephen confused? I find this very disturbing. Why didn't God inspire him to say everything correctly?

*Response:* Since Luke is writing under the inspiration of the Holy Spirit, we may be certain that Stephen said what Luke records. We can't blame any mistakes upon Luke. The most obvious possibility, therefore, is that Stephen indeed was confused. Nor would that fact reflect badly upon the Bible, much less prove that the Bible is not God's Word, as the skeptics would like to maintain.

---

Remember, the Bible records the words of many persons who were clearly not inspired of God: Adam's and Eve's excuses, Cain's lie about being innocent of Abel's murder, the lengthy speeches by Job's "comforters," Pharaoh's denunciations of Moses and Aaron, King Saul's fulminations against David, the High Priest's accusations against Jesus, and on and on. The Bible does not guarantee the truthfulness of every speech that it records unless it is clear that the person was speaking under the inspiration of God.

Stephen is not said to be speaking under the inspiration of the Holy Spirit any more than the many others whose words are recorded in Scripture. The Bible makes no attempt to hide the sins or errors of even its greatest characters, such as Abraham and David, so why should Stephen be protected from a slip of the tongue? However, let us look a bit deeper to see whether or not and to what degree Stephen was actually confused.

First of all, Stephen did not specifically state that *Jacob* was buried in Shechem. Here is that part of his speech: "So Jacob went down into Egypt, and died, he and our fathers, and were carried over into Sychem, and laid in the sepulchre that Abraham bought for a sum of money of the sons of Emmor the father of Sychem" (Acts 7:15,16). Stephen's reference to "our fathers" did *not* include Jacob ("he *and* our fathers") but rather his sons. It was the "fathers" who were buried in Sychem (Shechem). We know that Jacob was buried in the Cave of Machpelah next to the bones of Sarah, of Abraham, Isaac, and his wife, Rebekah, and of Jacob's wife, Leah. Do we know that *any* of Jacob's 12 sons, the "fathers" of the Jews, were indeed buried at Shechem? Yes.

We are told specifically that Joseph was buried at Shechem: "And the bones of Joseph, which the children of Israel brought up out of Egypt, buried they in Shechem, in a parcel of ground which Jacob bought of the sons of Hamor the father of Shechem for an hundred pieces of silver" (Joshua 24:32). This agrees with the statement that "Jacob came to Shalem, a city of Shechem . . . and he bought a parcel of a field . . . at the hand of the children of Hamor, Shechem's father, for an hundred pieces of money" (Genesis 33:18,19). If Joseph, one of the "fathers," was buried in Shechem, it could well be that some of his brothers who were also "fathers" of the children of Israel were buried there as well. The Old Testament doesn't tell us where they were buried, so we have no basis for saying that Stephen was inaccurate on that score.

## A POSSIBLE EXPLANATION

The only problem remaining is Stephen's statement that Abraham bought the field in Shechem. While there is no record that Abraham was ever in Shechem, he may well have passed through this centrally located city in his many travels. He could even have bought a field there and years later Jacob purchased an additional portion of it. Thus we cannot be dogmatic that what Stephen said was not true. He may have known then what we cannot know today.

On the other hand, it may be that Stephen made a slip of the tongue, and it was recorded in the Bible exactly as he said it. He had to be under tremendous pressure, surrounded by those who hated and were going to kill him. He had all the elements of the truth together but got them slightly and understandable confused. Stephen was only an ordinary mortal. He could make mistakes like the rest of us, and it is refreshingly honest that the Bible lets us know about such mistakes not only with him but with others.

Yes, we are told that Stephen was "full of the Holy Ghost and wisdom...full of faith and power [and] did great wonders and miracles among the people" (Acts 6:3,8). Thus we learn that to be filled with the Holy Spirit and to be inspired of God doesn't turn one into a mechanical robot incapable of human error—so long as one is not uttering prophecy, which must be without error.

## WHY WOULD GOD LET STEPHEN ERR?

If Stephen did make a blunder, why didn't God prevent him from doing so? Why should He? It made no difference. The rabbis didn't even react. One reason for allowing this mistake (if that is what it was) and recording it could be to teach us the very lesson we have just mentioned. Another reason, no doubt, is to strengthen the Bible's credibility in the eyes of honest seekers who are examining it to see whether or not they can trust it. In fact, the honest recording of this small inaccuracy is in the Bible's favor.

If the Bible had been put together by deliberate fraud centuries or even years later and this speech was simply manufactured as part of a fictitious story, the forgers would surely not have made such a blunder. They could have and no doubt would have looked up in the Old Testament anything they were uncertain of to make sure they had it right. The Old Testament is consistent and forgers surely would have stuck to that story and avoided this seeming contradiction.

The fact that this apparent mistake in Stephen's speech remains is one more proof that the Bible is an honest record. Furthermore, it shows us that no subsequent scribe dared to take it upon himself to "correct" the error. And that fact demonstrates once again the reverence with which the copyists handled what they knew to be God's infallible Word and refrained from tampering with it even when there seemed to be a mistake that needed correction.

## Is The Millennium The Ultimate Kingdom?

---

*Question:* Referring to Christ's prophesied future reign over this world from Jerusalem, the Bible says, "[Of] his government and peace there shall be no end..." (Isaiah 9:7). Yet the Bible also says that his reign will only last a thousand years and that it will end with a world war (Revelation 20:6-9). Which is it, forever or a thousand years; peace or war? It can't be both. How can anyone believe that the Bible is God's infallible Word when it contains so many contradictions, and particularly on such fundamental concepts as the reign of Christ, which is supposedly the culmination of all?

*Response:* There is a very simple and obvious explanation: the millennial reign of Christ is not the "government and peace" which the Bible says will never end. That fact is clear for a number of reasons. Certainly 1000 years is not endless, and war cannot be equated with peace. Yet most Christians imagine that the millennium is the "kingdom" for which we are to pray "Thy kingdom come" (Matthew 6:10), and which is the subject of so many biblical prophesies. In fact, it is not.

---

It is amazing that the obvious contradictions are ignored by Christians who persist in equating the millennium with Christ's eternal kingdom. The critics, however, who diligently search for every seeming contradiction they can find, have noted the problem, but in their eagerness to condemn the Bible they overlook the simple solution: The millennium is not the kingdom.

Christ said, "Except a man be born again, he cannot see ... [or] enter into the kingdom of God" (John 3:3,5). Clearly there will be many individuals living during the millennium who have not been born again or they would not follow Satan: "And when the thousand years are expired, Satan shall be loosed out of his prison, and shall go out to deceive the nations which are in the four quarters of the earth, Gog and Magog, to gather them together to battle, the number of whom is as the sand of the sea. And they went up on the breadth of the earth and compassed the camp of the saints about, and the beloved city; and fire came down from God out of heaven and devoured them" (Revelation 20:7-9). These rebels are obviously not born-again Christians! Yet only those who have been born again can be in the kingdom.

Moreover, Paul tells us that "flesh and blood cannot inherit the kingdom of God" (1 Corinthians 15:50). Yet the earth will be inhabited during the millennium by great numbers of "flesh-and-blood" people. Here then is another reason why the millennium cannot be the kingdom. (The unique role which the millennium plays will be discussed later.)

What then is the kingdom? That it is *eternal* indicates that it will exist in the new eternal universe that God will create after He has destroyed this one: "The day of the Lord will come as a thief in the night, in which the heavens shall pass away with a great noise and the elements shall melt with fervent heat; the earth also and the works that are therein shall be burned up.... Nevertheless we, according to his promise, look for new heavens and a new earth, wherein dwelleth righteousness" (2 Peter 3:10,13).

Obviously no kingdom nor anything else on this earth can be eternal until the present universe has been destroyed and a new one created. Only then will the kingdom have arrived which is eternal, whose peace will never end, which cannot be inherited by flesh and blood, and for which the entrance requirement is being born again. As Paul informed us:

> Then cometh the end [consummation], when he [Christ] shall have delivered up the kingdom to God, even the Father; when he shall have put down all rule and all authority and power....
>
> And when all things shall be subdued unto him, then shall the Son also himself be subject unto him that put all things under him, that God may be all in all (1 Corinthians 15:24,28).

*Every careful student and every thoughtful reader of the Bible finds that the words of the Apostle Peter concerning the Scriptures, that there are some things in them hard to be understood ... (2 Peter 3:16), are abundantly true.*

*Who of us has not found things in the Bible that have puzzled us, yes, that in our early Christian experience have led us to question whether the Bible was, after all, the Word of God? We find some things in the Bible which it seems impossible to reconcile with other things in the Bible. We find some things which seem incompatible with the thought that the whole Bible is of divine origin and absolutely inerrant....*

*[The Bible is] a revelation of the mind and will and character and being of an infinitely great, perfectly wise and absolutely holy God ... [but] the revelation ... [is] to finite beings who are imperfect in knowledge, and who are also imperfect in character and consequently in spiritual discernment.... There must, then, from the very necessities of the case, be difficulties in such revelation from such a source made to such persons. When the finite try to understand the infinite, there is bound to be difficulty....*

*It is not wise to attempt to conceal the fact that these difficulties exist. It is the part of wisdom, as well as of honesty, to frankly face them and consider them.*

—R.A. Torrey[1]

# 5
# Challenges to Faith

## HOW CAN GOD REPENT?

*Question:* In Genesis 6:6 we are told that "it repented the Lord that he had made man." Jonah 3:10 says that "God repented of the evil that he had said that he would do unto them." A number of other times throughout the Old Testament the same Hebrew word expresses a similar repentance on God's part. How can God, who is supposedly perfect, repent? And why would He need to if He knows in advance all that is going to happen and allows it?

*Response:* It is true, as you say, that if God is perfect and knows in advance all that will happen, then He could not possibly "repent" in the sense of having been wrong. In fact, there are so many verses in the Bible declaring that God cannot repent in this sense that we may be assured He never has and never will. For example: "God is not a man, that he should lie, neither the son of man, that he should repent; hath he said and shall he not do it? Or hath he spoken and shall he not make it good?" (Numbers 23:19).

Then what are we to understand when it says that God has repented or will repent? A number of verses provide the necessary insight. For example: "Therefore now amend your ways and your doings, and obey the voice of the Lord your God; and the Lord will repent him of the evil [judgment] that he hath pronounced against you" (Jeremiah 26:13). When God offers to "repent" of the judgment He has pronounced upon the wicked, if they turn from their wickedness, it is quite clear that His "repentance" is simply His gracious response to man's repentance. That fact is made clear by many Scriptures such as the following:

> If the wicked will turn from all his sins that he hath committed, and keep all my statutes, and do that which is lawful and right, he shall surely live; he shall not die (Ezekiel 18:21).

> At what instant I shall speak concerning a nation and concerning a kingdom to pluck up and to pull down and to destroy it, if that nation against whom I have pronounced turn from their evil, I will repent of the evil that I thought to do unto them (Jeremiah 18:7,8).

## A Change Of Action, Not Of Mind

Obviously if, after the conditions He has set forth are fulfilled, God then "repents," He has not changed His attitude or actions because He was wrong or because He didn't foresee the future. He has simply changed His action toward those who repented, exactly as He promised. There is neither remorse nor regret; nor is either of these possible for God. Such was the nature of His "repentance" in not destroying Nineveh, as Jonah had declared He would.

In each case where "repentance" is attributed to God, His action is quite consistent with the principle He has repeatedly laid down in His Word. Where there is repentance and turning from wickedness on the part of a person or nation, He will forgive and not execute the judgment which He has previously pronounced.

What then about God's "repentance" in Genesis 6? It is evidently the converse of the above. Instead of the wicked turning to good, and as a result God "repenting" of the judgment He had pronounced upon them, those whom God had created and pronounced good had instead turned to wickedness. Consequently, God "repented" of the blessing He had promised them. In fact, so great was their wickedness that the whole of mankind which He had made deserved to be destroyed.

Fortunately one man, Noah, "found grace in the eyes of the Lord" (Genesis 6:8). This fact tells us that although grace is free, as it must be, there are conditions for receiving it. God said, "My spirit shall not always strive with man" (Genesis 6:3). The time for judgment had come, but one man, in distinction to all the rest, was willing to repent and to obey God and thus could be a recipient of God's grace.

Parents need to pattern their discipline after God's example. There is a point of diminishing return and finally of no return in extending forgiveness to an erring child who always begs piteously for mercy. If there is never a punishment, then grace is meaningless and the required lesson is never learned. The grace which God extended to Noah had meaning only in relation to the judgment meted out upon all others. And so it is with the salvation God provides in Christ: It is meaningful and desirable only in light of the eternal judgment which we would otherwise have to endure for our sins.

### DID JESUS STUDY IN INDIA UNDER THE GURUS?

---

*Question:* The Gospels are silent about the approximately 18 years between the last time we hear of Jesus in the temple as a boy of 12 (Luke 2:41-52) and the beginning of His ministry at about 30 years of age (Luke 3:23). I have come across the report a number of times, not only in *The Aquarian Gospel,* but in newspapers as well, that during these missing years Jesus was in India studying under the gurus. The wisdom He acquired there supposedly became the basis for His ministry. Why not?

*Response:* The most widely circulated report involved an alleged Nicholas Notovitch, who claimed that while traveling in Tibet in the late 1800s he was told by Tibetan lamas that a record reporting the visit of Jesus existed in a Himalayan monastery. In the early 1900s another visitor to Tibet was allegedly told the same thing. However, no one capable of reading and translating such "records" ever saw them, no copy was brought to the West for examination, and now the story is that the "records" have been destroyed.[2]

---

If the Bible were based upon no better evidence than that, the critics would have justifiably dismissed it long ago. Yet such speculative claims are instantly given credence by those who demand proof for anything the Bible says. That double standard betrays an intense bias on the part of skeptics who claim to be interested only in the truth.

## All The Evidence Is To The Contrary

First of all, there is not a particle of historical or archaeological evidence that Jesus ever visited India, much less *studied* there. Moreover, this theory is refuted by everything that Jesus said and did during His ministry. The teachings which Jesus brought to the Jews were in agreement with all of their Scriptures (which He frequently quoted as authoritative) and without the slightest taint of either Hinduism or Buddhism. Had He studied under the Masters of India or Tibet, He would have been obligated to uphold their teaching and to honor His guru. In fact, His teachings were the very antithesis of Eastern mysticism of any kind.

Furthermore, the New Testament account, which holds together consistently, is not compatible with Jesus ever having made such extensive travels. The people in his hometown of Nazareth knew him as "the carpenter, the son of Mary, the brother of James and Joses and of Juda and Simon" (Mark 6:3). The implication certainly is that He was a familiar hometown personality who had grown up and continued in the local community, not that He was a Jewish Marco Polo who had traveled to exotic and distant places.

Friends and acquaintances were astonished when Jesus suddenly began to travel about Galilee and preach to great crowds. To family and neighbors it was a scandal for Jesus to present Himself as a religious teacher. They treated him with a contempt born of familiarity, not with the awe they surely would have given one who had traveled widely and studied in such far-off lands as India and Tibet.

Every guru who comes to the West lauds and honors his Master, for every Hindu, including the gurus themselves, must have a guru whom he follows. Yet the alleged "Guru Jesus" never referred to His guru or quoted any religious writings except the Jewish Scriptures. He claimed to have been sent not by some Master in the East but by His Father in heaven (John 5:23,30,36; etc.), a term unknown to the gurus and hated by the rabbis.

The gurus claim to be men who, through Yoga and ascetic practices, have attained to the mystical "realization" that "Atman [individual soul] is identical with Brahman [universal soul]" and have thereby become "Self-realized" gods. Had Jesus studied under them, He would have taught the same delusion. Yet in complete contradiction to that impossible dream and far from claiming to be a man struggling upward to godhood, Jesus presented Himself as the very I AM (Jahweh) of the Old Testament, the God of Israel who had stooped down to become a man:

> ....if ye believe not that I AM, ye shall die in your sins....Before Abraham was, I AM....Now I tell you [this] before it come to pass, that, when it is come to pass, ye may believe that I AM....A little while, and ye shall not see me...because I go to the Father....I came forth from the Father and am come into the world; again, I leave the world and go to the Father....*I and my Father are one* (emphasis added) (John 8:24,58; 13:19; 16:16, 28; 10:30).

## Irreconcilable Differences
## Between Christ And The Gurus

The gurus deny the existence of sin or of any absolute moral standards. Each person's *dharma* is different and an individual matter to be discovered on the mystical journey to union with Brahman. In complete contrast, Christ claimed to be the "light of the world" (John 8:12), whose very life exposed the evil in mankind. Moreover, He promised to send the Holy Spirit to convince the world of "sin, and of righteousness, and of judgment" (John 16:8). Jesus announced that He had come to call sinners to repentance (Mark 2:17) and to save them from eternal judgment by His sacrifice of Himself for the sins of the whole world.

Christ's life and teachings stand in the fullest contradiction to the Hinduism He would have learned in India had He studied there and which He surely would have practiced and taught to the Jews when He returned to Israel. This theory finds absolutely no support in the New Testament record given to us by eyewitnesses.

The gurus teach a continuing cycle of death and reincarnation, whereas Jesus was resurrected as He said He would be, and He promised the same deliverance from death to His followers. Reincarnation and resurrection are opposites; one cannot believe in both. The gurus teach a continual returning to this earth in life after life to work out one's supposed "karma," while Jesus taught forgiveness of sins by grace, thus fitting one for heaven. To the gurus, heaven is a mystical state of oneness with the Absolute. Jesus, on the other hand, taught that being in heaven is to dwell forever in His Father's house of "many mansions" (John 14:1-4). The gurus are all vegetarians. Jesus ate the Passover lamb, fed the multitudes with fish, and even after His resurrection ate fish as a demonstration to His doubting disciples that He was bodily resurrected and not a "ghost," as they supposed.

There have been thousands of gurus, but Jesus claimed to be the one and only Son of God, the only Savior of sinners. The gurus teach that there are many ways to God. Jesus declared: "I am the way, the truth, and the life; no man cometh unto the Father but by me" (John 14:6). Everything Jesus said and did opposes the teachings of Hinduism and Buddhism and disproves the false claim that He studied in India or Tibet.

This fraudulent theory demonstrates once again how impossible it would be to invent a fictitious history of Jesus and to make it fit into actual events on this earth. The erroneous theory that Jesus studied in India under the gurus simply won't fit into the New Testament record at all—and if it did, the New Testament would be incompatible with the Old, instead of being its fulfillment as it had to be. Nor would either the Old or New Testament records fit into the history of the world unless both were true. The perfect harmony of Scripture with established history is revealed by any careful and honest study of both.

## THE RELATIONSHIP BETWEEN MYTHOLOGIES AND THE BIBLE

*Question:* The Bible claims to have been inspired of God. Yet we find very similar accounts of some of the stories it records (Adam and Eve, the temptation in the Garden, Noah and the flood, etc.) in the myths of many ancient peoples scattered around the world. Some of these myths seem to be much older than the Bible. There are, for example, Assyrian tablets predating the books of Moses which tell of creation, the temptation in the Garden, the flood, and the tower of Babel in language very similar to the Genesis account. The first man in the Babylonian myths was called Adami. Is it not possible, then, that at least some of the Bible was derived from pagan mythology rather than from divine inspiration?

*Response:* To suggest that the Bible borrowed the Genesis accounts from pagan myths creates more problems than it could seem to solve. We are still left with two questions: What was the source of the pagan accounts, and what is the explanation for the close similarities in all accounts, including the Bible's? It is mathematically impossible that different races and cultures widely scattered around the world and without contact with one another would all develop independently such similar mythological accounts of mankind's origin and history. The odds against that happening are astronomical.

---

All accounts, therefore, including the Bible's, must have come from some *common source* which originated outside of any race or culture. There can be no doubt about it. That fact confronts us once again with the question of the *identity* of that common source and *how* all of these widely scattered peoples came in contact with it— or it came in contact with them.

Interestingly enough, the accounts themselves provide the only plausible explanation: that all peoples of every race and color are descended from one set of parents created by God and that there was a worldwide flood which again left one family from whom all peoples on earth today are descended. Mathematically, evolution is impossible, as we have already seen. Furthermore, if gradual evolution from apes to man had occurred over thousands of years it would have left millions of fossils of missing links (creatures that were neither ape nor man) scattered over a wide area, yet *not one* has ever been found. And if evolution were a fact, there would not be one pair of common parents for all peoples; there would be hundreds and perhaps thousands of such pairs and thus no explanation of how a single mythology became known to all peoples.

Adam and Eve, however, would certainly have passed the story of their creation, the serpent's deception, and their expulsion from the Garden of Eden on to their children, they to their children, and so on. That story would surely have been known by Noah's family, who would have passed it on to their descendants along with their account of the flood as they had experienced it. There is no other possible rational explanation for the worldwide existence of the common mythology recounting these events.

Furthermore, to this day, in Turkey, in the proximity of Mount Ararat, where the Bible says Noah's ark settled after the flood (Genesis 8:4), the native people living there still refer to that lofty summit as "the Mount of Noah." Even without the various accounts of those who claim to have seen a huge ship high in a glacier on Mount Ararat that could only be the remains of Noah's ark, we have compelling evidence. A local tradition of long standing agrees with a story that is known worldwide. Such confirmation speaks loudly and cannot be ignored.

### PERVERTED MYTHOLOGIES
### MAKE THE BIBLE SHINE BRIGHTER

Wherever archaeologists dig around the world, they find, in corroboration of the Genesis account, ancient representations of a woman, a serpent, and a tree in close relationship with one another. Therefore we know there is at least that core of truth in this widespread story. When we look at the nonbiblical accounts, however, there are obviously mythological elements perverting the transmission of what must have been a historical event. Of great significance is the fact (to which we will return in a later chapter) that the serpent is universally presented as the symbol of wisdom, or the Savior-god, exactly the opposite from what the Bible says.

In addition to perverting the role of the serpent, all pagan accounts embody obviously mythological and fantastic elements. The biblical account alone has the factual ring of history rather than myth. It fits the rest of the Bible and agrees with what we know of mankind's history to the present time. Thus the biblical account stands on one side and all of the others, in spite of their similarities to the Genesis story, stand together in opposition to it.

That distinction between the Bible and all other accounts is significant. It indicates that the biblical account was not borrowed from the others. Clearly, all non-biblical accounts originated from the same historical events, and their differences developed later. The pagan myths all vary from one another, so none can be trusted as authentic. They must have all become perverted in one way or another. Inasmuch as the biblical account is consistent with the rest of the Bible, it can claim the same infallibility of inspiration as all of God's Word. The pagan accounts are similar enough to confirm the biblical account, but different enough so that the latter stands alone as the only authentic record. The biblical account does not originate from oral tradition handed down from generation to generation (and thus it escapes the inevitable error inherent in such a process); but it was given by inspiration of God.

## What About Moving Mountains With Faith?

*Question:* Jesus very clearly said, "If ye have faith as a grain of mustard seed, ye shall say unto this mountain, Remove hence to yonder place, and it shall remove; and nothing shall be impossible unto you" (Matthew 17:20). I've never heard of a Christian moving a mountain yet, nor have I ever heard of a Christian to whom nothing was impossible. Yet there are absolutely no conditions; this promise is unequivocal. Either Matthew and Luke (who gives his own version—17:6) lied, or Jesus lied. Which was it? In either case the Bible is proven to be contradictory, is it not?

*Response:* Neither Matthew nor Luke nor Christ lied. Let us be careful to approach the Bible with due reverence. Even if we cannot quickly explain or reconcile every difficulty in the Bible, the corroborating evidence for the accuracy and authenticity of those passages which we are able to understand is overwhelming and points to its divine origin. R.A. Torrey reminds us:

What would we think of a beginner in algebra who, having tried in vain for half an hour to solve a difficult problem, declared that there was no possible solution to the problem because he could find none! ... The difficulties that confront one who denies that the Bible is of divine origin and authority are far more numerous and weighty than those which confront the one who believes it to be of divine origin and authority.[3]

In this case, the apparent conflict is created by a misunderstanding of faith. It is not some power that can be aimed at circumstances or people or things to move them into alignment with one's ambitions and desires. If that were the case, then Christ would be telling us that this hidden power of the mind is so incredibly strong that we only need a miniscule amount of it (the size of a tiny mustard seed) in order to effect whatever we desire. The universe would then be under man's control instead of God's. It would be terrifying if men had such power available to them. Fortunately they don't, nor did Christ promise it.

Faith is not a power one possesses, but complete trust in and dependence upon another person or object. *Faith must have an object.* Nor is there anyone or anything worthy of one's total trust except God. Jesus said, "Have faith in God" (Mark 11:22). What then is faith? It is a confident trust in the love and grace and power and wisdom of God.

It is easy to show the absurdity of "faith" as some power that man wields. Suppose two men want to move a mountain, but each in a different direction. Which one of them will manage to move the mountain when and where he wants it to go? The man with the most faith? That common misunderstanding is dispelled by Christ's statement that it only takes a very small amount of faith to move a mountain.

## GOD ALONE—NOT FAITH—CAN MOVE MOUNTAINS

The mountain (or whatever else) will not move by the power of *faith,* because faith has no power in and of itself. The mountain can only be moved by the power of *God.* It will, therefore, move only when and where God wants it to move.

Surely, then, no one can have faith that a mountain is going to move at a particular time and in a certain direction unless he knows such a move to be God's will. And how can one gain such insight and confidence? Obviously, only by getting to know God personally and learning to trust Him. It would be utter folly to trust a stranger or someone who has not yet demonstrated his reliability.

Faith puts man in touch with God, causing him to know and trust God and to know His will. By faith man can become an instrument in the effecting of God's will here on earth. Literal mountains rarely, if ever, require moving. That would be possible, however, if it were God's will. Jesus used the extreme example of a mountain being moved in response to one's faith in God to show that *nothing* is impossible to those who are in touch with God and who are the obedient channels of His purposes and power.

## Why Didn't Jesus Show His Resurrection To The Romans And Rabbis?

*Question:* Why didn't Jesus, if He really rose from the dead, show Himself openly to the rabbis and to the common Jews and to the Romans? Wouldn't that have established once and for all the fact that He had come back from the grave? And would not such a public appearance of Christ have converted the entire world of that day to Christianity? The fact that even the Bible admits He didn't do so is presumptive evidence against the alleged resurrection, is it not? If He really was alive, why didn't He prove it openly?

*Response:* You underestimate the proud stubbornness and evil in the human heart. There were many eyewitnesses in addition to Christ's disciples who testified to multitudes of friends and relatives and to the rabbis as well that Christ had raised Lazarus from the dead after his body had been in the grave for four days (John 11:43-46). There was no doubt that this incredible miracle had occurred. In fact, the rabbis admitted to one another in their council that Christ was doing "many miracles" (verses 47,48). That fact, however, did not soften their hearts nor make them willing to face the truth about Christ.

On the contrary, the fact that Christ had raised Lazarus from the dead before many witnesses (and that because of this undeniable miracle many of the people believed that He was the Messiah) only increased the rabbis' determination to kill Christ. And now they were determined to kill Lazarus also in order to prevent him from being a testimony to Christ's divine power (John 12:9-11)! Such fanatical opposition to Christ is not rational and therefore would not have been changed no matter what further facts had been witnessed.

No, it would not have changed the minds and actions of the secular and religious leaders at all had Christ Himself, the very One whom they had crucified, stood before them alive once again. And why should He have done so? Through His fulfillment of Old Testament prophecies, and in the miracles which had been confirmed by the many witnesses (who, like spies, had reported to the rabbis—John 11:46), Christ had given Israel's religious leaders more than enough evidence that He was the Messiah. Undoubtedly some of the rabbis themselves had witnessed Christ's miracles. But they still crucified Him.

### BOTH ROMANS AND RABBIS HAD MORE PROOF THAN THEY NEEDED

Furthermore, the rabbis had even more powerful evidence for the resurrection of Christ than the witness of the ordinary people who had testified that they had seen with their own eyes Lazarus come out of the grave "bound hand and foot with graveclothes . . . " (11:44). They had the eyewitness account of the trained and disciplined Roman soldiers who had guarded Christ's tomb and had reported their terrifying confrontation by the angel who rolled the stone away to expose the empty tomb. Yet in spite of this testimony of a platoon of tough and now badly shaken soldiers, so hard were the rabbis' hearts that they bribed the guards to say that the disciples had stolen the body while they slept (Matthew 28:13)!

Both the rabbis and the Roman authorities knew full well that Christ had risen from the dead. To supply further proof of the resurrection to those who were determined to deny it would not have changed anything. It would only have made their judgment all the more severe because of the additional evidence for which they would have been accountable. So Christ was actually merciful in not appearing to the rabbis and to the multitudes of others who would not have believed under any circumstances. Clearly He was following His own advice not to cast "pearls before swine" (Matthew 7:6).

As for the rest of the people, they were confronted by many resurrected individuals who undoubtedly testified to them of the resurrection of Christ: "The graves were opened, and many bodies of the saints which slept arose ... after his [Christ's] resurrection, and went into the holy city [Jerusalem] and appeared unto many (Matthew 27:52,53).

Thereafter both the rabbis and all the people had additional proof of the resurrection in the miracles which were done through the disciples in the name and power of Christ:

> With great power gave the apostles witness of the resurrection of the Lord Jesus, and great grace was upon them all (Acts 4:33).

> By the hands of the apostles were many signs and wonders wrought among the people ... ([and] the people magnified them. And believers were the more added to the Lord, multitudes both of men and women), insomuch that they brought forth the sick into the streets, and laid them on beds and couches, that at least the shadow of Peter passing by might overshadow some of them. There came also a multitude out of the cities round about Jerusalem, bringing sick folks and them that were vexed with unclean spirits; and they were healed every one (Acts 5:12-16).

The very transformation in the disciples, which the Pharisees acknowledged, was more than sufficient proof of the resurrection. The disciples, like the cowards they were, had abandoned Christ in the garden and had fled to save their own lives. Yet here they were, these "unlearned and ignorant men" (Acts 4:13), now no longer afraid, but boldly indicting the rabbis for having delivered Christ to be crucified. In spite of beatings and threats of imprisonment and death, these former cowards were now courageously standing up to the rabbis and with great conviction testifying that their Lord had risen from the dead. Moreover, in His name they were doing astonishing miracles which were convincing multitudes. No further proof was needed.

## A GROSS INJUSTICE?

---

*Question:* Some of my friends think that the teaching that Christ's death upon the cross paid the penalty for our sins, which is the very heart of Christianity, is itself reason for rejecting Christianity. They argue that it is unjust for an innocent party to suffer imprisonment or execution in the place of a criminal and that such a practice would encourage sin. I'm stumped. Can you help me?

*Response:* Their problem is a lack of understanding of what actually happened on the cross. First of all, Christ is absolutely unique. He is God and man in one Person, the only One who could die for the sins of others. Therefore, His death in our place is not to be taken as a suggestion that others should "suffer imprisonment or execution in the place of a criminal."

---

Furthermore, Christ did more than simply die in our place. If that were all that occurred, then Barabbas had the greatest "Christian" testimony of all time. It was literally true that Christ died in the place of Barabbas and thereby set him free. Yet Barabbas knew nothing of the true meaning of the cross. He did not, so far as we know, understand that Christ had died for his sins nor did he put his faith in Christ as his Savior. All Christ's death accomplished for that criminal was to set him free from prison to continue living his old sinful life. That is not the gospel!

Christ's work of redemption did more than simply pay for our sins. When Christ died, those who would trust Him as their Savior died in Him. The believer has accepted Christ's death as his very own and in that act of faith has given up life as he would have lived it so that the resurrected Christ can live in him. Giving his own testimony, Paul declared:

> I am crucified with Christ; nevertheless I live, yet not I, but Christ liveth in me, and the life which I now live in the flesh I live by the faith of the Son of God, who loved me and gave himself for me (Galatians 2:20).

So the believer does not merely escape from death, but is brought through death in Christ into resurrection life on the other side, a life which is no longer his but the life of Christ in him: "If one died for all, then were all dead [i.e. have died in Him]...that they which live should not henceforth live unto themselves, but unto him which died for them and rose again.... Therefore if any man be in Christ, he is a new creature: old things are passed away; behold, all things are become new" (2 Corinthians 5:14-17):

> For ye are dead, and your life is hid with Christ in God. When Christ, who is our life, shall appear, then shall ye also appear with him in glory (Colossians 3:3,4).

## AN INJUSTICE, YET THE ULTIMATE JUSTICE

Yes, in a sense it was an injustice for Christ to have died in our place. No ordinary person could have satisfied the demand of justice by taking the prescribed punishment for another person. Nor could any ordinary person have accomplished the glorious results of Christ's death for us by being imprisoned or executed in the place of some criminal.

It is often forgotten that in the death of the cross, Christ suffered not merely what *man* did to Him but the eternal judgment which *His own* righteousness had decreed against sin. He took our sins upon Himself. Thus the ultimate justice was accomplished because the penalty for sin was paid in full, a penalty which could not have been paid any other way.

Therefore, those who believe in Christ are given eternal life as a free gift of God's grace on a righteous basis. Such a transaction would not otherwise have been possible. In Christ we see a perfectly righteous and just forgiveness for sin which none of the world's religions can offer.

### WHY CAN'T THE GOSPELS AGREE?

*Question:* Christians try to explain away the contradictions in the narrative in the four Gospels as resulting from four different witnesses, each presenting his own perspective on what happened. But that could not account for the variations in the words attributed to Jesus. Did He use the words that Matthew records, or did He actually say what Mark writes, or what Luke or John offer us? Words can't be changed! If these writers really were eyewitnesses, why don't their memories agree? And if they were inspired by the same Holy Spirit, why the contradictions?

*Response:* First of all, there are no *contradictions* between the four Gospels. There are *variations* in the accounts, but they are exactly what one would expect from accurate independent eyewitnesses. Furthermore, as we and others have already noted, these variations prove that the Gospel writers were not in collusion nor were they copying from some common document, as the critics charge. They give us independent reports exactly as each claims.

The variations are actually an important evidence of the Bible's authenticity. They offer further proof that later copyists or translators did not alter the record in an attempt to make all the accounts superficially agree.

The very fact that seeming contradictions were left in the Gospels is verification that these records were considered by the church to be inspired of the Holy Spirit and therefore not to be revised but to be reverently left as they were. There was obviously not a "progressive revelation" or any "development" in the record, as the critics insist.

Why even have four Gospels? If the record is inspired of God, why do it this way? Why not just one account, which would have saved space and paper and reading time, since the four Gospels seem so repetitive? The Holy Spirit, who inspired these accounts, had good reasons.

One major purpose for having four separate Gospels is the very one we have just noted: to demonstrate the authenticity of the record in a way which could not have been accomplished otherwise. Four witnesses provide an attestation that a single witness could not. Moreover, to tell the story from four different perspectives presents a broader view of Christ's works and teachings than one account could give.

Nor were the disciples simply relying upon their faulty memories. If that were the case, we could have little confidence in the record they offer. Obviously they had no shorthand transcription, much less a tape recording to rely upon. They wouldn't dare pretend to give us the very words of Jesus unless they were relying upon the Holy Spirit's inspiration. Then why the variations in those words if those who report them have provided an accurate record under the inspiration of God?

There are several reasonable possibilities. Jesus surely gave similar teachings on certain subjects a number of times in different settings to different people. In such cases the wording would not and should not be exactly the same. Knowing the hearts of His listeners, Jesus no doubt introduced a particular variation in one place and a different innovation elsewhere.

There are, however, instances when such an explanation would not apply. Sometimes when the same teaching is given in different Gospels it is clear that the same location and occasion is being described by each; and yet there is a difference in the wording recorded in the different Gospels. How can that possibly be?

Here, as an example, is one of those instances which is given to us in each of the first three Gospels. John, who provides incidents and teachings not found in the other Gospels, doesn't mention this particular occasion. All three other Gospels record the same teaching and in the same setting—in the presence of publicans in the house of Matthew (also called Levi), whom Jesus had just called to be His disciple. The Pharisees criticized Jesus to His disciples for eating with sinners, and Jesus replied:

> They that be whole need not a physician, but they that are sick. But go ye and learn what that meaneth, I will have mercy and not sacrifice, for I am not come to call the righteous but sinners to repentance (Matthew 9:12,13).

> They that are whole have no need of the physician, but they that are sick; I came not to call the righteous but sinners to repentance (Mark 2:17).

> They that are whole need not a physician, but they that are sick. I came not to call the righteous but sinners to repentance (Luke 5:31,32).

## A REASONABLE EXPLANATION

While these three statements by Christ vary slightly in wording, they all have the same meaning. Matthew alone gives us something additional: "But go ye and learn what that meaneth, I will have mercy and not sacrifice...." Why don't the others record it? Why should they? Isn't once enough? It is ironic that the skeptics, on the one hand, criticize the Gospels for repeating the same incidents and teachings, yet when there is some legitimate variation they complain!

Matthew's account lets us know that Christ made a pointed remark for the Pharisees' benefit. He referred them to Hosea 6:6 as a rebuke for their lack of mercy. And He let them know that they needed to repent and that forgiveness of sin could only be on the same basis as physical healing—by God's mercy.

We have three accounts in perfect agreement. The only difference is that two of the three don't tell us *all* that Jesus said. In fact, perhaps none of them does. We don't really know. There is no contradiction in the three accounts, however, nor is there anything to suggest either collusion or tampering with the record or to deny the inspiration of the Holy Spirit. The same conclusion will be reached by thoroughly examining all of the Gospels. Personal research can verify this fact for all other apparent inconsistencies.

## What About That Old Sinner And Idolater, Solomon?

*Question:* We are told that "when Solomon was old" he worshiped false gods and goddesses, tried to kill Jeroboam (whom God had chosen as his successor), and did other evils. How then could God have inspired him to write parts of the Bible, how could he have been "the wisest man who ever lived," and how could it be said of him that he "slept with his fathers," which presumably meant that he went to heaven?

*Response:* Solomon began well. His heart was right with God and God loved him and blessed him abundantly (1 Kings 3:11-13). His God-given inspiration to write (Proverbs, Ecclesiastes, and The Song of Solomon) occurred long before he fell into sin. His downfall, which came in later life, was his love for beautiful women. He couldn't get enough of them:

King Solomon loved many strange [foreign] women, together with the daughter of Pharaoh, women of the Moabites, Ammonites, Edomites, Zidonians, and Hittites; of the nations concerning which the Lord said unto the children of Israel, Ye shall not go in to them, neither shall they come in to

you, for surely they will turn away your heart after
their gods; Solomon clave unto these in love....
  It came to pass when Solomon was old that his
wives turned away his heart after other gods....
For Solomon went after Ashtoreth the goddess of the
Zidonians, and after Milcom the abomination of the
Ammonites....Then did Solomon build an high
place for Chemosh, the abomination of Moab...and
for Molech, the abomination of the children of
Ammon.
  And likewise did he for all his strange wives,
which burnt incense and sacrificed unto their gods.
And the Lord was angry with Solomon....Where-
fore the Lord said unto Solomon...I will surely
rend the kingdom from thee, and will give it to thy
servant (1 Kings 11:1-11).

How could he be the wisest man (apart from Jesus
Christ) who ever lived and fall into such folly and gross
sin? Indeed, for that very reason Solomon serves as a
special lesson to us all: that a man so wise, far wiser than
anyone else could ever hope to be, could wander so far
from the God he loved ought to make us all the more
careful to heed Paul's admonition: "Let him that thinketh he standeth take heed lest he fall" (1 Corinthians
10:12).
  The reason for Solomon's sin is also sobering: He dis-
obeyed the Lord. How solemn to realize that one step of
disobedience leads to another, until one gathers such mo-
mentum on the downward path that there is little hope
of recovery!
  The very fact that the sins of Solomon and other major figures in the Bible are honestly presented in Scripture
is one more evidence of its authenticity. A fictitious
account would tend to glorify its main characters and
cover up their faults. Such was the nature of the accounts
written at that time about the Pharaohs and other rulers.
They were treated as deities. Moreover, the mention of
the sins of Solomon, David, and others raises questions
and creates conflicts which a fictitious account would

avoid. Here we have further evidence of authenticity and the impeccable integrity of the record.

As for the statement that "Solomon slept with his fathers" (1 Kings 11:43), that does not refer to being in heaven. No one is asleep in heaven. It refers to being in the grave with one's ancestors. For example, when Jacob was about to die he said to his sons, "I am to be gathered unto my people; bury me with my fathers in the cave that is in the field of Ephron the Hittite, in the cave which is in the field of Machpelah. . . . There they buried Abraham and Sarah his wife; there they buried Isaac and Rebekah his wife; and there I buried Leah" (Genesis 49:29-31).

Is Solomon in heaven or in hell? I think he is in heaven, but I do not know beyond doubt. Solomon is not mentioned in Hebrews 11 along with David his father and other heroes of the faith. However, that chapter honors those who were particularly triumphant in faith, so it is not surprising that Solomon would not be named among them.

## We Are All Sinners Who Need God's Mercy

It would be strange indeed if Solomon, who wrote some of the Bible under the Holy Spirit's inspiration and who built the original temple at Jerusalem, where the glory of God was manifested for so many years, went to hell instead of to heaven. God disciplined Solomon in this life more in the way He deals with His own than with unbelievers.

Solomon's sin was inexcusable and exceedingly grievous. In fact, it merited the death penalty under the law. But so did his father David's sin, yet God forgave him. And so did her adultery merit the death of the woman whom the Pharisees brought to Jesus. And yet in mercy He forgave her too. There is no doubt that God's mercy, made possible by the sacrifice of Christ upon the cross for the sins of the world, could also have been extended to Solomon.

Let us hear again and heed the words of Jesus to the Pharisees, who did not want any mercy for this adulteress:

"He that is without sin among you, let him first cast a stone at her" (John 8:7). John tells us, "And they... being convicted by their own conscience, went out one by one, beginning at the eldest even unto the last; and Jesus was left alone [with] the woman..." (John 8:9).

Whoever would himself receive the merciful pardon of God dare not withhold pardon from Solomon or from anyone else. The destiny of each of us is in God's hands alone. We rest in the assurance that "the Judge of all the earth" shall indeed "do right" (Genesis 18:25).

### ISN'T THE IMPORTANCE GOD GIVES MAN PREPOSTEROUS?

*Question:* In comparison with the almost-infinite reaches of the cosmos surrounding us, this planet which man calls home is but an infinitesimal speck of dust. In view of that fact, it seems the height of absurdity and self-importance (rather than the humility which Christians are supposed to embody) for such insignificant microbes to boast that God loves them and even came to this earth to become one of them and to die for their sins! Doesn't such a preposterous scenario seem the height of absurdity?

*Response:* On the contrary, God's love would not be genuine if He bestowed it upon us because we were so important as to merit it. In fact, love cannot be merited. It is the very nature of love to bestow itself upon the unworthy. That is difficult for the average person to comprehend today because of the popular acceptance of the deceitful Hollywood idea of love. One "falls in love" and just as readily "falls out of love" with that person and then "in love" with another person. That is not the love which the Bible presents.

If God's love for me were predicated upon how lovable, attractive, or worthy of His love He presently found me, I would feel insecure indeed. Being far from perfect, and subject to change, I would be fearful that I might change in some way that would cause God to love me no longer. But since my relationship to Him depends upon *His* love and faithfulness and unchangeableness and not upon my love or my appeal to Him, I am at peace. I have perfect assurance that His love for me will never wane and that I am secure in my relationship to Him eternally.

Moreover, our puny insignificance in relation to the vastness of the universe only makes God's grace and mercy all the more worthy of our praise and gratitude and thus all the more glorious. The more unworthy the object of love, the greater and purer must be the love that embraces it.

Throughout the vastness of the universe we see God's attention to the smallest detail, whether it be the design of a snowflake or the interior of an atom. Though He is infinite in might and knowledge and wisdom, nothing is too small for God's consideration. It is far from ludicrous or presumptuous for a Christian to believe that God loves him and sent His Son to die for him. On the contrary, that fact rings true to the character of God as we would expect Him to be, as the Bible depicts Him, and as the universe reflects Him.

## Did God Accept Jepthah's Sacrifice Of His Daughter?

*Question:* The Bible records some of the most horrible deeds ever perpetrated by men. There is, for example, Jephthah's vow to sacrifice his daughter to Jehovah, a vow which he then fulfilled. How can one reconcile a "God of love" with the acceptance of human sacrifices?

*Response:* This tragic story is told to us in Judges 11:30-40. Once again, of course, we see the honesty of the Bible in presenting not only the sin but the folly of its major characters. Let it not be forgotten, however, that the Bible never condones the sins which it faithfully records. God was no more pleased with Jephthah's rash vow and deed than with Solomon's idolatry or David's adultery with Bathsheba.

The vow itself was not only reckless but insane. He offered to sacrifice to the Lord as a "burnt offering" whatever first came out of the doors of his house to meet him when he returned victorious from battle. Did he even imagine that his daughter, the apple of his eye, his only child, might come out first? Surely not! Yet how could he have overlooked that possibility? Did he expect a sheep or a chicken or his favorite dog to be the first to come out to greet him?

Whatever his warped or confused thinking may have been, the vow was Jephthah's doing, not God's, and the latter is not to be blamed for it. Furthermore, it is not at all clear that Jephthah actually killed his daughter and offered her as a sacrificial burnt offering to God. Then why did she go about for two months mourning her virginity? Could that have meant that her father dedicated her to the service of the Lord as a virgin? We can't be certain.

It does say that after this period of mourning, Jephthah "did with her according to his vow which he had vowed" (verse 39). If in fact he actually offered her up as a human sacrifice, such an offering would have been an abomination to God and would not have been accepted by Him. In fact, it would have brought God's wrath upon him.

Jephthah's vow and act was not inspired of God, was not according to God's will, and certainly cannot be blamed upon God. Yet the Bible candidly records such follies and sins. That fact, rather than reflecting badly upon the Bible, is actually one further evidence of its authenticity and honesty.

## WHO REALLY KILLED GOLIATH?

*Question:* First Samuel 17 says that David killed Goliath, but 2 Samuel 21:19 says that Elhanan killed Goliath (if we eliminate the italics, which weren't in the original text). It does say Elhanan killed *"the brother of Goliath,"* but the words in italics were obviously added later to avoid the contradiction. That bothers me. I read a statement by a certain bishop who said that inserting *"the brother of"* in italics was a dishonest cover-up and proved that the Bible has been doctored up not only here but elsewhere as well. How do you respond to this charge?

> *Response:* First of all, we can quickly dismiss the charge of dishonest doctoring of the Bible. Would someone who was trying to change the meaning of a passage put his amendment in *italics*? That would be like a counterfeiter writing across the face of each of his phony bills, "This is a counterfeit." In fact, the italics are added by the translators to provide what is implicit but not expressed.

It often seems that a word or words were left out because of the lack of exact word equivalents between languages. In this case, however, it was necessary for the translators to insert "the brother of" for a number of reasons. First of all, because that was the only thing that made sense. Obviously this was not Goliath. To imagine that the original manuscript said it was Goliath is to accuse whoever wrote 1 and 2 Samuel of having an unbelievably bad memory. After all, the author, under the inspiration of the Holy Spirit, had already recorded some 34 chapters earlier that David had killed Goliath 45 years before this incident. One can only say to the skeptics at this point, "Me thinkest thou protesteth too loudly!"

One is sorely tempted to lose patience with the critics who have been dragging out this alleged contradiction in the Bible for at least 200 years. How can they search every page of the Bible so diligently as to come up with numerous apparent discrepancies and at the same time overlook the fact that 1 Chronicles 20:5 records the same incident and states, *without italics*, that the giant Elhanan killed was "the brother of Goliath"? Moreover, there we are given the name of this giant. His name was not Goliath, but Lahmi.

That Lahmi was Goliath's brother is not nearly as interesting as the fact that we learn from this passage that he was only one of four brothers of Goliath. So there were *five* of these fearsome Philistines living in Gath at the time David killed Goliath! One understands, then, why it was that when he went out to dispatch Goliath, David carefully chose exactly *five* smooth stones for his sling from the brook to take with him (1 Samuel 17:40)! That fact also gives us further insight into the incredible accuracy that David had with a sling—he only needed one stone for each giant.

## DID CHRIST RIDE AN ASS, ITS COLT, OR BOTH?

*Question:* The supposed prophecy in Zechariah 9:9 and the alleged fulfillment in Matthew 21:2-7 both say that Christ came riding into Jerusalem "sitting upon an ass, and a colt the foal of an ass." The accounts recorded in Mark 11 and Luke 19 mention only the colt, so there is an obvious contradiction. Furthermore, it is clearly absurd that Christ would ride upon both a colt and its mother at the same time. How can you make sense of this?

*Response:* Matthew simply quotes Zechariah 9:9. That statement is easily explained as a common type of poetic emphasis used in Old Testament times. The Messiah sits on an animal. It is an ass. More than that, it is a colt, the foal of an ass, meaning very young. That this expression, "upon an ass, and upon a colt the foal of an ass," was descriptive of the one animal on which the Messiah would sit is clear from the fact that both Mark (11:2) and Luke (19:30) replace that phrase with "whereon never man sat" and "whereon yet never man sat." It is highly unlikely that no man had ever sat upon the ass, but that statement was only true of her colt.

Mark and Luke are concentrating upon the animal upon which Christ sat. Neither of them quotes from Zechariah, where both the colt and its mother are mentioned, so there is no need to mention the mare. Matthew, who quotes Zechariah, then accounts for the mare as well. Matthew explains that the ass and its colt were tied together and were both loosed. It seems clear that the mare accompanied its colt because it was so young, apparently walking alongside, because garments were placed upon both. One can imagine Christ letting an arm rest upon the donkey as he rode its colt.

Far from being absurd, the picture shows two things. First of all, it reveals our Lord's control over nature and all created beings. A colt, so young that it has never been ridden and is even accompanied by its mother, willingly submits to carrying Christ, while its mother tags obediently along. Secondly, it emphasizes the meekness with which this One comes, exactly as Zechariah says: "lowly, and... riding upon...a colt...." This is no conquering king who has destroyed Israel's enemies and is riding triumphantly into Jerusalem at the head of an army, but upon a *colt* hardly able to support His weight. This is the Savior who has come to die for the sins of the world: "He is just, and having [bringing] salvation..." (Zechariah 9:9).

That the multitude would hail Him as Messiah, as the prophets had said, in spite of such a humble entry, is all the more remarkable. Of course, the same enthusiastic crowd that hailed Him on this occasion turned against Him and demanded His crucifixion a mere four days later. That fact was no less remarkable a fulfillment of prophecy, and we will have more to say about it later.

### LIBERALS MUST BLAME CHRIST HIMSELF

---

*Question:* One of the things I find most objectionable about Christians is the insistence that their particular formula for finding God is the only way. Such a narrow view does violence to the sincere beliefs of millions of followers of other religions. With such intolerance from Christians, what hope is there for peace among politicians and military leaders?

*Response:* It is not by virtue of some formula they have invented that Christians insist that Jesus Christ is the only way. Christ Himself said: "If ye believe not that I am [God the only Savior], ye shall die in your sins... [and] whither I go [heaven] ye cannot come....I am the way, the truth, and the life: no man cometh unto the Father but by me" (John 8:24,21; 14:6). So your quarrel is not with Christians but with Jesus Christ Himself.

---

It will do no good to suggest that Jesus didn't *really* make these claims, for we have the testimony of eyewitnesses. Furthermore, what Jesus said agrees with centuries of declarations by Hebrew prophets who all testified with one voice (though most of them didn't know one another) that only God could be the Savior of mankind and that in fact God Himself would come to this earth through a virgin birth to pay the penalty which His own justice demanded for mankind's sin. And the Bible is history's most fully established document, with hundreds (and in some cases thousands) of times more reliable manuscripts than any other ancient literature.

## LUNATIC, LIAR, OR GOD COME AS MAN?

There is no doubt about what Jesus said. The question which no one can escape, therefore, is whether or not He was telling the truth. If He wasn't, then there are only two other options: either He was a sincere egomaniac, so insane that He truly *thought* He was God come in the flesh and the only Savior of sinners, or else He was a deliberate deceiver who *knew* He was a fraud but who persisted in a masquerade so Machiavellian and clever that He deceived billions of people during the course of 20 centuries. In fact, neither of these two alternatives makes sense. He could only have been telling the truth.

The problem with many critics is that, far from having carefully examined the claims of Christ and honestly rejected them, they have a deeply ingrained (but totally irrational) prejudice against moral absolutes which will not allow them to seriously consider Christ's claims. They reject the very possibility that there may be only one way of salvation. They won't allow God to have any moral and spiritual standards even though it is clear that the physical universe couldn't function without precise direction. (The law of gravity, for example, is very narrow, with no exceptions. It operates whether one believes in it or not. And so it is with the laws of chemistry and physics.)

Nor can the way to heaven be any less definite. And since it has been fully paid for and is offered freely by God's grace to whoever will receive it, there is no valid basis for complaint by those who reject it. Furthermore, as His followers, Christians are obligated by duty and love and concern for the lost to remain true to Christ and to seek to persuade the lost that He is the only Savior of sinners.

*The essential marks of difference between true narrative of fact and works of fiction are unmistakable...the attributes of truth are strikingly apparent throughout the Gospel histories [in the New Testament]...*

—Simon Greenleaf,
Harvard Law School

*Imagine trying to crowd...the tremendous story of the Man of Calvary, if fiction, into a place in history already fully occupied with real and...inseparably linked happenings; and imagine the futility of the effort to remove this towering life and cataclysmic death [and triumphant resurrection] from the chain of events supporting the history and present condition of Christendom and of the world!*

—Irwin H. Linton in
*A Lawyer Examines the Bible*

# 6

# Evidences of Authenticity and Inspiration

## WAS PAUL IGNORANT OR SARCASTIC?

*Question:* In Acts 23, Luke tells us that Paul was brought before a council of the leading rabbis. Paul calls the presiding priest a "whited wall." When he is rebuked for that he apologizes and gives the excuse that he didn't realize that Ananias was the high priest. This reads like badly written fiction. Paul was supposedly an ex-rabbi. The high priest must have been wearing his robes and in charge of the proceedings. How then could Paul have been so stupid as not to know who the high priest was? Can you believe this scenario? And if not this, then how much else that Luke wrote?

*Response:* Once again this apparent flaw in the biblical record is in fact another convincing proof of its authenticity. The passage in question is found in Acts 23:1-5. Paul, who is a prisoner and allowed by Roman law to face his accusers, opens his defense by declaring to the rabbinic council, "I have lived in all good conscience before God unto this day."

Ananias, who is presiding over the proceedings as high priest, commands Paul to be struck on the mouth, presumably because he doesn't believe that anyone could always live in "good conscience before God." Paul, who knows the Jewish law and is far from being intimidated, retorts immediately, "God shall smite thee, thou whited wall, for sittest thou to judge me after the law, and commandest me to be smitten contrary to the law?"

Some of those standing around Paul exclaim in shock, "Revilest thou God's high priest?"

Paul then replies, "I wist not [didn't realize], brethren, that he was the high priest; for it is written, Thou shalt not speak evil of the ruler of thy people."

This is a most intriguing exchange. Yes, one might well wonder about it, but Luke simply presents the facts without explanation.

### Insight From Josephus

It becomes quite clear and all the more fascinating, however, upon reading Josephus. He tells us that Ananias had indeed *been* the high priest, but that he had been deposed. Subsequently his successor had been murdered and no replacement had been appointed for him. In the meantime, Ananias had stepped in and illegally usurped the office of high priest.

Knowing that background, the plot thickens. It is more than likely that under those conditions Ananias would not have been wearing the robes of the high priest, and so Paul could be excused for not recognizing him. Therefore it is entirely possible that Paul, who had been absent from Jerusalem for some time, was simply unaware that Ananias was acting as high priest at this time.

Knowing how astute Paul was, however, it is highly possible that, having spent a few days in Jerusalem upon his return after a long absence, Paul knew the status of the high priestly office. Paul was therefore speaking from knowledge rather than from ignorance. More than likely, then, and in keeping with his character, this man who had "turned the world upside down" (Acts 17:6) was using biting sarcasm to point out the uncomfortable fact that Ananias was *not* the legitimate high priest but a usurper and was thus without authority to sit in judgment upon him.

In any case, it should be obvious to any fair-minded person that this account could not have been written even decades, much less centuries, later, as the critics insist it was. It could only have been written by an eyewitness who was reporting accurately the proceedings and what Paul said. Moreover, this particular incident, far from discrediting Luke's testimony, was allowed of the Holy Spirit and recorded as one more unique and interesting proof of the authenticity of the New Testament record.

## ANSWERS TO THE CRITICS' FAVORITE LIE

---

*Question:* If the Bible is true and Christianity was founded by Christ as it states, then shouldn't there be at least some confirmation in the writings of non-Christian contemporaries? In fact, there is none. How do you account for that? How could Christianity have the impact that the New Testament claims for it and have been completely overlooked by all the writers of those times?

*Response:* On the contrary, there is overwhelming corroboration of the New Testament in the surviving non-Christian writings of that period, including even those of some of Christianity's sworn enemies. This false accusation of no evidence of Christianity's existence in contemporary writings outside the New Testament is repeated authoritatively by atheists, who even boast that this charge has never been answered. In fact, it has been answered by many Christian writers for at least a hundred years.

---

To show how long the evidence refuting this irresponsible allegation has been published, let me quote from one of the most brilliant educators and thinkers of a century ago, Mark Hopkins. President James A. Garfield declared that his idea of a college would be "a log with a

student on one end and Mark Hopkins on the other."[1]
Hopkins was not only a remarkable educator but an
earnest and effective apologist for the Christian faith. In
his 371-page book *Evidences* Hopkins writes:

> The *Talmud* [compilation of oral rabbinic tradi-
> tion dating to about A.D. 200]... speaks of Christ,
> and of several of the disciples, by name... of His
> crucifixion... that He performed many and great
> miracles, but imputes His power to... the magic
> arts which He [allegedly] learned in Egypt....
> [Flavius] Josephus [Jewish historian c. A.D. 37-
> 100] lived at the time many of these events... hap-
> pened and was present at the destruction of
> Jerusalem... [and] he confirms the accuracy of our
> books [New Testament writings]. Everything said
> in relation to the sects of the Jews, and the Herods,
> and Pilate, and the division of Provinces, and Felix,
> and Drusilla, and Bernice had just that agreement
> with our accounts which we should expect in inde-
> pendent historians.
> The account given by Josephus of the [strange]
> death of Herod is strikingly similar to that of Luke
> [Acts 12:21-23].... Josephus confirms all that is said
> [in the New Testament]... of Pharisees and Sad-
> ducees and Herodians... [and much about Christ
> Himself].
> [Cornelius] Tacitus [Roman historian c. A.D. 55-
> 117, governed Asia as proconsul 112-113] tells us
> that Christ was put to death by Pontius Pilate...
> under Tiberius, as a malefactor; that the people
> called Christians derived their name from him; that
> this superstition arose in Judea, and spread to
> Rome, where... only about thirty years after the
> death of Christ, the Christians were very numerous
> ... [and] that the Christians were subjected to con-
> tempt and the most dreadful sufferings... some
> were crucified; while others, being daubed over
> with combustible materials, were set up as lights in
> the night-time, and were thus burnt to death. This
> account is confirmed by Suetonius, and by Martial
> and Juvenal...

Pliny [the younger] was propraetor of Pontus and Bithynia [A.D. 112].... Many [Christians] were brought before him for their faith in Christ. If they remained steadfast, refusing to offer incense to the idols, he condemned them to death for their "inflexible obstinacy." [Some, to escape death] said they had once been Christians but had abandoned that religion... some even twenty years before... that they were wont to meet together on a stated day before it was light, and sing among themselves ...hymn[s] to Christ as God and to bind themselves by an oath not to commit any wickedness, nor to be guilty of theft, or robbery, or adultery, never to falsify their word... [and] to come together to a meal, which they ate in common....

How strong must have been that primitive evidence for Christianity which could induce persons of good sense, in every walk of life, to abandon the religion of their ancestors, and thus, in the face of imperial power, to persist in their adherence to one who had suffered the death of a slave!

We might also refer to Celsus, and Lucian, and Epictetus, and the Emperor Marcus Antoninus, and Porphyry— who all throw light on the early history of Christianity, and all confirm, so far as they go, the accounts in [the New Testament]... as do coins, medals, inscriptions.

One becomes a bit weary of the propaganda which is taught in universities and even in many seminaries and is promoted in books and the media by "experts" who pronounce falsehoods against the Bible with an air of indisputable authority. Unfortunately, the average person never takes the time (or may not have the resources) to check the accuracy of such derogatory statements and repeats these falsehoods trustingly. Just the small amount of data given in the quote above should be enough to show that Christ and Christianity were indeed mentioned and the New Testament record supported by secular writings of the same time or very shortly thereafter.

## ABUNDANT INTRIGUING VERIFICATION

Furthermore, some of these writers, supported by archaeological discoveries, provide additional evidence of a most interesting nature for the authenticity of the New Testament. Once again, more than a hundred years ago this evidence was well-known, and Mark Hopkins presented much of it in his *Evidences*. Here is a brief extract:

> Luke gives to Sergius Paulus a title belonging only to a man of proconsular dignity [*anthupatos*— Acts 13:7,8,12], and it had been doubted whether the governor of Cyprus had that dignity. A coin, however, has been found struck in the reign of Claudius Caesar (the very reign in which Paul visited Cyprus), and under Proclus, who succeeded Sergius Paulus, on which the very title applied by Luke is given to Proclus.
>
> Luke speaks of Philippi as a colony [*kolonia*— Acts 16:12], and the word implies that it was a Roman colony. It was mentioned as such by no other historian, and hence the authority of Luke was questioned. But a medal has been discovered which shows that this dignity was conferred upon that city by Julius Caesar. . . .
>
> There have also been found, in the catacombs of Rome, inscriptions which show, in a touching manner, in opposition to the insinuations of Gibbon and of some later writers, the cruelty of the early persecutions, and the number of those who suffered martyrdom. Much evidence of this kind might be added.[2]

Limited space prevents us from presenting the great amount of additional evidence that could be cited. The truth is that there is far more substantiation of the Bible's authenticity and accuracy to be found in early secular sources than we need. And in addition to supporting the biblical account, the secular writings of the time provide intriguing supplemental insights which prove that it was impossible for the New Testament to have been fabricated years after the events.

There is no way that a forger, putting together a counterfeit record that purported to be written by eyewitnesses of events that occurred centuries earlier, could have had the knowledge to put into the narrative the tidbits of information necessary to authenticate it. It makes far better sense to believe that Luke was indeed an eyewitness traveling with Paul at the time than to imagine that some forger centuries later just happened by chance to use the exact words to properly identify the unusual designations held by Sergius Paulus and the city of Philippi.

## A TESTIMONY TOO GOOD TO BE TRUE?

*Question:* The Antiquities of the Jews, by Flavius Josephus, is often cited by Christians as proof that Jesus Christ actually lived, did miracles, was crucified, and rose from the dead as the New Testament declares. However, I've been told that all of the real scholars agree that the section in Josephus referring to Christ is a forgery that was introduced later, probably by Eusebius, who was the first writer to cite it. This passage is not found in any of the older manuscripts. That such a forgery was necessary would indicate that legitimate supportive records did not exist. Isn't this an almost fatal blow to Christian apologetics?

*Response:* We have already shown that there was more than sufficient corroborative evidence of various kinds, including other contemporary writings, so there was no need for a forgery. Critics love to say that "all of the real scholars agree" to this or that when they really mean certain scholars of a particular bias. The fact is that the passage to which you refer is found in all ancient copies of the works of Josephus. It is accepted by most scholars and referred to as authentic by other ancient writers beside Eusebius. For that reason alone it could not have been added later as the critics want to believe and have unsuccessfully tried to establish.

Those who dispute this section in Josephus do not do so on the basis of any evidence but because what it says is so favorable to the cause of Jesus Christ. Here is the passage:

> Now there was about this time Jesus, a wise man, if it be lawful to call him a man; for he was a doer of wonderful works, a teacher of such men as receive the truth with pleasure. He drew over to him both many of the Jews and many of the Gentiles. He was [the] Christ.
>
> And when Pilate, at the suggestion of the principal men amongst us, had condemned him to the cross, those that loved him at the first did not forsake him; for he appeared to them alive again the third day; as the divine prophets had foretold these and ten thousand other wonderful things concerning him.
>
> And the tribe of Christians, so named from him, are not extinct at this day.[3]

No wonder anti-Christians don't want to admit that the above is authentic! If they face the evidence, however, they have no choice. In fact, there are *two* passages about Christ in Josephus. The authenticity of the second (which is also cited in ancient works) has never been disputed, yet it makes little sense unless the author had mentioned Jesus Christ previously in more detail. The second passage reads:

> Ananus [Ananias] assembled the Jewish Sanhedrin, and brought before it James the brother of Jesus who is called Christ, with some others, whom he delivered over to be stoned as infractors of the law.[4]

It is quite clear that Josephus has already mentioned and made some explanatory remarks about Jesus. Otherwise it would be unreasonable for him to make such a superficial reference to such a major figure, whom this passage itself admits was at least "called Christ." This is especially true inasmuch as Josephus mentions elsewhere in some detail several pretenders who claimed to be the Messiah. Thus his "silence" about Jesus in this brief passage would have been highly suspect had he not explained something about Him previously.

## VERIFICATION OF JOSEPHUS BY HIS CONTEMPORARIES

At the end of his translation of *The Life and Works of Flavius Josephus*, published in 1737, William Whiston includes "Seven Dissertations [appendices] concerning Jesus Christ, John the Baptist, James the Just . . . etc." In these he cites numerous secular and Christian writers from A.D. 110 to the end of the fifteenth century who quoted Josephus as authoritative concerning what he said about Jesus, John the Baptist, and other persons and events named in the New Testament.

One further comment by Professor Hopkins is in order. He explains why it would have been impossible for the contested passage to have been forged by Eusebius or anyone else:

> Had such a forgery been attempted, it would unquestionably have been detected by some of the acute and inveterate enemies of Christianity; for both Josephus and his works were so well received among the Romans that he was enrolled a citizen of Rome, and had a statue erected to his memory. His writings were also admitted into the Imperial Library.
>
> The Romans may further be considered as the guardians of the integrity of his text; and the Jews, we may be assured, would use all diligence to prevent any interpolation in favor of the Christian cause. Yet it cannot be discovered that any objection was ever made to this passage by any of the opposers of the Christian faith in the early ages; their silence therefore concerning such a charge is a decisive proof that the passage is not a forgery. Indeed, the Christian cause is so far from needing any fraud to support it that nothing could be more destructive to its interest than a fraud so palpable and obtrusive.[5]

There is at least one spurious attestation to Jesus attributed to Josephus. This is found in *Josephus—The Jewish War*, translated and with an introduction by G.A.

Williamson (Penguin Books, 1959). Unfortunately, this bogus account has been promoted by overzealous Christians because it is longer than the above and seems to more fully testify to the divinity, miracles, and resurrection of Jesus, even claiming that His tomb was guarded by 30 Roman soldiers and 1000 Jews! The latter claim is obviously not true, since Jews would not stand guard on a Sabbath, especially the high Sabbath of Passover. Moreover, the spurious passage contains other embellishments which conflict with the New Testament, whereas the authentic account quoted above agrees fully with the accounts in the four Gospels.

## WHAT ABOUT MISSING BOOKS OF THE BIBLE?

*Question:* There were at least 15 apostles. That only four of them [Peter, James, John, Paul] would be "inspired" to write the New Testament seems rather odd. One would logically expect many others to have written "inspired" accounts. How do we know there weren't several other records written which were lost—or even that all of the genuine works were lost or destroyed and that the ones we have are frauds substituted in their place?

*Response:* Don't forget Matthew, Mark, and Luke, the first an apostle, the other two sincere disciples. Why should there be any other divinely inspired written record? The New Testament is complete in itself and needs no further inspired witness. As for how we know the ones we have are the true record, we are answering that legitimate question from many different angles with overwhelming evidence throughout these pages. Another observation by Mark Hopkins from the last century deals with this issue:

That such a movement as Christianity . . . involving the origin of so many new institutions and such ecclesiastical and social changes should have originated at such a time and in such a place, and that no written documents [true account] should have been drawn forth by it, is incredible. And that the true account should have perished, leaving not a vestige behind it, and that false ones, and such as these, should have been substituted, is impossible. Of the origin of such institutions we should expect some account. That of our books [New Testament] is adequate and satisfactory. There is nothing contradictory to it, for even spurious writings confirm the truth of our books, and there is no vestige of any other.[6]

Yes, there is one other book which claims to be an inspired record of early Christianity: the Book of Mormon. It purports to give an account of Christ appearing in America to natives who were allegedly the descendants of certain Jews who supposedly sailed the Atlantic to the new world and built large cities, fought wars, etc. Here we have a classic example of outright fraud, and it provides a most striking contrast to the Bible. The Book of Mormon is pure fiction, like the Bhagavad-Gita, the Hindu Vedas, and much of the content in the sacred writings of other religions. The Church of Jesus Christ of Latter-day Saints has spared no archaeological effort in its attempt to authenticate this spurious account and has utterly failed, as must be the case with every such fabrication.

## THE BOOK OF MORMON: AN INSTRUCTIVE COMPARISON

The ruins of cities mentioned in the Bible have been located and their inhabitants identified and their histories verified in proof of the biblical accounts. Secular museums around the world contain vast quantities of ancient inscriptions, documents, coins, utensils, and weapons dating back to Bible times and which thoroughly confirm its pages. This plethora of evidence verifies beyond any question the authenticity and accuracy of the historical record found in the Bible concerning peoples, cultures, places, and events.

In striking contrast, *no evidence of any kind* has ever been found to support the Book of Mormon. This remains the case today, in spite of decades of the most aggressive archaeological exploration throughout

North, Central, and South America. This Herculean effort, supported by the vast wealth and determination of the Mormon Church, has left no stone unturned in the search for verification of the Book of Mormon but has come up empty-handed. Not one piece of evidence has ever been found to support the Book of Mormon—not a trace of the large cities it names, no ruins, no coins, no letters or documents or monuments, nothing in writing. Not even one of the rivers or mountains or any of the topography it mentions has ever been identified!

The Book of Mormon provides an excellent example of the impossibility of fabricating a make-believe scenario and then trying to convince the world that it really happened. Fiction simply doesn't fit into history, and no evidence can be found to support it. For a full exposé of Mormonism we recommend *The God Makers*, both the book and the video.

### A Purely Logical And Irrefutable Authentication

*Question:* I have friends who have been convinced by university or seminary professors that the New Testament is not historically accurate but is a fictional story written long after the events supposedly took place. They can't prove that to me, but neither can I prove them wrong. Is there some simple way, without going into a detailed study of archaeological evidence and historical research, to help them to see that Christianity began as the New Testament says it did?

*Response:* Yes. There is a purely logical argument made famous by Mark Hopkins, though not originated by him, which should be helpful. In his *Evidences* he referred to an earlier writing titled *Short and Easy Method With the Deists*, by Leslie. That author presented four essential criteria which, if met by any event recorded in writing, would establish it as truly historical: "1) That the matter of fact be such that men's outward senses, their eyes and ears, may be judges of it; 2) That it be done publicly, in the face of the world; 3) That not only public monuments be kept up in memory of it, but some outward actions be performed; and 4) That such monuments, and such actions or observances, be instituted, and do commence from the time that the matter of fact was done."

---

Leslie explains that "the first two rules make it impossible for any such matter of fact to be imposed upon men *at the time*, because every man's eyes and ears and senses would contradict it." We know that the Gospels and most of the epistles were written within a few years after the events recorded therein. Thus there were many people still alive who would have refuted what was written if it had not offered a true account of events witnessed by them. For example, the account of Christ calling Lazarus from the grave, if not true, would have been rejected and exposed as fraud by numerous friends and relatives who would have responded indignantly either that Lazarus had not yet died and been laid in any grave or, if he had, that he was still dead and buried.

It is unthinkable that anyone, in the small country of Israel and so soon after the supposed events, would dare to publish fictitious reports of alleged miracles, naming persons and places. Multitudes of people who were still alive from those days and from those regions would have rejected the accounts as lies. Rather than helping to authenticate Christianity, such false accounts would have become known as frauds and the new movement would have been promptly and publicly discredited.

## "ON-THE-SPOT" AUTHENTICATION

Remember, Christianity began right there in Jerusalem. It was based upon the claim that this Jesus, the carpenter from Nazareth turned prophet, who was acclaimed as the Christ by multitudes and whose miracles were spoken of all over Israel and whom the Romans had crucified, was alive, having died for the sins of the world. The very fact that 3000 people converted to

Christ on the day of Pentecost in the heart of Jerusalem and that thousands more in Jerusalem continued day after day to join this "new faith" is irrefutable evidence that these events really happened. *The opposition did not deny the facts.* Christianity was opposed only because it contradicted the authority and teachings of the rabbis.

There is no escaping the fact that this was not a political movement based upon arguable ideologies, nor was it a religious movement based upon emotional attraction to unprovable spiritual theories. Christianity was based upon *events* which had happened in the small country of Israel and had been consummated right there in Jerusalem. The claims could not have been presented (that Jesus of Nazareth had healed the sick, opened blind eyes, raised the dead and Himself rose from the dead, leaving behind an empty tomb) right there in Jerusalem and throughout Judea unless these events had actually occurred. It was for this reason that Jesus told His disciples to begin their preaching in Jerusalem, to establish the church there first of all, and only then to spread the word to a wider audience.

Obviously, the multitudes who heard Peter and the other apostles preach knew the facts and could not refute the message. That short walk outside the city wall to verify that the tomb which all Jerusalem well knew had been guarded by Roman soldiers was indeed empty must have been taken by many skeptics. The word quickly spread in confirmation of this greatest of miracles, a miracle which seemed to put the final stamp of approval by God Himself upon the claims of Jesus Christ.

## WHY CHRISTIANITY COULDN'T HAVE BEEN INVENTED LATER

Leslie then points out that deception would be possible only if the tale were "invented some time after, when the men of that generation wherein the thing was said to be done are all past and gone, and the credulity of later ages might be imposed upon to believe that things were done in former ages which were not." This was clearly not the case with Christianity, for it was proclaimed openly in Jerusalem from the very beginning.

How can we be sure, without checking historical and archaeological records, that Christianity began as it is claimed at the very time of Jesus and the apostles? Leslie points out that the last two criteria he prescribes prevent the fabrication of a fictitious story years after the supposed date of the alleged event being foisted upon later generations as though it were true. He goes on to explain:

> For, whenever such a matter of fact came to be invented, if not only monuments were said to remain of it, but likewise that public actions and observances were constantly used ever since the matter of fact was said to be done, the deceit must be detected by no such monuments appearing, and by the experience of every man, woman and child who must know that no such actions or observances were ever used by them.
>
> For example, suppose I should now invent a story that for the past thousand years every man at the age of twelve years had a joint of his little finger cut off... it is impossible I should be believed...because everyone could contradict me as to the mark of cutting off the joint of the finger; and that being part of my original story, must demonstrate the whole to be false.

Applying this line of reasoning to the New Testament and its testimony of Jesus Christ and the founding of Christianity, Hopkins then argues:

> For any man to have invented the New Testament after the time of Christ, and to have attempted to cause it to be received, would have been as if a man had written an account of the [American] Revolution, and of the celebration of this day [July 4, 1776] from the first, when [in fact] no revolution was ever heard of, and no one had ever celebrated the Fourth of July. Nor, when such a festival was once established, would it be possible to introduce any account of its origin essentially different from the true one.

> But the case of . . . Christian[ity] is even stronger;
> because we have several different institutions which
> must have sprung up at its origin; because baptism
> and the Lord's Supper have occurred so much more
> frequently; and because the latter has always been
> considered the chief rite of a religion to which men
> have been more attached than to liberty or to life.[7]

## No Escape From The Truth

There is no refuting these arguments. That Christianity involves established customs, churches, and a history going back to its very foundation by Christ is beyond dispute. That secular historical evidence supports these claims as far back as we are able to trace cannot be called into question. Furthermore, it can be shown that at many stages in history, disputes have arisen as to what the true practice of Christianity ought to involve. In each case the disputants have gone back to the Bible as the authority.

Even today, when some practices differ widely between Catholics and Protestants, between various Protestant denominations and among factions in the Roman Catholic Church, the appeal is continually both to Scripture and to history. While Protestants look to the Bible alone as the final authority, Catholics look to tradition as well, which they claim goes back to Christ, and to the decisions of Church Councils which have maintained this continuity. Hopkins then concludes the argument:

> We have seen that it was impossible that the
> apostles should have been either deceivers or de-
> ceived, and that the books [New Testament] could
> not have been received, either at the time they pur-
> port to have been written, or at any subsequent
> time, if the facts recorded had not taken place.[8]

The testimony of the New Testament highlights the very logic in the above arguments. On more than one occasion we have the account of the accusations made by the Jewish religious leaders who wanted Paul executed, and we have Paul's defense. The complaint against Paul had to do with Christianity being contrary to Judaism. Never was there the accusation that it was based upon fraud or that any of the facts Paul presented were simply false.

Paul appealed to the knowledge that the Roman officials had of the facts. We are told that Governor Felix had "perfect knowledge of that way" (Acts 24:22)—i.e. of Christianity. Indeed, far from seeing anything contrary to the facts in Paul's testimony, "Felix trembled" as Paul reasoned with him (verse 25). And when he defended himself before Felix's replacement, Festus, and King Agrippa, Paul declared:

> The king knoweth of these things, before whom also I speak freely; for I am persuaded that none of these things are hidden from him, for this thing was not done in a corner (Acts 26:26).

## THE CHALLENGING MYSTERY OF LIGHT

*Question:* I've had several atheists challenge me with the very first chapter of Genesis—not with the usual arguments about the universe being created in six literal days, for which I think there are scientific answers, but with one I can't solve. Verses 14-19 say that God created the sun, moon, and stars on the fourth day. Yet on the very first day, "God said, Let there be light, and there was light.... And the evening and the morning were the first day" (verses 3-5). Where did the light come from on the first day if the sun, moon, and stars weren't created until the fourth day?

*Response:* These are among the favorite verses used by the critics as one more "proof" that the Bible contains contradictions and thus could not be the Word of God. As usual, however, they are too eager to come to such a conclusion. In fact, this passage presents one more unique evidence of the Bible's authenticity and inspiration. Let us think about this problem logically for a moment.

If this is indeed a contradiction, it is certainly so obvious that whoever penned these words would have become immediately aware of it and revised the order of creation to correct it. And if the original writer inexplicably failed to take care of it, then that inexcusable blunder would surely have been "corrected" by a later scribe. But neither revision occurred. The very fact that this apparent contradiction remains in the text to this day forces upon us a logical conclusion.

Obviously Moses, who originally wrote these words and certainly was too perceptive and intelligent not to notice the problem, must have believed he was inspired of God and therefore put the account of creation down exactly as it was revealed to him even though he probably did not understand all that he recorded. Moreover, as we have already noted, the subsequent scribes, too, who painstakingly copied and preserved this ancient record must have been so certain that it was the Word of God that they dared not tamper with it, even leaving intact what might seem to be a number of blatant "contradictions."

Whether or not Moses himself fully understood what God inspired him to write is a question about which we need not concern ourselves. The prophets whom God inspired to record His Word dared not second-guess God on the basis of their imperfect understanding or of the myths current in their day. For example, at the time of superstitious explanations of earthquakes, from the belief that the earth was sitting upon the shoulders of the god Atlas to the theory that it was resting upon a tortoise floating in a huge sea, the Bible declared that God "hangeth the earth upon nothing" (Job 26:7). The Bible, unlike other religious or even ancient scientific and philosophical writings, far from reflecting the limited knowledge and popular superstitions of the culture and time in which it was written, contains truth and understanding neither known by nor available to mankind at the time of the writing. That fact alone is one of the great proofs that the Bible was inspired of God.

## REVEALING KNOWLEDGE BEYOND THE TIMES

Furthermore, the Bible contains hidden wisdom (1 Corinthians 2:7) which was not fully revealed even to those "holy men of God" (2 Peter 1:21) who were inspired to write it. Though its writer probably didn't understand what he had been inspired to declare, Hebrews 11:3 stated centuries before science came to that conclusion that the universe was made out of something invisible. We are specifically told that those who wrote the Old Testament announced things which they didn't fully understand (Romans 1:1,2; 16:25,26; Ephesians 3:3-5). So Moses, too, may not have understood all that was meant when he wrote, "And God said, Let there be light, and there was light."

In keeping with the mystery surrounding light in Scripture, to this very day science has been unable to explain it. Light acts like both a wave and a particle, which is impossible—but it's true. What is light? We still don't know.

We are given a glimpse of a truth in these first few verses of Genesis which is only revealed more fully in the last chapters of the Bible. The secret of the "light" which surrounded the earth prior to the creation of the sun, moon, and stars is made known in this description of the new creation after this present universe (with its sun, moon, and stars) will have been destroyed and replaced:

> I saw a new heaven and a new earth, for the first heaven and the first earth were passed away .... And I John saw the holy city, new Jerusalem, coming down from God out of heaven....
>
> And the city had no need of the sun, neither of the moon, to shine in it, for the glory of God did lighten it, and the Lamb is the light thereof. And the nations of them which are saved shall walk in the light of it....
>
> And there shall in no wise enter into it anything that defileth, neither whatsoever worketh abomination or maketh a lie, but they which are written in the Lamb's book of life....

> And there shall be no night there; and they need no
> candle neither light of the sun, for the Lord God giveth
> them light... (Revelation 21:1,2,23,24,27; 22:5).

The Bible tells us that "God is light, and in him is no darkness at all" (1 John 1:5). That light pervaded the universe from eternity past. Before sin entered the world and until the celestial bodies were created, that supernatural light was apparently directed by God to illuminate this earth. After sin has been removed, the light which God is, and which Christ, who is God, also is, will fill the new universe once again.

## WAS SAUL/PAUL SINCERE BUT DELUDED?

---

*Question:* The conversion of Saul of Tarsus, a rabbi, to Christianity, seems to be the strongest argument that Christian apologists can muster for the resurrection. Even if we accept it as having been written by Luke, the book of Acts presents an account of Saul's conversion that is less than convincing. Yes, he *claimed* he saw Jesus Christ alive on his way to Damascus; and, yes, he was willing to die for this belief. That does not prove, however, that Paul actually saw Christ. It only proves that he *sincerely thought* he saw Him alive years after His crucifixion. He could have imagined that he saw Christ. He could have hallucinated due to a sense of guilt for having persecuted Christ's followers. How can Christians make so much out of Saul's conversion when it stands on such flimsy ground?

*Response:* First of all, it is rather doubtful that a man of Paul's obvious intellect and emotional stability could have experienced such a vivid hallucination and allowed it to change his life. Furthermore, the event was accompanied by visible phenomena—a supernatural light at midday brighter than the sun (Acts 9:3; 26:13), and a voice from heaven—which those accompanying Paul also saw and heard (Acts 9:7). Paul's companions would have refuted his story if they had not also witnessed these things.

---

There was also Paul's sudden blindness and miraculous recovery through a disciple in Damascus who could confirm the facts. Many witnesses must have seen Paul led into Damascus totally blind. Had there been any flaw in Paul's testimony, refutation discrediting him would have followed from many quarters. Yet no one disputed his testimony when he declared it before religious and secular leaders and crowds of Jews who opposed his message on religious grounds. The evidence is compelling.

Saul of Tarsus had been the chief enemy of the church at its very beginning, arresting and imprisoning many believers and persecuting some even to death. This course so diligently pursued must have made him very popular among the religious Jews. As a young rabbi, Saul was already a hero well known for his zeal against Christians. He had everything to live for in remaining true to Judaism. That he would forfeit a brilliant future and become one of those whom he had persecuted, knowing that the same beatings, imprisonment, and eventual martyrdom would befall him as well, is indeed powerful evidence that he was convinced beyond doubt that Jesus Christ was alive and that he had personally met Him. Hallucination simply doesn't fit the known facts.

## CONVINCING EVIDENCE OF ANOTHER KIND

Even more convincing is the leading role which Paul quickly assumed in the explosive growth of early Christianity. He had inside knowledge and taught new doctrines completely at odds with his years of training and practice in Judaism, doctrines which he couldn't possibly have acquired except from Christ Himself. Yet Paul had never met Him prior to His crucifixion. He claimed to have learned all he knew of this new faith directly from the risen Christ. Paul wrote to the Corinthians:

> I have *received of the Lord* that which also I delivered unto you, that the Lord Jesus the same night in which he was betrayed took bread; and when he had given thanks, he broke it and said, Take, eat; this is my body which is broken for you; this do in remembrance of me.

After the same manner also he took the cup,
when he had supped, saying, This cup is the new
testament in my blood; this do ye, as oft as ye drink
it, in remembrance of me (1 Corinthians 11:23-25).

Paul wasn't present on that occasion, so how did he
know what happened at that final intimate meeting between Christ and His 12 disciples? Why was it left to Paul
to explain what happened at the Last Supper and its
meaning? Why not Peter or James or John, who were
there? Clearly the Holy Spirit had Paul write these words
as part of the proof of Christ's resurrection. He testifies
that he "received of the Lord" all that he is now teaching.
We repeat: Everything that he knows about this new faith
and now teaches with such authority Paul claims to have
received personally and directly from the resurrected Lord
Jesus Christ Himself. Nor is there any other explanation.

Unquestionably, Paul had never studied under Christ
with the other disciples. He was a rabbi *opposed* to Christ
during the latter's life. Yet suddenly he became not only the
chief spokesman for Christianity but its chief authority. He
even rebuked Peter to his face and Peter had to acknowledge that Paul was right and he was wrong (Galatians 2:11-
14). Whence this sudden authoritative knowledge?

Of course the skeptics suggest that Paul had hur-
riedly gone to the apostles and said, "I'm a believer in
Jesus now, but I don't understand this Christianity
thing. I want to preach it, so you'd better give me a
crash course. Otherwise I could make some horrible
blunders!" Could that be true? Did Paul learn what he
knew of Christianity from Peter or from other apostles
and Christians?

UNDENIABLE INTERNAL PROOF

On the contrary, it was three years after his conversion that Paul finally came to Jerusalem. And when he attempted "to join himself to the disciples... they were all
afraid of him, and believed not that he was a disciple"
(Acts 9:26). Paul solemnly testifies:

> I certify you, brethren, that the gospel which was preached of me is not after man. For I neither received it of man, neither was I taught it, but by the revelation of Jesus Christ....I conferred not with flesh and blood; neither went I up to Jerusalem to them which were apostles before me, but I went into Arabia. . . .
>
> Afterwards I came into the regions of Syria and Cilicia, and was unknown by face unto the churches of Judaea which were in Christ; but they had heard only that he which persecuted us in times past now preacheth the faith which once he destroyed. And they glorified God in me (Galatians 1:11-24).

That he is telling the truth is clear from the fact that Paul was the revealer of truths unknown to the other apostles. It was Paul to whom Christ made known by revelation (Ephesians 3:3-10) "the mystery, which was kept secret since the world began" (Romans 16:25) and gave to him the privilege of preaching it (1 Corinthians 15:51; Ephesians 5:32; Colossians 1:25-27). He became the leading apostle and authority on Christianity, and the other apostles had to admit that he knew more than they and that he had indeed learned it directly from the risen Christ.

Paul wrote most of the epistles, more than all of the original apostles combined. It was he who stood up against the false doctrine being taught by the Judaizers who came from Jerusalem, where the apostles still resided. Paul confronted the apostles and church leaders in Jerusalem with this heresy (Acts 15) and changed the thinking of the church.

There was no explanation for Paul's knowledge except that Christ had indeed risen from the dead and had revealed Himself and His teachings to this former enemy. Hallucination cannot account for such knowledge and authority.

## MARTYRS' TESTIMONY, AND OF THE MOST CONVINCING KIND

---

*Question:* I don't deny that the early Christians were thrown to the lions, crucified, burned alive, and otherwise killed for their faith. But I object to using their willingness to endure such treatment as proof of Christianity. The followers of many other religious leaders, even of cult leaders later proven to be frauds or evil, have been willing to die for their faith. Look at the 900 followers of Jim Jones lying dead in the jungles of Guiana. Muslims (suicide bombers and other terrorists, for example) are willing to sacrifice themselves for Allah and Mohammed. How can you say that the martyrdoms of Christians prove Christianity any more than the martyrdoms of others prove their religions?

---

## AN ESSENTIAL DISTINCTION

---

*Response:* There are huge differences between the martyrdom of Christians and the others you mention. Most of those who died with cult leaders such as Jim Jones and David Koresh had little or no choice. Therefore their martyrdoms cannot be compared with that of Christians who were given the chance to save their lives if they would deny Christ, yet persisted in their faith in Him though it meant torture and death.

---

Islam, which was spread with the sword, is now maintained by the same means. Today one must be a Muslim to be a citizen of Saudi Arabia. It is the death penalty there and in other Islamic nations for a Muslim to convert to any other religion. Try to imagine what it would be like if one had to be a Southern Baptist or a Methodist (or member of any other religious group) to be a citizen of the United States and that the death penalty would be carried out upon anyone who converted to another religion! (In fact, such will be the case if Islam ever accomplishes its goal of making the United States and every other nation Islamic countries.)

Loyalty to Islam is maintained under the threat of death, whereas loyalty to Christ is maintained by love. Jim Jones and other cult leaders tricked their followers into dying. They were not killed for their faith by persecutors. And they submitted to the death in the belief that not to do so would be to miss heaven. So it is with Muslims who sacrifice their lives in *jihad*. They are taught that this is the only sure way to paradise, so they give their lives to gain eternal life.

In contrast, the followers of Christ are assured of heaven without any required good works or sacrifice on their part. Christ has paid the full price for their salvation. They know they have eternal life and need not die to obtain it. Their submission to persecution and death is out of love for their Lord and their unwillingness to deny Him or to compromise what they believe is the truth.

## DYING FOR FACTS VERSUS LOYALTY TO A RELIGION

To recognize the greatest distinction between Christian martyrs and all others, however, one needs to go back to the apostles themselves and to the early Christians. They died not out of loyalty to a religion but for *testifying to the resurrection of Jesus Christ*. The importance of that fact seems to be overlooked by the skeptics. For example, the famous nineteenth-century atheist Robert Ingersoll wrote:

> All the martyrs in the history of the world are not sufficient to establish the correctness of an opinion. Martyrdom, as a rule, establishes the sincerity of the martyr—never the correctness of his thought. Things are true or false in themselves. Truth cannot be affected by opinions; it cannot be changed, established, or affected by martyrdom. An error cannot be believed sincerely enough to make it a truth.

What he says is true as far as it goes, but he misses the distinction of Christian martyrdom. The apostles and early disciples died for insisting that Christ had risen from the dead; and they insisted upon it not merely as a religious dogma but as an event in real time to which they themselves had been eyewitnesses. Ingersoll admits that people generally won't die for what they know is a lie, yet all of the apostles (except perhaps John) died as martyrs. Not one backed off at the point of death and bought his freedom by confessing that the apostles had dreamed up the story of the resurrection and that it hadn't really happened—or that maybe they weren't really sure they had seen Him alive but perhaps had only thought they had.

We know for certain, even by Ingersoll's standards, that the apostles were sincere—and not just concerning their belief that Jesus was the Messiah, but that they had spent 40 days with Him after His resurrection and He was indeed alive. That is the point. To disprove their solemn testimony, one would have to show that they had simply all imagined that Christ had spent those 40 days with them, showing Himself alive "by many infallible proofs" (Acts 1:3). For such an imagined tale they would all die? Never!

### Eyewitnesses Of The Resurrection

The apostles suffered almost unbearable persecution and then went to their graves as martyrs still affirming that the *events* which they had witnessed had actually occurred. They all testified, to the very death, when they could have bought their freedom by denying it, that Christ's miracles, His teachings, and His resurrection were *factual events* which they themselves had witnessed and therefore could not deny. Greenleaf argues:

> From these absurdities [of men willing to die for a lie] there is no escape, but in the perfect conviction and admission that they were good men, testifying to that which they had carefully observed and considered and well knew to be true.[9]

It is often forgotten that not only those to whom Christ appeared during that historic 40 days but *all Christians* testify to the resurrection of Christ. The very heart of Christianity is the certainty that one is in personal contact with the resurrected Christ, resident in one's heart. Linton picks up that fact when, as a fellow lawyer, he pursues an argument similar to Greenleaf's:

> Nothing in history is better established than the fact that the Gospel writers, and those who believed their report and became Christians, were subjected

to lifelong persecution, frequent torture, and ultimate death. This occurred both at the hands of the Jews, who were incensed at being told that they had slain their own promised Messiah, and of the pagans, who were enraged at being told that all the gods in their Pantheon were but myths and the Pontifex Maximus at Rome but the perpetrator of a hoax, and that the only true God was the One who became incarnate as a Jew and died on a cross.

Now as surely as the human frame shrinks from pain and death, no man ever lied when the natural and sole result of his lying was to incur all the evils possible to suffer in this life and punishment for his lie in any possible life to come.[10]

Therein lies the great distinction. The apostles died for testifying to the resurrection, a question of *fact*, not merely of faith. They were convinced of an *event*. And their willingness to die in attestation of that event is far more convincing than the willingness of others to die for a mere belief or because of loyalty to a religion or religious leader. As Linton points out, "Christ is the only character in all history who has four contemporary biographers and historians, every one of whom suffered persecution [and martyrdom] in attestation of the truthfulness of his narrative."

## PROPHECY, THE GREAT PROOF

*Question:* In several of your books you offer prophecy fulfilled as proof that God inspired the writing of the Bible. But that's proving the Bible by the Bible, which is circular reasoning. Any religion can offer similar "proof" by using their Scriptures in the same way.

*Response:* There is overwhelming evidence of many kinds for the inspiration of Scripture. Prophecy is only part of the evidence. Nor is there anything wrong with "proving the Bible by the Bible" any more than with proving a mathematical theorem by mathematics. However, prophecy fulfilled proves the Bible not by itself but by verification from secular history that what the Bible foretold did indeed occur. As for suggesting that "any religion can offer similar 'proof' by using their Scriptures the same way," that is simply absurd.

---

Give me just one example of a prophecy for the coming of Buddha, Confucius, Zoroaster, Krishna, or Mohammed, much less one that was fulfilled! There simply aren't any. Yet there are scores of *specific* prophecies for the Jewish Messiah throughout the Old Testament. Moreover, we have documentation for the detailed fulfillment of every one of these prophecies in Jesus both from the eyewitnesses who recorded the events and from Josephus and others. There is far more evidence for the events of the life, death, and resurrection of Jesus than for any of the Caesars, for Plato, for Alexander the Great, or for any other ancient historical character. The skeptic rejects Jesus Christ out of personal prejudice rather than from thorough and unbiased investigation and evidence.

Scores of specific prophecies foretold unique events that literally were fulfilled to the letter in the factual history of the Jews as a people. There is no parallel in the history of any other race or ethnic group. We have dealt with the proof provided by biblical prophecies in detail in other books.

*We have heard talk enough. We have listened to all the drowsy . . . vapid sermons that we wish to hear. We have read your bible and the works of your best minds. We have heard your prayers, your solemn groans and your reverential amens. All these amount to less than nothing.*

*We want one fact. We beg at the doors of your churches for just one little fact. . . . We know all about your mouldy wonders and your stale miracles. We want a this year's fact . . . and we demand it now. Let the church furnish at least one, or forever after hold her peace.*

*Praying has become a business, a profession, a trade. A minister is never happier than when praying in public. Most of them are exceedingly familiar with their God. Knowing that he knows everything, they tell him the needs of the nation and the desires of the people, they advise him what to do and when to do it.*

—Robert Green Ingersoll, *famous nineteenth-century lawyer, agnostic, orator*

# 7

# What About Prayer?

## REASONS FOR UNANSWERED PRAYER

*Question:* Jesus promised, "If two of you shall agree on earth as touching anything that they shall ask, it shall be done for them of my Father which is in heaven" (Matthew 18:19). I have never seen it demonstrated that any two Christians getting together can have anything from God upon which they agree. Was Christ's promise, then, not true?

*Response:* Perhaps nothing is more badly misunderstood by the average person, both Christian and non-Christian, than prayer. It is generally thought to be a means of persuading God to fulfill one's dreams and ambitions and to satisfy one's desires. But a moment's reflection should quickly dispel that deadly delusion.

The basic problem in the world is the conflict of wills and the resulting competition for power and supremacy. Prayer, then, would only make matters worse if it released a supernatural power that each person could call upon in order to impose his will upon others and upon the universe. Rather than bringing unity and peace, prayer would then only increase division and conflict by

175

giving each person the power to enforce his will upon others. God must remain in charge of His universe. Of course, there is much that is done that is not according to God's will because He has indeed given man the power of choice. God will not, however, become an active partner in effecting the will of man. He will not lend His power to merely fulfill our selfish desires. Prayer must be according to God's will: "If we ask anything *according to his will* . . . we have the petition" (1 John 5:14,15). Prayer must also meet certain other conditions in order for God to grant the request.

The agreement of two or more together is only *one* of the conditions for prayer being answered. Here are a few of the others presented in the Bible: "Whatsoever ye shall ask in prayer, *believing*, ye shall receive" (Matthew 21:22); "If ye *abide in me, and my words abide in you*, ye shall ask what ye will, and it shall be done unto you" (John 15:7); "Ye ask and receive not because ye ask amiss, that ye may consume it upon your *lusts*" (James 4:3); "Whatsoever we ask we receive of him, because we *keep his commandments and do those things that are pleasing in his sight*" (1 John 3:22).

These are not all of the conditions for answered prayer. These are enough, however, to suggest why so many prayers are not answered in spite of the earnestness of those who meet together to petition their heavenly Father for whatever it is they desire.

### THREE CONDITIONS FOR PRAYER TO BE ANSWERED

*Question:* I have been a Christian for many years and have attended hundreds, perhaps thousands, of prayer meetings. I have heard many earnest prayers for good purposes but rarely have I seen an answer. This is rather shattering to my faith. *Why are so few prayers answered?*

*Response:* First of all, you admit that you have personally seen at least *some* prayers answered. In addition, you have surely heard or read the testimony of others who unquestionably have had miraculous answers to prayer. Consider, for example, George Müller, whose life was an amazing testimony to answered prayer. He housed, clothed, and fed thousands of orphans, made it a point never to ask for any financial help from man but only from God, and recorded in his diary literally thousands of specific answers to prayer. Müller wrote:

Now if I, a poor man, simply by prayer and faith, obtained *without asking any individual*, the means for establishing and carrying on an Orphan-House, there would be something which, with the Lord's blessing, might be instrumental in strengthening the faith of the children of God, besides being a testimony to the consciences of the unconverted, of the reality of the things of God.

This, then, was the primary reason for establishing the Orphan-House. I certainly did from my heart desire to be used by God to benefit the bodies of poor children, bereaved of both parents, and seek in other respects, with the help of God to do them good for this life.... [and] to be used by God in getting the dear orphans trained in the fear of God—but still, the first and primary object of the work was (and still is) that God might be magnified by the fact that the [thousands of] orphans under my care are provided with all they need, only by *prayer and faith* without anyone [other than God] being asked by me or my fellow-laborers [for help or funds]....[1]

We could multiply other examples to show that God does answer *many* prayers. Robert Ingersoll, who was the epitome of agnosticism and ridiculed Christians for praying, demanded "just one little fact" proving that prayers are answered. There are facts by the thousands that he and other agnostics and atheists have refused to accept—not because it could not be proved that prayers are answered, for that has been proved repeatedly, but because their prejudice wouldn't allow them to face the truth.

In fact, an entire library could be filled with testimonies of answers to prayer that cannot be explained away as mere coincidence. The issue, then, is not whether God is able to, or ever does, answer prayer but why His answer to so many prayers is *no*. There are, according to the Bible, at least three factors that determine whether a prayer will be answered or not: 1) whether it is God's *will* to answer it; 2) whether it is God's *time* to answer it; and 3) whether those praying are living in such a relationship with God that it would be *appropriate* for Him to answer the prayer.

We can thank God that many of our prayers are not answered. We are supposed to pray at all times, "Not my will but thine be done." Yet many of our prayers are not in that spirit at all but are actually attempts to persuade God to do man's will, to bless or bring to pass man's plans. Since we are far from perfect in wisdom, it could bring disaster upon us if God always did what we asked.

There is the matter of timing as well. Consider, for example, Hannah's prayer for a son. It was years before the Lord gave her the son for whom she had prayed. At last Samuel was conceived and brought into the world. It must have seemed a long and inexplicable wait to his parents-to-be; but Samuel had to live at a certain time in order to accomplish a particular mission in Israel.

Or consider Nehemiah's prayer for the rebuilding of Jerusalem. We are told of one occasion when he "wept, and mourned certain days, and fasted and prayed before the God of heaven" (Nehemiah 1:4) for the restoration of Jerusalem. The implication is clear, however, that Jerusalem was on his heart continually and that he must have prayed for months and probably years without any answer. The answer came in God's time, and how important that timing was! It had to occur on a specific day foreordained of God. From that date, 69 weeks of years (483 years) would be counted to determine the very day that Jesus would ride into Jerusalem on a donkey and be hailed as the Messiah (Daniel 9:25). Yet Nehemiah may not have even suspected the importance of this timing, although the prophecy of Daniel declaring this remarkable fact had already been recorded.

Finally, an affirmative answer to prayer, when it comes, is at least in part a blessing from God which indicates that the petitioner is living according to God's will

(1 John 3:22). How does one get to know God's will? Based upon his life and experience of many years of walking with God, George Müller gives us some advice as he explains one of the secrets to answered prayer:

> I never remember, in all my Christian course, a period now (in March, 1895) of sixty-nine years and four months, that I ever *sincerely and patiently* sought to know the will of God by *the teaching of the Holy Ghost*, through the instrumentality of the *Word of God*, but I have been always directed rightly.
>
> But if *honesty of heart* and *uprightness before God* were lacking, or if I did not *patiently* wait upon God for instruction, or if I preferred *the counsel of my fellow men* to the declarations of *the Word of the living God*, I made great mistakes (emphasis in original).[2]

Prayer is not a one-way street on which we get everything we want and God gets nothing. Prayer, in fact, is designed to conform us to God's will. For God to answer the prayers of those who are not willing to take time to know His will and are careless about obeying Him in their daily lives would only encourage them to continue to live in disobedience.

### DISCIPLINE AND MATURITY THROUGH PRAYER

*Question:* It is my understanding that Christians should pray "according to God's will." Why doesn't God just do His will without being advised how to do it? And if He knows everything, why does He need anyone to tell Him what needs to be done? If God "cares for His own," as I have so often heard preached, then why do "His own" ever have to cry to Him to supply their needs?

*Response:* No one who truly understands prayer believes that by this means one advises God of anything He doesn't already know, or of how or when to do His will. Prayer is the expression of our desire to God, but true prayer is not an insistence upon that desire. Nor would anyone who knows God want to persuade Him to do anything that is contrary to His will, even if such persuasion were possible. After all, God is wiser than we are. To express in prayer as Christ did as a man, "Not my will, but thine be done" (Luke 22:42), is to acknowledge one's finite understanding and to surrender one's desires to God's infinite wisdom and love, knowing that His way is best.

---

Then why pray at all? Let's look at a specific example. Suppose a person is seriously ill. Prayer for that person's healing is an expression of one's love and concern. It is also an admission that healing is in God's hands and a confession of utter dependence upon Him. Suppose the person recovers so miraculously that there can be no doubt that God intervened. Would God have healed the person without prayer? Inasmuch as full recovery was clearly God's will, we may be certain it would have occurred without prayer, but perhaps not in an obviously miraculous manner.

So what was the point of prayer, if basically the same effect could have occurred without it? All prayer that is not self-centered is an opportunity first of all to praise and thank God and to express one's love to Him. Paul said, "With thanksgiving let your requests be made known unto God" (Philippians 4:6). So worship, thanksgiving, and praise to God come first in prayer and are certainly more than sufficient reason to pray.

Prayer is also an opportunity to express to God one's love and concern for others and at the same time to obediently submit to His will. Prayer can have a powerful effect in molding one's character and bringing one closer to God. The godly person's prayers begin to reflect more and more the will of God as He changes the character and thoughts and deeds of the one praying to conform to His will and plan in all things. God's Spirit moves us to pray for the very thing that He is going to do. Thus the petitioner becomes God's partner in the working out of His will on earth.

As for why those who are His own and for whom God cares should ever have any needs, there are several reasons. First of all, as any wise parent on earth would do for his children, our heavenly Father may be teaching patience and molding character by delaying answers to prayers for certain needs. There also may be conditions which must be met in one's life before God sees fit to meet some needs.

A child will never learn self-control and self-discipline and the other essential lessons in life if the parents instantly give him everything he wants. Knowing this and being confident of God's love and care, one does not despair when prayers are not answered, but seeks to learn what God is teaching. Of course, there is also the difference between what we may *think* are real needs and those things which God, in His wisdom, considers to be unnecessary or even harmful desires. Thankfully, we wait in vain for Him to provide those for us.

PRAYER IS MUCH MORE THAN ASKING

---

*Question:* Jesus said we are not to use "vain repetitions" in prayer nor will we be heard for our "much speaking"(Matthew 6:7). Yet He also said that we should persist in prayer. That seems to be a contradiction. Why isn't it enough to ask God once? He's either going to grant the request or not. Why repeat a prayer?

*Response:* Prayer is communion with God and thus involves getting to know Him intimately in a relationship of heavenly love. Understandably, then, He does not respond to casual inquiry but to the passion of the heart. In the Old Testament God said, "Ye shall seek me, and find me when ye shall search for me with *all your heart*" (Jeremiah 29:13). In the New Testament God says He is "a rewarder of them that *diligently* seek him" (Hebrews 11:6). Prayer requires diligent and passionate persistence. Nothing less shows the fervor of sincerity and love that God desires in our relationship with Him.

---

Jesus said that we should always persist in prayer and not give up (Luke 18:1). He said that a characteristic of God's elect is that they "cry day and night unto him" (Luke 18:7). He encouraged us to keep asking, seeking, and knocking at the door of God's mercy and grace until we receive our petition from Him (Luke 11:5-10). Such persistence is not the "vain repetition" which Christ condemned.

The latter need not come from the heart but can be recited mechanically without any thought, much less passion. As Christ said, vain repetition operates on the premise that God will hear us because of the sheer volume of our words—i.e., quantity instead of quality. This is the "much speaking" which He rejected. To repeat a prayer again and again because of passion, however, is not "vain repetition" but reflects the sincerity and earnestness that God loves to reward.

Why isn't it enough to ask once? Often it is. David asked only once for God to defeat "the counsel of Ahithophel" (2 Samuel 15:31). That defeat was the key to victory over those who, led by David's own son Absalom, had chased him from his throne. But Jesus indicated that God sometimes listens long to the cry of His elect without responding (Luke 18:1-8). The implication is that He delays not because He doesn't want to answer their cry, but because He desires to mature and mold them to His will.

**"IN THE NAME OF JESUS": WHAT DOES IT MEAN?**

---

*Question:* Jesus said, "If ye shall ask anything in my name, I will do it" (John 14:14). I've heard thousands of prayers that were offered, in reliance upon that promise, "in the name of Jesus" or even "in the *mighty* name of Jesus," sincere prayers from simple people that were never answered. Wouldn't these many unanswered prayers offered "in the name of Jesus" prove that Christ doesn't or can't keep His word?

*Response:* "In the name of Jesus" is not a magic formula like "Open Sesame," which merely had to be spoken once in order for the secret door to the thieves' treasure to swing wide open. Merely repeating the words "in the name of Jesus" doesn't make it so. For a prayer to be truly "in the name of Jesus," it must be as He would express it if He were praying. It must be for the furtherance of *His*

interests and to *His* glory. His name must be stamped on
the character and engraved on the heart and life of the
one praying "in His name."

---

Many years ago I managed the affairs of a multimillion-
aire. In order to do so, I had been given the authority to act in
his name. Powers of attorney giving me the right to sign his
name and to conduct business in his name were registered in
various counties and states. There was nothing on the face of
the documents that would prevent me from making out a
check for a million dollars, signing his name to it, and de-
positing it in my own bank account. Had I done so, however,
he could have recovered from me in a court of equity.

Though the documents didn't state it explicitly, it
was understood that I had the power to use another
person's name only for his good and in his best interests, not my own. And so it is with our Lord. There are
no restrictions stated in His promise that He will do
whatever we ask in His name. It is understood, however, that to pray in His name is to ask as He would ask
for His interests and glory.

Tragically, all too many Christians imagine that "in the
name of Jesus" are magic words which, if added to a prayer,
no matter how self-seeking, will enable a person to get from
God whatever he or she desires. When the desired response
doesn't come from God there is often great confusion as to
why earnest prayers aren't answered, and even at times re-
sentment against Christ for not keeping what is perceived
to be His promise. James explained it well:

> Ye ask [in prayer] and receive not because ye
> ask amiss, [not to God's glory, but] that ye may
> consume it upon your lusts (James 4:3).

## How To "Believe That You Receive" When Praying

---

**Question:** Christ promised, "What things soever ye
desire, when ye pray, believe that ye receive them, and ye
shall have them" (Mark 11:24). There are no conditions

stated such as abiding in Christ, being obedient, asking according to God's will, or anything else. Do you know any Christians for whom this promise is fulfilled in that they always get whatever they ask for in prayer? I've never met one for whom that is true. How can you explain away Christ's failure to fulfill this promise?

*Response:* One must first of all understand exactly what "believe that ye receive them" actually means. Christ's phrase "when ye pray" is all-important. Prayer is to *God*. Obviously, then, if the prayer is going to be answered, *God* must answer it. So to "believe that ye receive them" means to believe that *God* will grant or do that for which one is praying. Clearly, to attempt to *believe* that God would do anything which one is not certain is God's will would be presumptuous.

---

On what basis, then, could one have *whatever one desires* by *believing* that one receives these things? Is there some mysterious power of the mind which is activated by "believing" and which literally creates what one "believes"? That idea has been at the heart of occultism for thousands of years. That teaching has been popularized in the secular world by a variety of motivational speakers and writers such as Claude Bristol (*The Magic of Believing,* etc.), Denis Waitley (*Seeds of Greatness,* etc.) and others. The same belief in the magical power of *belief* has even become popular in the church through the writings of Norman Vincent Peale (*The Power of Positive Thinking,* etc.) and the many books on *The Power of Possibility Thinking* by Peale's chief disciple, Robert Schuller. The latter states:

> ... through possibility thinking ... [an] amazing power will unfold in your life.... [3]
> You don't know what power you have within you ...! You make the world into anything you choose. Yes, you can make your world into whatever you want it to be! [4]

So we can take God's world and reshape and remake it to whatever we wish through possibility thinking? Here we have a serious and deadly contradiction. If what we pray for comes to pass because we *believe* it will, then God has no real part to play in the answer to our prayers. Instead, we are producing the results by the power of our own *belief.*

There is a vast difference between believing that what I'm praying for will happen *because I believe it will happen* and in believing that *God will make it happen* in response to my *faith in Him.* To recognize this difference (which is as wide as the distance between heaven and hell) is crucial in understanding the promise of Jesus quoted above.

If *believing* does not in and of itself *create* the answer to prayer, might it not at least *cause God to answer the prayer?* It takes little thought to realize that we cannot make God do something merely by "believing" He will do it. If we could, then we rather than God would be in charge of our lives and even the entire universe.

Genuine faith (in contrast to the power of belief) is a gift of God (Ephesians 2:8). We can only conclude that Christ was speaking of true faith in God. When God gives the faith to know for certain that He is going to grant our request, then and only then can we *believe* that we receive our request from Him. Wonderfully, we find that our desires more and more coincide with His will.

CAN CHRISTIANS ALWAYS EXPECT TO BE HEALED?

---

*Question:* How is it that Christians as a class do not live any longer or healthier lives than the average person, yet so many prayers go up for their health and healing?

*Response:* I don't know of any authoritative survey which has established that Christians don't live longer on the average than any other segment of society. However, there is no reason (other than a healthier diet and lifestyle) that they should. The Bible doesn't promise greater longevity to believers, so there is no biblical basis for praying for it. Rather, Christians are promised persecution and martyrdom.

---

There is a popular teaching within the Pentecostal and Charismatic movements that a Christian who is filled with the Spirit and walking in faith should never become ill or feel pain. It is alleged that "healing is in the atonement," an idea which is derived from Isaiah's declaration "with his stripes we are healed" (53:5). Peter, however, lets us know that this statement doesn't refer to healing from disease but from sin:

> Who [Christ] his own self bore our sins in his own body on the tree, that we being dead to sins should live unto righteousness, by whose stripes ye were healed (1 Peter 2:24).

It is verse 4 in Isaiah 53 that deals with the healing of physical ailments: "Surely he hath borne our griefs and carried our sorrows...." Furthermore, that promise was fulfilled in the healing ministry of our Lord upon earth and thus does not relate to a continuing healing of our bodies today. That interpretation is stated for us clearly:

> When the even was come, they brought unto him [Christ] many that were possessed with devils; and he cast out the spirits with his word, and healed all that were sick, that it might be fulfilled which was spoken by Esaias the prophet, saying, Himself took our infirmities and bore our sicknesses (Matthew 8:16,17).

Of course, every blessing we have is "in the atonement." The truth is that through Christ's atoning death and resurrection we have the promise of something far better than the perpetual healing of these corruptible bodies of sin in order to lengthen our lives here in this "present evil world" (Galatians 1:4). We have the promise of new bodies like Christ's resurrected, glorified body and eternal life in a new universe without sin or suffering.

All those who have taught "healing in the atonement" as the guarantee that Christians need never be ill or even die are themselves dead or dying. Not one of them has been able to lengthen his life substantially. One would think that if this teaching were true, then at least some of its advocates surely would have lived remarkably longer lives than average, but that is not the case.

As for prayers for the ill and dying, many of these are miraculously answered by God. But all people eventually die, and usually at an age not much beyond the allotted "threescore years and ten." That is what the Bible teaches.

## JESUS NEVER PRAYED THE LORD'S PRAYER

*Question:* In his famous "Lord's Prayer," Jesus prayed "and lead us not into temptation" (Matthew 6:13). Yet we are told that He was in fact "led up of the [Holy] Spirit into the wilderness to be tempted of the devil" (Matthew 4:1). So even His own prayer wasn't answered! How can you explain this?

*Response:* First of all, the "Lord's Prayer" is misnamed. This was not a prayer that the Lord Himself prayed, nor was it to be repeated word-for-word by anyone. It was a *pattern* for prayer—"*After this manner* therefore pray ye" (Matthew 6:9)—that He taught His disciples in response to their request "Teach us to pray" (Luke 11:1). It ought to be called the "Disciples' Prayer."

In giving them this pattern or model prayer, Jesus said to His disciples, "*When ye pray*, say, Our Father which art in heaven, Hallowed be thy name...etc." (Luke 11:2). There is no suggestion that Christ Himself ever prayed this prayer. Indeed, it would be entirely inappropriate for Him, because the prayer includes the phrase "And forgive us our sins" (Luke 11:4), something which Jesus, being sinless, would never have prayed. So in responding to your question, I am doing so with the understanding that this is a prayer for His *followers* to pray, but not for Christ. That fact takes care of the question about the phrase "lead us not into temptation," as far as Christ is concerned.

What about this phrase for His followers? No one who asks God "Lead us not into temptation" is guaranteed immunity from being, like Christ Himself, tempted by Satan. That phrase, like all the rest of the prayer, comes in the context of the affirmation "Thy kingdom come; thy will be done on earth, as it is in heaven." Thus the person repeating this prayer is ready to submit to God's will, whatever that may be, even including being tempted by Satan.

Then why ask not to be led into temptation? It is the voice of humility acknowledging our own frailties. It is the opposite of praying proudly, "Lead us into all the temptation You want, Lord, because we're ready to handle it!" Praying the biblical phrase acknowledges the appropriateness of Paul's warning, "Let him that thinketh he standeth take heed lest he fall" (1 Corinthians 10:12). At the same time it is the voice of trust in God in case temptation should come.

## WHAT AND WHY DID CHRIST PRAY?

---

*Question:* Luke tells us that Christ "went out into a mountain to pray, and continued all night in prayer to God" (6:12). If Jesus is God, yet it says He prayed to God, did He pray to Himself? And if He is God, why did He pray at all—especially all night? That sounds like He was desperate for help, which doesn't reflect well upon Him as the supposed Savior of the world!

*Response:* Prayer is primarily communion with God in worship and praise and love. Unfortunately, most people (and that would include most Christians) think of prayer almost exclusively as begging some favor or intervention or help from God, and they only pray to this end. That is not what prayer is mainly about. Nor would Christ's continuing in prayer all night indicate that He was desperate for help. It would rather indicate the depth and closeness of His communion with His Father.

---

Although Jesus was God in the flesh, He was indeed flesh, a real man. That fact is impossible for us to comprehend. In fact, Paul calls it a *mystery*: "Without controversy great is the mystery of godliness: God was manifest in the flesh, justified in the Spirit, seen of angels, preached unto the Gentiles, believed on in the world, received up into glory" (1 Timothy 3:16).

When Christ prayed to the Father, He did not do so as the eternal Son of God, one with the Father, but as a man who repeatedly said, "I can of mine own self do nothing. . . . I seek not mine own will, but the will of the Father which hath sent me" (John 5:30). And again, "The words that I speak unto you I speak not of myself [on my own initiative]; but the Father that dwelleth in me, He doeth the works" (John 14:10).

Yes Christ also prayed out of deep need and weakness as a man. In the Garden of Gethsemane He cried out in agony so intense that His "sweat was as it were great drops of blood" (Luke 22:44): "O my Father, if it be possible, let this cup [of bearing the sins of the world] pass from me; nevertheless not as I will, but as thou wilt" (Matthew 26:39). But He never prayed, "Lead me not into temptation."

### WHAT IS "THE PRAYER OF FAITH"?

---

*Question:* The Bible very clearly states in unmistakable language with no conditions attached, "The prayer of faith will heal the sick" (James 5:15). Yet thousands of such prayers for healing have gone up to God unanswered. How can one reconcile the promise with the results?

*Response:* Once again, the key is in understanding that "faith" is not some power we aim at God to get Him to do our will. On the contrary, true faith is complete and total trust in God, which by very definition must include submission to His will. That fact helps us to understand what the Bible means by "the prayer of faith." It obviously means absolute and total trust in God to heal the sick and the complete assurance that He will do so.

---

On what basis could such a prayer be offered to God? Obviously only if the one who is praying had complete faith that God was going to do what was being asked. How would one have such confidence without knowing that it was the will of God to do so? There is no verse in the Bible that promises anyone a healing every time it is asked or that says it is always God's will for every Christian to be healed of every instance of illness.

Thus the kind of faith Christ is talking about could only come as a gift from God. I have experienced this on rare occasions, sometimes for others and sometimes with regard to myself when I was ill. At those times, when praying for a sick person (or for my own healing), I had complete confidence that healing would occur instantly — and so it happened.

No one can "work up" this kind of faith. It would be presumptuous to try to "believe" that God was going to heal someone unless one was absolutely certain that it was God's will to do so. The so-called "faith healers" teach that healing can be claimed at all times for anyone and everyone. Their failure to put this into practice, however, on TV and in large rallies is so evident that one wonders how they continue to gather large crowds. The complete assurance that healing will take place in any given situation in response to prayer can come only by direct revelation from God.

Then should we not pray for the sick unless we have received such a revelation? No. Christ said that "men ought always to pray, and not to faint [i.e. give up]" (Luke 18:1). There are many examples in the Bible of godly people (and even Christ Himself) praying for something that God refused to grant. We may always ask God to do what we believe would be for the good of others and to His glory. And we should persist in asking until we know it is not God's will to grant the request.

## WHERE IS GOD'S WILL IN FAITH AND PRAYER?

---

*Question:* I've heard a number of preachers on Christian TV say that to ask for something in prayer and then to say, "If it be Your will, Lord," or "According to Your will, Lord," will destroy one's faith. I tend to agree. What do you say?

*Response:* While there is much good, unfortunately there is also an abundance of heresy on Christian TV. Far from being supported by the Bible, this teaching contradicts it. After making a request of His Father in heaven in prayer, Jesus added, "Nevertheless, not as I will but as thou wilt" (Matthew 26:39). That sounds very much like "If it be Your will, Lord" or "According to Your will, Lord." The words are only slightly different, but the meaning is exactly the same.

---

Instead of submission to God's will being a *hindrance* to faith, it is the only way to *have* faith. Faith in God causes one to trust Him and to want His will above all and thus to obey Him. Would you desire, even if you could, to persuade God to do something against His will? We have dealt with this question in some depth earlier, so I won't go into it again.

---

*Question:* Jesus told His disciples to pray, "Our Father, who art in heaven ... thy kingdom come, thy will be done.... " Isn't God going to do His will without our asking? Why ask Him to bring in his kingdom? Isn't that His plan anyway?

*Response:* Prayer is all about asking God to do what He has planned to do. Prayer is entering into partnership with God so that our desires reflect His. To pray "Thy kingdom come; thy will be done on earth as it is in heaven (Matthew 6:10) is to affirm our longing that God's plans be fulfilled and His purposes realized throughout the universe to the furtherance of man's joy and hope. What could be a better prayer than this?

---

### CHRIST'S UNANSWERED PRAYER IN GETHSEMANE

---

*Question:* I think the classic example of unanswered prayer is the one Jesus supposedly prayed in Gethsamene on His way to the cross: "If it be possible, let this cup pass from me" (Matthew 26:39). We are told that the "cup" He feared (of going to the cross) didn't pass from Him. Why was He so afraid of the cross? Thousands were crucified by the Romans, many bearing it bravely and some even defiantly. Doesn't the fact that Christ was so afraid and that His prayer wasn't answered disprove the claim that He was God in the flesh?

*Response:* Jesus did not fear the cross. It was not the thought of the intense physical suffering He faced that made His sweat seem like drops of blood. Instead, His holy soul shrank from becoming the very thing He hated: sin. As Paul explained, "He [God] has made him [Christ] to be sin for us, [he] who knew no sin, that we might be made the righteousness of God in him" (2 Corinthians 5:21).

---

As for this being the classic example of unanswered prayer, you are not far wrong. The fact that Christ's prayer was not answered speaks volumes to us. We thereby know that there was no other possible means for our redemption. Had there been any other way, God would not have insisted upon the cross.

We are assured that not even God's infinite love for His Son could cause Him to go back upon His promise to save the world from the penalty which His own righteous law demanded for sin. The cross which Christ endured in obedience to His Father and out of love for mankind stands forever as proof of God's love and assures us that we can never be lost. For as Paul said:

> I am persuaded that neither death nor life, nor angels nor principalities nor powers, nor things present nor things to come, nor height nor depth nor any other creature shall be able to separate us from the love of God which is in Christ Jesus our Lord (Romans 8:38,39).

## DO CATHOLICS REALLY PRAY TO THE "SAINTS"?

---

*Question:* I can't seem to get a straight answer from my Catholic friends concerning prayers to the saints.

They seem ambivalent on the subject. Some admit they pray to Mary, while others deny it. What is the truth?

*Response:* It is not surprising that you have found ambivalence. Roman Catholic apologists generally deny that prayers are offered to Mary and the saints and insist that they only ask Mary and the saints to pray for them, just as one might ask of a friend. This deceit is promoted widely and vigorously to counter valid criticism from Protestants on this vital subject.

------

For example, a recent major article featured on the cover of the official magazine of the Christian Booksellers Association made this statement: "Catholics only ask saints to pray for them—just as we ask the living to pray for us." [5] The author, himself a Catholic and university professor, surely knew that he was not telling the truth. And why would the Christian Booksellers Association, an evangelical body, pass along such misinformation?

Here are just a few of the facts. Consider first of all "The Holy Father's [Pope's] Prayer for the Marian Year [1988]." This was the official prayer for all Catholics *to* Mary for an entire year and came from the highest authority in the Roman Catholic Church. In it Pope John Paul II never once asked Mary to *pray for* Catholics. Instead, he asked her to *do* what she would have to be God to *do*: to comfort, guide, strengthen, and protect "the whole of humanity...." His prayer ended, "Sustain us, O Virgin Mary, on our journey of faith and obtain for us the grace of eternal salvation."

## MARY: AS GREAT AS GOD AND MORE SYMPATHETIC?

For Mary to guide and protect the whole of humanity and sustain all Catholics on their journey of faith, she would have to be omnipotent, omniscient, and omnipresent. What supernatural powers would it take on her part to hear millions of prayers simultaneously in hundreds of different languages and dialects, to keep them all in her memory, and to answer them all by her power! Furthermore, it is blasphemy of the worst kind to ask Mary to obtain the salvation which Christ alone has already provided through His death and resurrection and now offers freely by His grace to all who will believe in Him.

In Denver, at the close of the Sunday Mass for the August 1993 World Youth Day, John Paul II consigned all youth and the entire world to Mary's *protection* and *guidance*. Here again was a prayer by the Pope *to* Mary asking her to *do* what she would have to be deity to accomplish:

> Mary of the New Advent, we implore your protection on the preparations that will now begin for the next meeting [World Youth Day]. Mary, full of grace, we entrust the next World Youth Day to you. Mary, assumed into heaven, we entrust the young people of the world . . . the whole world to you![6]

Catholics only ask Mary to *pray for* them? If one asks prayer of a friend one doesn't say, "I implore your protection and entrust the whole world to you"! Yet such requests that only God could fulfill are typical of Catholic petitions of Mary, who is exalted to omnipotence and credited with caring for all who trust in her.

Both the new *Catechism of the Catholic Church* (approved by the Vatican) and the Second Vatican Council (Vatican II) refer to Mary as "the Mother of God to whose protection the faithful fly in all their dangers and needs." [7] Why fly to her protection when God's protection is available? And if this Catholic Mary can indeed protect all Catholics from all dangers and supply all their needs, then she must be at least as great as God. Moreover, she is apparently considered to be more sympathetic than God, because at least a thousand times as many prayers are offered to Mary as are offered to God and Christ combined.

Mary is the "Mother of God"? Yes, Jesus is God and she is His mother. She is only His mother, however, through His *incarnation*. She is the mother of the *body* which Christ took when He came into the world. Obviously, however, she can't be the mother of the eternal Son of God (Christ as God before He became man), for He existed an eternity before Mary was born. Yet prayers to Mary, including for salvation, are based upon her imagined status as Queen Mother of heaven.

## SALVATION THROUGH MARY?

The most authoritative book written on Catholicism's "Virgin Mary" is by Cardinal and Saint Alphonsus de Liguori. Titled *The Glories of Mary*, it is a virtual compendium of what the great "saints" of the Roman Catholic Church have had to say about Mary down through the centuries. The chapter headings are staggering, crediting Mary with attributes, abilities, titles, and functions that belong to Christ alone: Mary, Our Life, Our Sweetness; Mary, Our Hope; Mary, Our Help; Mary, Our Advocate; Mary, Our Guardian; Mary, Our Salvation." Here is a sampling of Liguori's quotes of what the leading Roman Catholic "saints" down through the centuries have said about Catholicism's Mary, but which in fact are true only of Christ:

> Sinners receive pardon by ... Mary alone. He falls and is lost who has not recourse to Mary. Mary is called ... the gate of Heaven because no one can enter that blessed kingdom without passing through her. The way of salvation is open to none otherwise than through Mary ... the salvation of all depends on their being favored and protected by Mary. He who is protected by Mary will be saved; he who is not will be lost ... our salvation depends on thee.... God will not save us without the intercession of Mary.... who would receive any grace, were it not for thee, O Mother of God ...?[8]

It should be quite clear that Roman Catholics are taught to look to Mary not only for the supernatural protection and guidance and help which only God could provide, but also for that very salvation which only God through Christ could provide and, in fact, has already provided. Here is a typical prayer, once again *to* Mary, taken from a popular booklet of Marian prayers, which is obtainable at any Catholic bookstore:

> In thy hands I place my eternal salvation, and to thee do I entrust my soul.... For, if thou protect me, dear Mother, I fear nothing; not from my sins,

because thou wilt obtain for me the pardon of them; nor from the devils, because thou art more powerful than all hell together; nor even from Jesus, my Judge himself, because by one prayer from thee, he will be appeased. But one thing I fear; that, in the hour of temptation, I may neglect to call on thee, and thus perish miserably. Obtain for me, then, the pardon of my sins.... [9]

## THE ROSARY: MOST REPEATED PRAYER TO MARY

As one final example from the hundreds that could be given, consider the Rosary. This is the best-known and most recited Catholic prayer, repeated millions of times by the faithful worldwide each day. It concludes with this final petition:

Hail, holy Queen, Mother of Mercy! our life, our sweetness, and our hope! To thee do we cry, poor banished children of Eve; to thee do we send up our sighs, mourning and weeping, in this valley of tears. Turn, then, most gracious Advocate, thine eyes of mercy toward us; and after this our exile show unto us the blessed fruit of thy womb, Jesus; O clement, O loving, O sweet Virgin Mary.

Quite clearly, Catholics do not merely ask Mary to *pray for* them. They pray *to* her. And why not, if she is all that the Rosary says she is: our *life* and our *hope*? The Bible, however, says that *Christ* is "our life" (Colossians 3:4) and "our hope" (1 Timothy 1:1)! Again Paul declares that the "blessed hope" of the Christian is "the glorious appearing of the great God and our Savior, Jesus Christ" (Titus 2:13). Peter confirms that the Christian has been given a "living hope by the resurrection of Jesus Christ from the dead" (1 Peter 1:3). Never does the Bible suggest that Mary is also our life or hope! Christ is more than enough!

Do Mary's "eyes of mercy" actually see everyone in the world? Isn't that capability an attribute of God alone? Is she really the "Mother of Mercy"? Didn't God's mercy exist long before Mary was even born? We read of the "God of my mercy" (Psalm 59:17) and are encouraged to trust in the mercy of God (Psalm 52:8; Luke 1:78; etc.), but we never read a word in the entire Bible about Mary's mercy toward mankind. Those who know God's mercy have no need of Mary's.

Regardless of what any individual Catholic may believe, the teaching of the Roman Catholic Church and the practice of the vast majority of her members elevates Mary to a position where she is at least equal in power to God and is considered to be far more sympathetic than He. No wonder, then, that Roman Catholics by the hundreds of millions perpetually offer prayers *to Mary* for every need and desire.

## WHO HAS THE "KEYS" TO "BIND AND LOOSE" TODAY?

*Question:* Jesus said, "I will give unto you the keys of the kingdom of heaven, and whatsoever you shall bind on earth shall be bound in heaven." That sounds as though we have the authority not just to ask God for something in prayer, but to command Him. Why can't we make this work today?

*Response:* You have mixed two Scriptures. The promise "I will give unto thee the keys of the kingdom of heaven, and whatsoever thou shalt bind on earth shall be bound in heaven: and whatsoever thou shalt loose on earth shall be loosed in heaven" (Matthew 16:19) was given to Peter individually, the singular "thee" and "thou" making that clear. Shortly thereafter, the same promise of binding authority (minus the statement about the "keys of the kingdom of heaven") was repeated word for word to all of the disciples: "Whatsoever ye shall bind on earth shall be bound in heaven, and whatsoever ye shall loose on earth shall be loosed in heaven" (Matthew 18:18). The plural, "Ye," makes it clear that on this occasion the promise was given to all the disciples.

How do we understand the "keys of the kingdom of heaven" given to Peter individually? That Peter did not have a "key" or "keys" by which he alone could open the door into the kingdom for *all* who would enter is very clear. One enters the kingdom by believing the gospel and as a result being born again by the Holy Spirit (John 3:3-5). That gospel was preached by Christ (Luke 4:43), and He commissioned all of His disciples to preach it as well (Luke 9:2) long before the "keys" were given to Peter. Christ said that Abraham, Isaac, and Jacob would be in the kingdom (Luke 13:28), but they certainly were not given entrance by Peter, having entered it centuries before he was born. Many entered the kingdom through the preaching of Philip (Acts 8:12) and Paul (Acts 14:22; 19:8; 20:25; 28:31) and, by implication, through the preaching of the other apostles when Peter was neither present nor referred to as holding any required "key."

## When The Keys Were Used

The only unique actions by Peter which could be associated with opening the kingdom to anyone were on the day of Pentecost and at the home of the Roman centurion Cornelius. These were historic occasions on which Peter undoubtedly used the "keys of the kingdom": one key to open the kingdom through the gospel to the Jews (Acts 2:14-41) and the other key to open the kingdom to the Gentiles (Acts 10:34-48). Although Paul was "the apostle to the Gentiles" (Romans 11:13), Peter was the first to preach the gospel and offer salvation to non-Jews. He reminded the church leaders of that fact when they gathered in Jerusalem to discuss the status of Gentiles:

> Men and brethren, ye know how that a good while ago God made choice among us, that the Gentiles [the household of Cornelius] by my mouth should hear the word of the gospel, and believe. And God, which knoweth the hearts, bore them witness, giving them the Holy Ghost, even as he did unto us, and put no difference between us and them, purifying their hearts by faith (Acts 15:7-9).

Obviously these keys given to Peter by Christ, one for the Jews and the other for the Gentiles, needed to be used only once. The door of the kingdom having been opened to all mankind, the "keys" had served their purpose. The Roman Catholic Church, however, teaches that the "keys" bestowed a unique and lasting authority upon Peter which then passed to his alleged successors, the popes. There is no support for this belief either in Scripture or in history. Peter never again used "keys" during his lifetime. Obviously, having served their purpose, they were no longer needed. Nor is there a word about Peter's alleged successors or subsequent use of the "keys." That the popes were not by any stretch of the imagination successors to Peter is very clear from both the Bible and history, a fact which we document thoroughly in *A Woman Rides the Beast*.

### SUCCESSORS OF THE APOSTLES TODAY?

Furthermore, it is clear that *all Christians* are the "successors" to Peter and the other apostles. Jesus told His disciples, "Go ye into all the world, and preach the gospel" (Mark 16:15). He commanded them to teach those who believed the gospel "to observe all things whatsoever I have commanded you" (Matthew 28:19,20). That would obviously include teaching all new disciples to preach the gospel and make disciples, who in turn would be likewise taught. Those of us who are believers today have heard the gospel from others, who in turn heard it from others, and so forth all the way back to the original disciples of Christ. Thus we (and all others who have believed the gospel from the day of Pentecost until now) are bound to obey everything that Christ commanded the original 12 disciples. That would include the command He gave His disciples regarding "binding and loosing" in His name and by His power. No exception is made for anything the apostles were commanded to do.

Roman Catholicism claims that the bishops are the successors of the apostles and therefore they alone can "bind and loose." Similarly, some Charismatics try to make some special power out of "binding and loosing" available only for certain "prophets" or those who have this special gift. Note, however, that the "binding and loosing" in Matthew 18:18 is linked with the promise "Where two or three are gathered together in my name, there am I in the midst of them" (Matthew 18:20). That applies to *all* Christians, and so does every other promise and command given to the disciples.

As for "binding and loosing," the context and the entire tenor of Scripture make it clear that Jesus was not handing His disciples some unique power which they could wield as they please. He was telling them that as His representatives they were to act in His name alone. This is not different from His promise that "whatsoever ye shall ask the Father in my name, he will give it you" (John 16:23). Invoking God's name in prayer is not a magic formula whereby we receive automatic answers to our requests. The same is true with "binding and loosing." Whether binding demonic spirits in a certain situation or loosing someone from the power of sin in their lives, it must be in Christ's name, as He would do it, to His glory, through His Word, and in the power of the Holy Spirit.

*A man of thought and sense does not believe in the existence of the Devil. He feels certain that imps, goblins, demons and evil spirits exist only in the imagination of the ignorant and frightened. . . . Back of this belief there is no evidence, and there never has been. . . .*

*Now take the Devil out of the New Testament, and you also take the veracity of Christ; with that veracity you take the divinity; with that divinity you take the atonement, and when you take the atonement, the great fabric known as Christianity becomes a shapeless ruin.*

—Robert Green Ingersoll

*We [devils] are really faced with a cruel dilemma. When the humans disbelieve in our existence we lose all the pleasing effects of direct terrorism and we make no magicians. On the other hand, when they believe in us, we cannot make them materialists and skeptics. . . . I have great hopes that we shall learn in due time how to emotionalise and mythologise their science to such an extent that what is, in effect, a belief in us (though not under that name) will creep in while the human mind remains closed to belief in the Enemy [God]. . . .*

*If once we can produce our perfect work—the Materialist Magician…veritably worshipping what he vaguely calls "Forces" while denying the existence of "spirits"—then the end of the war will be in sight.*

—SCREWTAPE to WORMWOOD
in *The Screwtape Letters* by C.S. Lewis

# 8

# What About Evil, Satan, and Demons?

## WHAT IS THE SOURCE OF EVIL?

*Question:* Isaiah 45:7 seems to state that God creates evil. How can this be possible if God is totally good? And if He does create evil, why does He do so and what form does it take?

*Response:* Let's examine this verse: "I form the light and create darkness; I make peace and create evil. I the LORD do all these things." How does God create darkness? Darkness is really nothing. It is not a "thing" that God created; it is simply the absence of light. No one would know he was in the dark if he had never seen light. Thus by creating light God exposes the absence of it as darkness.

In the same way, God's perfection exposes all else as evil. Sin is therefore defined as falling "short of the glory of God" (Romans 3:23). In His presence the angels cry continually, "Holy, holy, holy is the LORD" (Isaiah 6:3; cf. Revelation 4:8). God's perfection is the blaze of light in contrast to which all else is darkness and evil. Indeed, we are told that God dwells "in the light which no man can approach unto"(1 Timothy 6:16).

How then does the perfection of God reveal evil if no man can approach unto the light of holiness in which He dwells? Because He has written His law in the consciences of all mankind (Romans 2:14,15) causing us to recognize evil in ourselves and in others.

## DUALISM AND WORLD RELIGIONS

In fact, the biblical explanation of evil is unique. The author of *The Dead Sea Scrolls and the Bible* points out that "the Jewish religion, unlike other theologies, considered the one and omnipotent God to be the author of both good and evil, the master of the world."[1] The very idea that one Supreme Being could be responsible for both good and evil contrasts sharply with the beliefs of the world's religions during Old Testament times, which tended toward dualism.

Manly P. Hall, an expert on the occult and non-Christian religions, reminds us: "In all the ancient Mysteries, matter was regarded as the source of all evil and spirit the source of all good."[2] The mysteries emanated from two irreconcilable opposites: Absolute Spirit and Absolute Substance. For the Gnostics, it was the "positive and negative" principles. In polytheistic mythology, of course, there were both good and evil gods who fought with one another. Isaiah's statement that the one true God of the Hebrews is responsible for both good and evil stands apart from all the world's religions and provides one more piece of evidence that the Bible came from a source of inspiration independent of the culture or religion surrounding its writers.

## WHAT MAKES EVIL POSSIBLE?

In the Bible, evil is associated with the power of choice and could not exist apart from it. Only beings capable of choice can have moral responsibility; and this very power of choice makes evil not only possible but inevitable. It is a foregone conclusion that creatures who, though made "in the image of God" (Genesis 1:26,27), are less than God (as any creation of God must be), will think thoughts and do deeds unworthy of God and thus evil by very definition.

That being the case, why would God give mankind this exceedingly dangerous ability to choose? Why would God, who is only good, allow evil of any kind or even of the smallest degree in His universe? The answer, of course, is obvious: God wanted to have a meaningful and loving relationship with mankind. Without the ability to choose to love or to hate, to say yes or to say no, it would be impossible for mankind to receive God's love and to love Him in return, for real love must come from the heart. Nor could there be genuine praise and worship unless it were voluntary.

It would hardly be glorifying to God for robots, who cannot choose to say or do otherwise, to continually sing His praises. And for such beings to be programmed to say repeatedly "I love you" would be meaningless. The love and praise of God must come from beings who have the choice of not loving and praising but even of hating and denigrating Him, beings whose hearts have been captured by His love and who genuinely love Him in return. That is why, if Islam, through threats of terrorism and death, could force the entire world to submit to Allah—or if Communism through similar threats and force could take over the world today—it would not be a victory for either totalitarian system. Rather, such a world conquest would be the greatest defeat, for it would have failed to win the love and loyalty of its alleged "converts."

Of course, while giving man the power of choice made love possible, it also opened the door to all manner of evil. It is by our own personal choice that we think evil thoughts and do wicked deeds. God did not cause Lucifer or any angels or any of us to do evil. That tragedy came about by our individual volition. We choose to satisfy our own selfish desires rather than to glorify God, and thus we come short of His glory and demonstrate ourselves to be sinners.

How wonderful, then, that in His love and wisdom God was able to pay the penalty for our sins and thus to forgive us and make it possible for us to be in His presence, loving and praising Him eternally! And surely His love has captured our hearts and created in us a love that is real and eternal. As 1 John 4:19 says, "We love him because he first loved us." That can only be said meaningfully by beings who are also capable of choosing not to love.

## WHAT ABOUT SATAN?

*Question:* The Bible blames evil on a mythological figure it calls the devil, or Satan. There is absolutely no evidence that imps and gnomes and gremlins and devils even exist. Furthermore, we don't need that hypothesis. Everything can be explained without it. Name one evil in our world which man is not capable of committing without any help from the so-called devil or his demons!

*Response:* The Bible never mentions such imaginary creatures as imps, gnomes, fairies, gremlins etc., nor do these products of superstition have anything whatsoever to do with Christianity. The perverse attempt on the part of critics to pretend that Christians believe in such entities (Ingersoll's quote at the beginning of the chapter, for example) betrays their proud prejudice. That they find it necessary to resort to ridicule and overstatement also reveals how weak the skeptics' position really is. Let the critics at least be honest and stick to the facts.

The Bible does *not* blame all evil on Satan or demons. In fact it actually says, "Every man is tempted when he is drawn away of his own lust and enticed" (James 1:14). Of course man is capable of all the evil being committed in the world; he is the one who is actually doing it. That does not prove, however, that there may not be an outside influence at work. A young man who robs a bank is clearly capable of doing so, but that doesn't nullify the fact that his partner in crime initiated the idea and goaded him into joining him.

Eve was certainly capable of eating the forbidden fruit, and actually did so. That did not, however, negate the possibility that Satan, speaking through the serpent, put her up to it. Nor would the fact of Satan's involvement excuse Eve. She was held accountable by God for her sin. Far from forcing mankind to sin, Satan plays rather the part of tempter, teasing man with evil desires to which he is not only susceptible but inclined.

It is not man's duty to fight off Satan but to rest in the victory Christ has won and to trust in Him both for salvation and for victory over sin and temptation. While we acknowledge Satan's existence, we resist the seductive impulse to become fascinated with him or to imagine we can directly engage him in battle. As C.S. Lewis said:

> There are two equal and opposite errors into which our race can fall about the devils. One is to disbelieve in their existence. The other is to believe, and to feel an excessive and unhealthy interest in them. They themselves are equally pleased by both errors and hail a materialist or a magician with the same delight.[3]

### THE COLLAPSE OF SCIENTIFIC MATERIALISM

*Question:* I need no further argument against the existence of Satan and demons than the fact that no one in the history of the world has ever seen such creatures. They exist only in mythology. The Bible tries to get around this obvious problem by claiming that they are not physical and are thus invisible spirit beings. Wasn't this old-fashioned superstition about "spirits" abandoned long ago by thinking people? Surely if Satan existed there ought to be some scientific proof. Where is it?

*Response:* Belief in "spirits" has not been abandoned. Instead, the scientific community is now endorsing it. Materialism is dead. No longer do the great thinkers imagine that this physical universe is all there is or that everything, including human consciousness, can be explained in physical terms. In his book *Quantum Questions: The Mystical Writings of the World's Great Physicists,* Ken Wilbur has compiled statements made by the greatest physicists of all time which show that they all believed in a spiritual dimension of existence. In full agreement, Sir John Eccles, Nobel prize winner for his research on the brain, writes:

---

If there are bona fide mental events—events that are not themselves physical or material—then the whole program of philosophical materialism collapses.

The universe is no longer composed of "matter and a void" but now must make (spaceless) room for (massless) entities [i.e. *minds*].[4]

Ideas are obviously not physical. Evil itself is not physical. It may involve physical *acts*, but it begins in the mind with nonphysical thoughts. Morals and ethics are nonphysical things. It would be folly to ask someone to describe the texture, color, or taste of *truth* or how much one would have to pay for a pound of *justice* or *mercy*. As Sir Arthur Eddington said, "'Ought' takes us outside chemistry and physics."[5]

All purposeful acts begin with a thought that does not exist as a physical part of a bodily organ, the brain. Ideas are held in the mind. The brain is physical but the mind is not. Quite clearly, thoughts *precede* and *cause* neural activity in the brain. They do not *result* from anything happening in the physical brain, nor can thinking be explained on that basis. Thoughts about truth or justice, for example, could not originate through any physical stimulus (and thus could not result from any evolutionary process), because they are totally unrelated to any physical quality such as weight, texture, taste, or smell.

The human brain does not initiate thoughts, decisions, or plans. If it did, we would be the prisoners of this bit of matter in our skulls. Moreover, if evolution were true and our brains the result of random, impersonal chance processes over billions of years, then our thoughts could only be the result of the same random processes and would thus be meaningless. The same would apply to the theory of evolution, which by its own affirmations could only be the result of chance motions of atoms in the brain. Expressing logic's necessary rejection of materialism and evolution, C.S. Lewis wrote:

> If minds are wholly dependent on brains and brains on biochemistry, and biochemistry (in the long run) on the meaningless flux of the atoms, I cannot understand how the thought of those minds should have any more significance than the sound of the wind in the trees.[6]

## SPIRIT BEINGS?

Based upon years of brain research, world-famed neurosurgeon Wilder Penfield declared, "The mind is independent of the brain. The brain is a computer, but it is programmed by something that is outside itself, the mind."[7] The brain is a computer of such complexity that human genius cannot duplicate it; and, like any computer, it requires someone to operate it. That is the function of the human spirit, which uses this "brain/computer" to interface with the physical dimension of life in which our bodies function.

Inasmuch as our own minds are nonphysical, how foolish to deny the possibility of the existence of other minds or even to insist that they must all be attached to physical bodies! Robert Jastrow, one of the world's leading astronomers, and certainly highly regarded by his colleagues in that field, suggests that evolution could have been in process on other planets 10 billion years longer than here on earth and may have produced beings as far beyond man on the evolutionary scale as man is beyond a worm. We are not promoting the false theory of evolution but simply observing that Jastrow sees nothing about this materialist theory that would deny the existence of spirit beings. In fact, Jastrow suggests:

> Life that is a billion years beyond us may be far beyond the flesh-and-blood form that we would recognize. It may . . . [have] escaped its mortal flesh

to become something that old-fashioned people
would call spirits.
And how do we know it's there? Maybe it can
materialize and then dematerialize. I'm sure it has
magical powers by our standards. . . .[8]

That spirit beings, whatever their origin, do exist has
been acknowledged by many other top scientists in addition to Jastrow, Eccles, and Eddington. Among them are
not a few Nobel Prize winners: Nobelist Eugene Wigner,
one of the greatest physicists of this century; Sir Karl Pop-
per, the most famous philosopher of science of our age;
mathematician John von Neumann, who has been called
"the smartest man who ever lived"; and many others. So
the skeptics' derisive accusation that only uneducated and
superstitious people believe in spirits is nothing more than
the bluster of wishful thinkers.

It would only be logical that nonphysical beings, if they
did exist, could think and even communicate with our
brains by the same means that our own spirits use. C.G.
Jung, the famous Swiss psychiatrist, had a personal spirit
guide, Philemon, which seemed to demonstrate the powers
of materialization suggested by Jastrow and with whom he
had lengthy and very real conversations. Jung wrote:

> Philemon represented a force which was not
> myself. . . . It was he who taught me . . . the reality
> of the psyche . . . he seemed quite real. . . . I went
> walking up and down the garden with him. . . . [9]

Jung wanted desperately to believe that Philemon
and other entities who literally appeared to him and
conversed with him were nothing more than psychic
extensions of his subconscious mind. Eventually, however, the mounting evidence forced Jung to conclude
that they were independent beings. He confessed, "On
the basis of my own experience . . . I have to admit that
the spirit hypothesis yields better results in practice
than any other."[10]

## THE CASE FOR EVIL SPIRITS

In view of the evil of which our own minds are capable, it would be extremely naive to imagine that all other minds in the universe must be benevolent. Some of Jung's experiences were so terrifying that he became convinced that at least some of these entities were exceedingly evil. Jung discussed this topic at length with James Hyslop, Columbia University professor of logic and ethics. Hyslop expressed his own convictions:

> If we believe in telepathy [which Hyslop considered fully demonstrable], we believe in a process which makes possible the invasion of a personality by someone at a distance.
>
> It is not at all likely . . . that sane and intelligent spirits are the only ones to exert [such] influence . . . there is no reason why others cannot do so as well.[11]

In view of the above conclusion based upon evidence which convinced Jung, Hyslop, and many other investigators, there is no reason for rejecting the idea that a being of such evil genius as Satan could exist. Indeed, there is much experimental verification of the existence of demons and of Satan, evidence which has been accepted by non-Christian psychiatrists and scientists, not because the Bible said so but on the basis of their own experience. Many examples could be given, but let us conclude with the experience of someone who in recent years has become known as an expert on the subject of "evil," psychiatrist M. Scott Peck.

While Peck was Assistant Chief of Psychiatry under the Army Surgeon General, he served as chairman of a special committee of psychiatrists appointed by the Army Chief of Staff to study the "psychological causes of [the massacre in Vietnam at] My Lai, so as to prevent such atrocities in the future." In the process, Peck became involved in attempted exorcisms. He refers to two specific cases that convinced him of the reality of demonic possession. He even declared with awe that he had "personally met Satan face-to-face."[12] Peck writes:

> When the demonic finally spoke clearly in one case, an expression appeared on the patient's face that could be described only as Satanic. It was an incredibly contemptuous grin of utter hostile malevolence. I have spent many hours before a mirror trying to imitate it without the slightest success. . . .
>
> When the demonic finally revealed itself in the exorcism of [another] patient, it was with a still more ghastly expression. The patient suddenly resembled a writhing snake of great strength, viciously attempting to bite the team members.
>
> More frightening than the writhing body, however, was the face. The eyes were hooded with lazy reptilian torpor—except when the reptile darted out in attack, at which moment the eyes would open wide with blazing hatred. Despite these frequent darting moments, what upset me the most was the extraordinary sense of a fifty-million-year-old heaviness I received from this serpentine being.
>
> Almost all the team members at both exorcisms were convinced they were at these times in the presence of something absolutely alien and inhuman. The end of each exorcism proper was signaled by the departure of this Presence from the patient and the room.[13]

The conclusion arrived at by Peck and his team is not a matter of "scientific proof," but an intuitive conviction of conscience arrived at by careful observation. Nor could it be otherwise when one confronts the spirit realm. Eddington points out that if a physicist should try to apply scientific methods to the study of thought by examining the brain, "all that he discovers is a collection of atoms and electrons and fields of force arranged in space and time, apparently similar to those found in inorganic objects... [and thus] might set down thought as an illusion. . . . "[14]

Human personality surely exists, yet it cannot be defined or demonstrated scientifically. So it is with the manifestation of demonic power. Unfortunately, though increasing numbers of psychologists and psychiatrists are now acknowledging the reality and horror of demonic possession, their attempt to discover a "scientific" explanation undermines their understanding of evil. If there is a *psychological* explanation for evil, then moral choice and personal responsibility are no longer involved. Furthermore, if evil can be explained as psychologically programmed behavior, then what was the *presence* that Peck said he and his team could palpably "feel" and whose exit could be felt as well?

## WHAT ABOUT SATAN AS SERPENT?

---

*Question:* I think one of the great evidences against the authenticity of the Bible is its treatment of the serpent. In the Bible the serpent is the embodiment of evil, whereas ancient myths and religions give exactly the opposite view. The Bible equates the serpent with the devil, but the most ancient religions, some of which are even practiced to the present time, almost universally identify the serpent as the Savior or at least as benevolent and to be worshiped. How can the Bible be true and at the same time be so much out of touch with what is clearly the common intuition of humanity?

*Response:* This is a fascinating subject, and its implications go beyond our ability to understand fully. There is no doubt that the Bible repeatedly identifies Satan both as the serpent and the dragon, not only in Genesis 3 but elsewhere. For example, "And the great dragon was cast out, that old serpent called the Devil and Satan, which deceiveth the whole world" (Revelation 12:9). In view of the usual human revulsion and fear of both dragons and serpents, one would think that Satan would do everything possible to deny such a connection, yet the opposite seems to be the case, for some strange reason. How intriguing it is that both are so closely associated with nearly all pagan religions! The dragon is found on thousands of temples throughout Asia, while the serpent permeates and even dominates the religion of India.

---

In view of the natural human revulsion for these creatures, this association could hardly be of human origin and would require another explanation. The biblical indication that Satan is the "god of this world" and thus the originator of all false religions would seem to offer that explanation. Furthermore, archaeologists and explorers continue to uncover ancient representations of a woman, a serpent, and a tree in close association, a connection which undoubtedly reflects the Genesis story of the temptation in the garden. Even today, one finds ancient Hindu temples deep in the jungles in northern India bearing centuries-old faded wall frescoes in which one can still make out the woman, serpent, and tree. When asked the meaning of these symbols, the villagers, who worship the serpent, explain that the serpent brought them salvation.

SERPENT WORSHIP EVERYWHERE

In the temples of ancient Egypt and Rome the body of the god Serapis was encircled by the coils of a great serpent. In Hinduism one of the three chief gods, Shiva, has serpents entwined in his hair. Yoga is symbolized as a raft made of cobras, and its goal is to awaken the kundalini power coiled at the base of the human spine in the form of a serpent. Numerous other examples could be given, from the plumed serpent Quetzalcoatl, the Savior-god of the Mayas, to the annual snake dance of the Hopi Indians. One of the greatest authorities on the occult (himself a practitioner of occultism) has written:

> Serpent worship in some form permeated nearly all parts of the earth. The serpent mounds of the American Indian; the carved-stone snakes of Central and South America; the hooded cobras of India; Python, the great snake of the Greeks; the sacred serpents of the Druids; the Midgard snake of

Scandinavia; the Nagas of Burma, Siam and Cambodia . . . the mystic serpent of Orpheus; the snakes at the oracle of Delphi . . . the sacred serpents preserved in the Egyptian temples; the Uraeus coiled upon the foreheads of the Pharaohs and priests—all these bear witness to the universal veneration in which the snake was held. . . .

The serpent is . . . the symbol and prototype of the Universal Savior, who redeems the world by giving creation the knowledge of itself. . . . It has long been viewed as the emblem of immortality. It is the symbol of reincarnation . . .[15]

In Greek mythology a serpent was wrapped around the Orphic egg, the symbol of the cosmos. Likewise at Delphi, Greece (for centuries the location of the most sought-for and influential oracle of the ancient world, consulted by potentates from as far away as North Africa and Asia Minor), the three legs of the oracular tripod in the inner shrine of the temple were intertwined with serpents. As one further example, consider the Greek and Roman god of medicine, Aesculapius, whose symbol was a serpent-entwined staff, from which the symbol of modern medicine, the caduceus, was derived.

In the temples erected in his honor, Aesculapius was worshiped with snakes because of an ancient myth which said that he had received a healing herb at the mouth of a serpent. Here again we have the Genesis story perverted: The serpent is not the deceiver and destroyer but the Savior of mankind, replacing Jesus Christ. At graduation ceremonies of medical schools around the world, where prayers to the God of the Bible or to Jesus Christ would not be allowed, graduates, upon receiving their M.D. degrees, still repeat loudly in unison the Hippocratic oath. It begins, "I swear by Apollo, by Aesculapius, by Hygeia and Panacea, and by all the gods and goddesses. . . . "

Surely the Bible's depiction of Satan as a serpent and dragon, the deceiver and destroyer of mankind, and then as the god of this world who originates pagan religions, fits the evidence. Furthermore, the very fact that the Bible stands alone against all ancient religions provides further evidence that all of them have a common source and that the inspiration behind the Bible is, exactly as it claims, independent of theirs. In fact, the two sources of inspiration are obviously diametrically opposed.

## Why Should Satan Exist?

*Question:* Why would God, knowing all the evil that would follow, create a being that would become Satan? What could be the purpose of Satan's existence? The biblical devil, in fact, is presented as so powerful that he seems to be God's equal. If not, why has it taken God so long to conquer him?

*Response:* No one reading much of the Bible could come to the conclusion that Satan is God's equal. Moreover, the reason for his existence and why he has not already been locked away becomes clear as we understand the issues involved. God's desire is to capture the hearts of those whom He created in His image. He wants to have them in His presence for eternity, where He will fully demonstrate "the exceeding riches of his grace in his kindness toward us through Christ Jesus" (Ephesians 2:7).

For God to genuinely win man's heart, there must be no coercion. Man must have complete freedom to reject God and to choose to worship another being or object. Satan presents man with the ultimate alternative to God, and he convinces billions of people to reject God and to give their allegiance to him. Such an alternative is essential in determining man's true desire. To have in heaven those who really didn't want to be there is hardly God's intention and would be counterproductive to His eternal purpose.

## Satan As The Competitive Suitor

We can illustrate the point like this. Suppose a king wants to marry the most beautiful woman in his realm.

In order to be certain of winning her heart, he expels from his kingdom all men who might be his rivals for her affection. Obviously, that is not the way to be assured of her sincere love; she must have the freedom to choose someone else. Only when she has that freedom and, having rejected all others, consents to marry the king, can he be assured that he has indeed captured her heart.

For the same reason, God has not locked Satan away but allows him to continue to entice mankind with his false promises. As the most powerful and brilliant being next to God, Satan provides the ultimate alternative. The battle between God and Satan for the soul of man is very real. It would hardly be any credit to the world's heavyweight boxing champion to defeat a four-year-old in the ring; the opponent must be worthy. Satan is the strongest opponent, God's ultimate competition in the battle for the hearts and minds of mankind.

Yes, as far as raw power is concerned, God could immediately throw Satan into the "bottomless pit" (Revelation 20:1-3) so that he could no longer deceive mankind. In fact, that will be the case during the millennial reign of Christ upon earth, when it will be fully proved that man is an evil rebel in his own right without any influence from Satan. In the meantime, however, the battle for the souls of mankind is not to be fought with raw power, for the issues involved are not of that nature. It is a contest for the heart's affection and loyalty; and to that end Satan must be allowed full freedom to tempt mankind with every ploy he can devise.

Satan is not only the "god of this world" (2 Corinthians 4:4), but its kingdoms belong to him (Matthew 4:8-10). He is able to reward those who follow him with great riches and success in this world. However, Satan is doomed, and those who give their allegiance to him will share in that doom eternally.

In the battle for man's soul and destiny, God is completely open and honest, while Satan misrepresents and deceives. Thus the battle is presented in the Bible as between the truth of God and the lie of Satan. God wants those who choose to receive Christ as Savior and Lord to do so on the basis of the facts. If Satan has more to offer, if his way is best, then let mankind follow him.

## Satan's Fall

---

*Question:* I was always taught from Isaiah 14 that Satan was a fallen angel originally named Lucifer. Recently I've learned that this isn't so, for the one being spoken of in Isaiah 14 is obviously "the king of Babylon" (verse 4). Then was Satan created by God as he is now, the most evil of creatures?

*Response:* Satan was not created by God as he is now. God does not create evil beings. Satan was originally as the Bible describes him in Isaiah 14 and Ezekiel 28 and elsewhere. He is a fallen cherub with great power and cunning. The cherubim seemed to be the angels closest to God, guarding even His very presence—and Satan was originally the chief cherub. Psalm 99:1 says of God, "He sitteth between the cherubims." (See also Genesis 3:24; Exodus 25:20; 37:9; Ezekiel 10; Hebrews 9:5; etc.)

---

Yes, the king of Babylon is being addressed in Isaiah 14. However, what is said about him could not apply solely to him but ultimately only to Satan. For example, when did the king of Babylon have a position in heaven from which he fell? At times the Bible addresses Satan through ungodly earthly rulers to show that he is the real power behind them, just as he will be the power behind Antichrist, of whom it is said, "The dragon [Satan] gave him his power and his seat and great authority" (Revelation 13:2). In fact, all these despotic and evil rulers are types or symbols of Antichrist.

That Satan is being addressed through such kings is clearer in Ezekiel 28:2-19. Here the "prince of Tyrus" is being addressed: "Thou hast been in Eden the garden of God; every precious stone was thy covering.... Thou art the anointed cherub [highest order of angel] ... and I have set thee so.... Thou was perfect in thy ways from the day that thou was created till iniquity was found in thee" (verses 13-15). Obviously, none of this was true of the literal "prince of Tyrus" but only of Satan, who inspired and directed him in his ungodly activity.

Note the similarities in Ezekiel 28 to what is said of "the king of Babylon" in Isaiah 14: "I am a God, I sit in the seat of God.... Thou [hast] set thine heart as the heart of God," etc. Clearly Satan is being addressed as the power behind both the king of Babylon and the prince of Tyrus. Isaiah 14 does indeed present Satan's fall.

Satan is "the god of this world" (2 Corinthians 4:4). Christ did not dispute his claim to ownership of the world system when, in the temptation in the wilderness, Satan offered to give the kingdoms of the world to Christ if He would bow down and worship him (Matthew 4:8,9). Isaiah 14 and Ezekiel 28 carry the same message.

## WHAT ABOUT SATAN IN GOD'S PRESENCE?

*Question:* Evil is supposedly not allowed in God's presence because He is so holy. Yet Satan still appears before the throne of God, according to the book of Job. How can that be?

*Response:* Yes, Satan still appears before the throne of God (Job 1:6; 2:1) as the "accuser of our brethren" (Revelation 12:10). The day is yet future when "that old serpent called the Devil" will be cast out of heaven (Revelation 12:9). Until then, he continues to accuse the believers "before our God day and night" (Revelation 12:10).

Before his fall Satan had been given a position of power and authority, and he will retain some residue of that until the battle for the soul and destiny of man has been fought to its finish. The challenge which Satan has presented to God can only be fully answered and Satan fully defeated by the redemption of mankind through the blood of Christ. Until that time, the relationship of God to evil is one of hatred and rejection, not of complete separation. For example, we know that God is "of purer eyes than to behold evil, and cannot look upon iniquity"

(Habakkuk 1:13); yet He sees everything that happens in the earth and must know all evil or He could not be the judge thereof.

Evil was conceived in the heart of Satan even though he dwelt in the very presence of God. The Bible speaks of the "*mystery* of iniquity" (2 Thessalonians 2:7). That evil could originate in God's presence and that it could begin on earth in the perfect environmental paradise of the Garden of Eden is indeed a mystery. And this mystery only deepens when we consider that sin involves rebellion against the infinite, almighty Creator of all. That both Satan and man would be so blinded by self as to embrace the impossible dream of defeating God is mystery indeed.

Satan's continuing appearances before God's throne do not implicate God in evil any more than the fact that creatures whom God created (and whose every thought, word, and deed He knows) have turned to evil by the billions. The day is coming, however, when God will create a new universe "wherein dwelleth righteousness" (2 Peter 3:13), and from that time on "there shall in no wise enter into it anything that defileth" (Revelation 21:27).

## What Was The First Sin?

---

*Question:* We are told in the Bible that sin entered into the world when Adam and Eve took of the forbidden fruit. Yet Eve wanted it and must have looked upon it with desire before she actually ate of it. Was it sin for her to do so, even to touch it and pick it? If so, there was sin before Adam sinned.

*Response:* You may be technically correct. However, the Bible looks upon the temptation, Eve's desire and eating of the forbidden fruit, and Adam's partaking of it as one act. In fact, Adam is blamed: "Wherefore, as by one man sin entered into the world, and death by sin . . . " (Romans 5:12).

---

It seems clear that Adam's sin was even greater than Eve's. She was deceived, but Adam was not (1 Timothy

2:14). Apparently Adam knew what he was doing and did it in order not to be separated from his wife. He was determined to share her fate, even though he knew that to do so he was rebelling against the God who had created him.

## WHAT ABOUT SPIRITUAL WARFARE?

*Question:* There is a new teaching in the church called "spiritual warfare" which is rapidly growing in popularity. It is even taught that by "binding" in the name of the Lord the "territorial spirit" controlling a city, Christians can take over that city for God. The reference in Daniel 10 to the prince of Persia withstanding the angel Gabriel seems to support this teaching. What is your response?

*Response:* Today's teaching about "spiritual warfare" has no biblical basis, either by precept or example. Yes, "the prince of the kingdom of Persia" prevented the angel (presumably Gabriel) for three weeks from coming to Daniel (Daniel 10:12,13). Daniel, however, was seeking prophetic insight, not the "binding" of the "territorial spirit" over Persia. Nor did the angel instruct him to wage such "warfare." In fact, nowhere in the entire Bible is the idea even suggested that certain demons have special authority over certain cities or territories and that they must be "bound."

The angel's mission was to inform Daniel of last-days events affecting Israel (10:14)—information which would become part of Scripture and which the "prince of Persia" tried to keep from Daniel. There is no hint that "binding" this demon would have delivered Persia from satanic influence or that Gabriel's victory over this demon (with the help of Michael the archangel) had any effect upon the spiritual climate in Persia or aided in the salvation of a single Persian.

Paul never tried to "bind territorial spirits" in bringing the gospel to the world of his day, so why should we? And although the apostles "turned the world upside down" (Acts 17:6), there is no hint that a single city was ever "taken for God," as some preachers are falsely promising today. In Corinth, for example, where Paul spent 18 months, God gave him special protection and blessing because He had "much people in this city" (Acts 18:9,10). The issue was not one of *delivering Corinth* but of *calling a company of believers out of it*. Nor did Paul's success change the destiny of Corinth, or of any other city or nation. Such teaching simply has no basis in the Bible but comes from the imagination and ambition of men.

## Why Does God Harden Hearts?

*Question:* I have been greatly troubled by two statements in the Bible: 1) that God hardened Pharaoh's heart (Exodus 4:21; 7:13,14; etc.; and 2) that God will give people a "strong delusion that they should believe a lie, that they all might be damned who believed not the truth" (2 Thessalonians 2:11,12). This seems so obviously unjust that it has shaken my faith! Furthermore, it seems to make God responsible for evil or at least a partner in it. Can you help me?

*Response:* First of all, let's get the facts straight. Before God ever hardened his heart, Pharaoh refused a simple request to let the people of God go "three days' journey into the desert" to offer a sacrifice to their God (Exodus 5:1-9). This desire to worship was hardly unreasonable coming from people who had been enslaved and prevented from offering the prescribed sacrifices to their God for centuries. They needed to remove themselves from Egypt because their sacrifice of animals to God would have been highly offensive to the Egyptians (Exodus 8:26). Yet Pharaoh's response was not only to sternly deny this request but to viciously increase the rigors of the Israelite's slavery.

We must remember that God did not force Pharaoh to do anything that he had not already determined to do. God simply helped Pharaoh to persist in the path he had firmly chosen. God "hardened Pharaoh's heart," not by changing his will but by strengthening him in his resolve not to let the people go. In dealing with this same question, R.A. Torrey wrote:

> The facts of the case are these: Pharaoh was a cruel and oppressive tyrant, subjecting the people of Israel to most awful bondage, suffering and death. God looked down upon His people, heard their cries, and in His mercy determined to deliver them (Exodus 2:25; 3:7,8). He sent Moses as His representative to Pharaoh to demand the deliverance of His people, and Pharaoh in proud rebellion defied Him and gave himself up to even more cruel oppression of the people. It was then and only then that God hardened his heart.
>
> This . . . [is] God's universal method of dealing with men . . . if man chooses error, to give him up to error (II Thessalonians 2:9-12). This is stern dealing, but it is just dealing.[16]

We can better understand what it meant to "harden Pharaoh's heart" by considering why it was necessary. The plagues of God's judgment upon the false gods of Egypt became so unpleasant in their consequences and so obviously supernatural in their cause that Pharaoh was terrified. His heart was not changed, but he no longer had the courage to persist in his desire to keep the people of God in bondage. However, God was not yet ready to terminate His judgments upon Egypt's false gods. Therefore God helped Pharaoh to continue in his refusal to let the people of Israel go until He had completed His exposure and punishment of the false gods that served as a front for Satan in his deception of the Egyptian people.

It is also important to understand that the hardening of Pharaoh's heart proceeded precisely because of each new request by Moses and Aaron to let the people go. Each time he was given the choice of submitting to God and refused, that very refusal was a hardening of his heart by which Pharaoh continued to dig himself ever deeper into the pit of rebellion. Each act of rebellion and rejection of God hardens the heart that much more.

So it will be with all those who have refused to accept the truth which God has made known to them. How can it be unjust for God to help them believe the lie which they themselves have determined to believe? No, it is only just to do so; and that is the solemn lesson we learn here.

### Is God Fair In His Demands For Obedience?

*Question:* The Bible says that we must obey God because this is His universe. Doesn't that make Him a tyrant? You say He gave man freedom to choose good or evil, but hasn't He stacked the deck so that man is forced to go God's way or be damned? Is that fair?

*Response:* The command that God gave to Adam and Eve simply forbade them to eat of a particular tree in the garden. There is no conceivable command that could have been easier to obey. There must have been thousands of trees of every variety in that lush garden of perfection. The tree of which God told them not to eat was no doubt one of hundreds of trees bearing that same kind of fruit. The fruit of the tree did not have magical powers that imparted sin and death to Adam and Eve. It was their disobedience in eating of it in defiance of God's prohibition that constituted sin and brought death upon them and all of their descendants to this day.

We must agree, then, that there was nothing unreasonable about God's very first commandment to mankind. Nor can we find any way to excuse Adam and Eve for their disobedience. The same is true of all sin and all sinners.

In the first sin of mankind we see the truth about all sin. The act itself may not seem so bad. Simply eating some fruit isn't evil in itself. A couple committing fornication may excuse themselves by saying they are only expressing their love to each other. The evil lies in defying

God, who as our Creator not only has the right to establish laws governing our behavior but only does so for our good.

Furthermore, that defiance is both a rejection of God's authority and a denial that He really loves us and that His way is best. It is man's egotistical and self-centered assertion that he can be his own god, that he can decide his own fate. Such rebellion cannot be allowed in God's universe any more than the referees on a football field or basketball court can allow the players to violate the rules of the game. In the case of Adam and Eve we also see the horrible consequences of an individual's sin upon future generations. That awesome fact should be enough to make us all shrink from sin.

## Two Logical Alternatives

Let me illustrate the point. Though it occurred about 30 years ago, I vividly remember two young men visiting me late one night. One of them was angry at God because he was being shipped out to Vietnam the following morning. His friend had brought him to me to see if I could answer some of his complaints against God.

"I didn't ask to be created," the one going to Vietnam said bitterly, "but here I am without choosing to be here. And now God dangles me over the flames of hell and says, 'Turn or burn. Do it my way or I'll drop you in!'" Hostility seemed to be consuming him.

"Let's look at it like this," I suggested. "Suppose you have just come into existence somewhere in the universe and you have the authority and power to create your own destiny. After spending 3 or 4 billion years planning your ultimate Utopia you put the finishing touches on your blueprint for life and sit back rather pleased with yourself. God immediately lays His blueprint for your life beside yours and you look it over carefully. Now tell me, which blueprint would be better?"

He looked at the floor, then the ceiling, then the fire in the fireplace, and finally at me with an unhappy expression. "I guess I'd have to be the greatest egotist in the world to say my plan would be better than God's," he admitted at last.

"Precisely," I said. "God is infinitely wiser than you and truly loves you. Therefore His plan would obviously be far better than yours. That being the case, what's this about 'Turn or burn, do it my way or I'll drop you in'? What you ought to say is, 'God, thank You that though I've been such an egotistical fool as to imagine that my way is better than Yours, and though I have rebelled against You, You sent Your Son to pay the full penalty for my sin and now offer to me as a free gift of Your grace Your perfect blueprint of life in exchange for mine. Thank You, Lord!'"

I tried to persuade this troubled young man to receive Christ as his Savior and to trust himself to God's love and grace and protection. There is no other way to have real peace in our hearts. Tragically, he was not willing to give up his complaints and to let God be God. I do not know what became of him or whether he ever returned safely from Vietnam. Years later the other young man who had brought his friend made himself known to me at the end of a meeting where I was speaking. He had become a pastor.

"God was dealing with me through what you said that night," he told me. "As a result, I surrendered my life fully to Christ."

The facts are clear: Evil and Satan are indeed real and exist in opposition to God. There is a genuine and fierce battle for our souls and destiny. Each of us has a solemn and eternal choice to make, one which will determine the outcome for good or evil of that battle.

Nor can there be any doubt that the only intelligent choice we could possibly make would be to let God have His way fully in our lives. Nothing else makes sense. It is no "sacrifice" to obey God; it is a great *privilege* to become His child through faith in Christ and to begin already in this life to enjoy the eternal blessings He has prepared for those who love Him.

*If this universe was created by an all-wise, omniscient, omnipotent deity, then that deity knew what he was about when he created the universe and is therefore responsible for all that is and for all that will be; and therefore he is responsible for all the suffering in the universe. He made it. He is the author of it, and toward any such God I have only feelings of the utmost abhorrence. I hate him. I detest him. I scorn him.*

*Any God who makes one particle of suffering is worthy of our condemnation even as a man who willfully makes suffering is worthy of condemnation, for if God makes suffering he willfully makes it. God, by the very definition, is not the creature of circumstances. He is omnipotent . . . and therefore when he makes suffering he does that which he was not obliged to do.*

—Samuel P. Putnam, *leading ninteenth-century atheist*[1]

# 9

# What About
# Suffering and Hell?

## IS GUILT ACTUAL OR MERELY
## A FIGMENT OF THE MIND?

---

*Question:* The pain and suffering caused by crime is
bad enough. Christianity, however, has added to that
pain and suffering by convincing mankind that it has rebelled against God and broken His laws. Consequently,
the threat of eternal punishment haunts everyone who
has come under Christianity's influence. Wouldn't the
world be better off without these delusions to trouble it?

*Response:* It is not true that Christianity has created
the feeling of moral guilt and coming judgment that
haunts mankind. Man is an incurably religious creature,
and the religious practices which are found in every race
and culture around the world all involve a sense of guilt
and the attempt to erase guilt through some kind of sacrifice. Such is the case worldwide. It can be traced back in
every culture through thousands of years and thus cannot be blamed upon Christianity at all.

---

The same is true even of those brought up in a so-called
"Christian country" such as the United States. While their

sense of guilt may have been reinforced through contact with Christianity, that contact is certainly not the sole source. The universal guilt that haunts even primitive man would also haunt Americans even if Christianity were unknown here. Jacques Ellul calls the idea that Christianity is to be blamed for guilt a "trite notion" and points out:

> Sacrifice, found in all religions, is propitiatory or else is a sacrifice for redemption or forgiveness. In any case, the sacrifice is substitutionary and proceeds from a deep sense of guilt. . . .
> As far as situations that create guilt are concerned, you can find nothing better than the tangles of prohibitions among so-called primitive peoples. . . .[2]

In fact, it is Christianity alone which can deliver man from the guilt that otherwise haunts him. Turning over a new leaf and vowing to live a morally upright life in the future cannot deliver one from the guilt of past sins. True deliverance from guilt can only come through faith in Christ as the One who paid the full penalty for one's sins and has effected a full pardon on a righteous basis. It is only then that we realize the magnitude of our guilt and can thus thank God all the more for our salvation. Ellul put it well:

> We must also remember constantly that...biblically, and in truly Christian thought, sin is known and recognized for what it is only *after* the recognition, proclamation, and experience of forgiveness. Because I have been pardoned, I realize how much of a sinner I was. Sin is shown to be sin through grace, and not otherwise, just as the abruptly freed slave realizes, as he sees his chains, how great his misery was.[3]

## GOD IS NOT A SADIST

*Question:* The Bible claims that God knows the future. Surely, then, He knew that Adam and Eve would sin and that immeasurable evil and suffering would follow.

The Bible's God must have known every rape and murder and war and every bit of pain and sorrow that would follow. Since He went ahead and created man anyway, how can He be anything but a monster or a sadist?

*Response:* The unreasonable and blasphemous idea that God is cruel can be dismissed immediately. For one thing, there is far too little evil and pain in the world to sustain that theory. If God were the fiend that the skeptics make Him out to be, life would be infinitely worse than it is. There would be no pleasure at all mixed with the pain, but all of life would be a torment. Instead of joy and ecstasy there would be only depression and misery; sex would not be exquisitely enjoyable but horribly painful even while irresistible. Linton expressed it like this:

---

[If God were a sadist], He could give us infinitely more pain than we do suffer. He could force us to eat, as the drug addict is forced to the use of his drug, by the pain of abstention instead of by the pleasing urge of healthy hunger. All physical functions could be forced by pain instead of invited by pleasure.

If God were indifferent, why the variety of fruit flavors for the palate, the invariably harmonizing riot of colors in flower and sunset, the tang of salt air and power to vibrate in joy to these things? Why the subtle joys and utter sense of well-being that a believer in Christ often experiences which he cannot even name or describe?

If God loves His creatures all is explained, except death, pain, and sorrow, and these things would indeed present, as they do present to all but believers, an insoluble problem. But the Bible's explanation is as clear as crystal: "Death came by sin," and the glorious end is as succinctly put as the explanation, "And God shall wipe all tears from their eyes."[4]

---

The universe was clearly not designed by a sadist. We must abandon that theory as a legitimate possible explanation of evil and suffering. Nevertheless, the illogical and unreasonable complaint against God, blaming Him for evil and suffering, has been expressed repeatedly for centuries by atheists. Here is how Samuel Putnam phrased it in the last century:

> In the place of that suffering he [God] could have made happiness. Of his will, and without compulsion, he made suffering. What is he, then, but an almighty fiend? His good acts cannot excuse his evil acts, any more than the good acts of a murderer can condone his crime...God must be all good, or else not good at all.[5]

Putnam was seemingly an intelligent man. How then could the obvious folly of his argument escape him? Could he be blinded by prejudice? I dare say that Putnam (and if not he, then certainly many atheists who have raised the same objection) had children. Did he not know that the children which he and his wife brought into the world would suffer pain and eventual death? Did he not know that it was entirely possible that one or more of his children, like those of many parents, might even become criminals and do great harm to others? Of course he did. Common sense would tell him that.

## God Is Not The Author Of Evil

Is Putnam, therefore, responsible for all the evil and suffering that may have been inflicted upon his children and/or for that which they may have inflicted upon others? Of course not. Was there any way that Putnam and his wife could have been absolutely certain that all of their children would experience only pleasure and never pain, only joy and never sorrow? Certainly not. Could they be certain that all of the children they brought into the world would turn out to be honest and good in all their deeds and never cause harm to others and never be worthy of imprisonment or even execution for their crimes? Again the answer is clearly no.

Any honest person must conclude that neither Put-nam nor any other parents who raise this objection against God could be certain of what kind of lives their children would live, whether good or evil, or of what suffering they might endure or inflict upon others. They could, however, be absolutely certain that their children would suffer at least *some* sickness and pain and sorrow. Therefore, are not these critics and all other parents just as guilty as God of bringing suffering upon others? If God is a sadist for creating man, are not all parents equally sadists for bringing children into the world?

The difference, it is argued, is that God is in control of the world, and He could make it what He wants it to be. Is He? Can He? On the contrary, has not the world, as it is today, been created not by God but by the willful thoughts, ambitions, lusts, and foul (and often brave and good) deeds of mankind down through history? It is a world as man has made it, not as God made and intended it. If blame is to be attached to anyone, then the pain and sorrow and evil in today's world must be charged to man. Sin and suffering are not God's doing, but man's!

Could God force everyone even against their will to be wise and good and happy, any more than earthly parents could force their children to behave precisely the way they determine? Obviously not, so long as man is allowed to retain the power of choice. And if he were robbed of that power he would no longer be man but some lesser species of moral cripples no more responsible for their own actions than puppets on a string. Would Putnam or any other atheist want that? Surely not. Then let them cease from unjustly blaming God for the evil in this world!

## God's Parental Lament

The prophet Isaiah, inspired of the Holy Spirit, expresses God's grief over the actions of men, actions which are so contrary to His benevolent desire for them. Listen to God's lament:

> Hear, O heavens, and give ear, O earth, for the LORD hath spoken. I have nourished and brought up children, and they have rebelled against me.
>
> The ox knoweth his owner and the ass his master's crib, but Israel doth not know, my people doth not consider.
>
> A sinful nation, a people laden with iniquity, a seed of evildoers, children that are corrupters; they have forsaken the LORD, they have provoked the Holy One of Israel unto anger, they are gone away backward (Isaiah 1:2-4).

These are not the words and sentiments of a sadist who has willfully brought pain and sorrow upon the world. On the contrary, it is the lament of a God of love who desires the best for those whom He has created and grieves that they have chosen to bring pain and death upon themselves by their own evil actions.

Surely any parent could identify with God's expression of grief at the conduct of those whom He calls His children. Were there ever parents who did not have some regrets for the behavior, at least at some times and in some degree, of their children? And what could be the solution? Could the parents, having brought the child into the world, force him or her to obey? Could they compel the child to behave according to their dictates? Obviously not.

Yet even if parents could accomplish that task, it would not solve the problem that plagues mankind. The child must respond of his own free will or the "obedience" forced upon him would be meaningless. So it is with God. He has given us the power of choice so that we could love Him, and to deprive mankind of that right would destroy man as God has made him and as man wants to be. Evil is not God's doing but man's, through a self-centered and thus malignant use of the power of choice bestowed upon him.

## "To Be Or Not To Be; That Is The Question"

---

*Question:* A friend who used to claim to be a Christian but who now calls himself an atheist presented a problem to me that I couldn't solve. He is willing to concede (for sake of argument, though he doesn't believe it) that sin comes by man's wrong use of the power of choice given to him. Even then, however, he insists that we can't exonerate God because, knowing the evil and suffering that would follow, God nevertheless chose to create man. Even worse, God created billions of beings that He not only knew would suffer on this earth but whom He knew He would consign to suffer eternally in the lake of fire! Can you help me answer him?

*Response:* The implication of your friend's thesis (which is simply another variation on an overworked theme) is chilling: It favors the nonexistence of the human race as beings capable of choice. One cannot have real human beings without the possibility of evil. So the issue is the existence or nonexistence of the human race: "To be or not to be." The only way to have forever eliminated evil and suffering on this earth would have been not to create man at all. Though that would eliminate all suffering and sorrow, think of the beauty and joy and love it would have eliminated as well.

---

Let's assume purely for illustrative purposes this impossible scene: A million years ago billions of as-yet-uncreated humans in hypothetical precreation spirit form parade before the throne of God demanding not to be created. "We are all going to be in hell and the lake of fire!" they scream in protest. "Therefore we demand the right not to be created! It would be sadism of the worst sort if you bring us into existence, knowing the torment we will suffer eternally!"

God's reply would have been something like this: "You inevitably must be the mothers and fathers, the aunts and uncles, the children and grandchildren and cousins of millions upon millions who will believe in Christ and therefore whose destiny is the eternal bliss and joy of heaven. If you do not come into existence then neither can they. I will not allow your selfish desire for nonexistence to eliminate the existence and eternal delight of billions of souls who will be redeemed by the blood of My Son and will therefore spend eternity in My presence where there is 'fullness of joy' and 'pleasures for evermore'" (Psalm 16:11).

"Then you are consigning us to the torment of the lake of fire for all eternity!" they continue to protest. "Your enemies will therefore be able to say that You are not a good God of love, but a fiend who creates men for hell."

"On the contrary," God would have replied, "the lake of fire was made 'for the devil and his angels' (Matthew 25:41) and if any of mankind ever enters that place of eternal torment it will be contrary to My will. My Son is going to die in payment of the penalty My justice demands for any sin that any human being will ever commit. The provision for everyone to be in heaven, where I want all to be, will be fully made. If anyone goes to hell instead, it will be due to his willful refusal of the salvation I have provided."

"But we'll suffer eternally!" the protesters insist.

"If so, that will be your doing, not mine," God would have replied. "I will not rob billions of redeemed souls of eternal joy just to cater to your obstinate rebellion."

### Did God Create Man To Suffer?

---

*Question:* There is no way God can be exonerated from the accusation that He is a sadistic fiend. He says He doesn't want anyone to suffer, yet we do suffer both in this life and are warned that our suffering will be even worse in eternity. In fact, the suffering that God has planned for eternity is horrible beyond words. How can you say that a God who creates man to burn in the fires of an everlasting hell is good?

*Response:* God did not create man for such a fate, and when man by his own self-will rejects the salvation from that fate which God so graciously offers, it grieves God. The Bible clearly says that God is "not willing that any should perish" (2 Peter 3:9) but that He wants "all men to be saved" (1 Timothy 2:4).

---

The Bible tells us clearly that Christ paid the penalty for the sins of the whole world, even for the sins of those who reject Him: "Behold the Lamb of God, which taketh away the sin of the world" (John 1:29); and again, "He is the propitiation for our sins; and not for ours only, but also for the sins of the whole world" (1 John 2:2).

We may rest assured that no one will suffer in hell who could by any means have been won to Christ in this life. God leaves no stone unturned to rescue all who would respond to the convicting and wooing of the Holy Spirit. Paul makes that clear: "For whom he did foreknow [would respond to the gospel]...them he also called [with the gospel]; and whom he called, them he also justified; and whom he justified, them he also glorified" (Romans 8:29,30). Let me try to illustrate.

## LIKE A FISH OUT OF WATER

A fish sees a man on the shore sitting on a chair with legs crossed, smoking a cigar and holding a fishing pole. The fish decides that it is missing out on real life and determines to be like the man. It manages to jump out of the water, flips itself up on a chair, crosses its fins, and lights up a cigar. But before it can manage to grasp a fishing pole it runs out of oxygen and, its life expiring, falls from the chair, and flops around in dirt and gravel, gills opening and closing rapidly in a vain attempt to pull oxygen from the air.

An atheist walking by exclaims in derision: "What kind of a God would create a fish to suffer like that?"

The obvious truth, of course, is that God never made the fish to suffer like that. He created fish to swim in exuberant freedom in rivers, lakes, and oceans. This horrible suffering, which is contrary to God's will, came about because the fish rebelled against the purpose God had for it. Rebelling in his own way against God, man too is like a fish out of water.

God made man to swim in the ocean of His love and to enjoy the full life and freedom of expression of those who do God's will. It would have been so beautiful, but man chose to rebel against God and to do his own thing. Human egos that have rebelled against God find themselves, as a consequence of their selfishness, in conflict with one another as well. What one self-willed person wants to do inevitably conflicts with what other self-willed persons want to do, bringing anger, jealously, hatred, and all the evils which follow. But don't blame God for this. He created all things in beauty and perfection. It is man who has perverted that perfection and is wreaking destruction upon God's creation.

## WHY MUST THE DAMNED BURN IN FIRE?

*Question:* I am distressed by the very thought of anyone suffering eternally. It is particularly troubling to my faith that just as God created man with the capacity for joy, He also gave him the horrible, and I should think unnecessary, capacity to suffer, not only in this life but in eternity. And the suffering that awaits the damned is of the most horrible kind: burning forever in what the Bible describes as a "lake of fire." How can you reconcile this with God's goodness?

*Response:* Many people have suffered the excruciating pain of being terribly burned in this life. By your reasoning, God is to blame for their suffering because He constituted the human body with nerves that could feel pain. Yet those nerves were designed to warn of disease or other destructive forces at work in the body, and thus to save life.

More than one leprous person in primitive societies has had part or all of a foot burned off by a campfire before noticing what was happening because he couldn't feel the pain. Any doctor will tell you that pain is one of the marvels that help to preserve the body, that pain and life are so inextricably linked as to be inseparable. Pain sends a vital message that we need to heed.

## THE "BURNING" OF UNQUENCHABLE "THIRST"

The "fire" of hell and the "burning" torment of the doomed and damned are consistently likened to thirst. When we look at it in that way we come to a better understanding: that the suffering of hell exists not because of God's desire to punish but because of His love. He loved man so much that He made him an eternal being capable of knowing Him and dwelling with Him forever. In His love, He so constituted man that fellowship with God is no mere option and thus of little enjoyment. No, it is vital to his very being and thus brings infinite pleasure and satisfaction.

If God made us to have fellowship with Him and to draw our life and purpose from His direction over us, then the moment we divorce any part of life from Him, whether it be knowledge or love, it becomes polluted and perverted, a caricature of what was intended. That fact is observable everywhere. Man may not experience the thirst for God in this life when he is surrounded with like-minded friends and the pleasures of this world. He is like a man in the Sahara desert who, early in the morning, refuses to take the water offered to him; but in the heat of the day he is dying for lack of the water he earlier despised.

That the Bible likens separation from God's life and fellowship to a burning thirst provides a metaphor which helps us to understand in some measure what both heaven and hell will be like. Following that analogy, we realize that hell's suffering will be so excruciatingly painful for the very same reason that heaven will be so exquisitely joyful. That is the way with thirst un-quenched—or satisfied.

It is easy to understand that the person dying of thirst *burns* with torment for the same reason that a drink of cold water quenching one's thirst tastes and feels so good. Our insight becomes even clearer when we remember that thirst burns and torments, and quenching that thirst soothes and exhilarates, because water is absolutely essential to life. In like manner, hell will feel so bad and heaven so good because the intimacy and fullness of God's presence and love is as essential to our spiritual life as water is to our physical life.

Those in hell will burn with an unquenchable thirst for the love of God for which they were made and from which God never intended them to be separated. There is absolutely no quenching of this moral and spiritual thirst for those in hell because they have by their own choice cut themselves off from God for eternity.

## What About "The Lake of Fire"?

---

*Question:* As I understand it, the Bible says there will be two resurrections: one of the saved and the other of the lost. The latter stand before God in their physical resurrected bodies and are cast into a place of torment called "the lake of fire" (Revelation 20:15). What is the point of eternally tormenting the lost?

*Response:* The Bible describes the damned who stand before God at the Great White Throne judgment and are cast into the lake of fire in these terms: "I saw the dead, small and great, stand before God ... and the dead were judged ... according to their works" (Revelation 20:12). Although their appearance before God is said to be a *"resurrection* of damnation" (John 5:29), it seems clear that they do not stand before God in physical bodies which have been reconstituted from their decayed and consumed remains. The fact that they are twice referred to as "dead" would seem to indicate rather that they are disembodied spirits.

---

In fact, the Bible tells us that the pain suffered by the damned has nothing to do with bodies and nerves. That Christ's description of the rich man and beggar, the one in hell and the other in paradise, is no mere parable is evident from the fact that the beggar's name is given us, so he must have been a real person. Note Christ's words:

The rich man also died and was buried; and in hell he lifted up his eyes, being in torment ... and cried ... send Lazarus that he may dip the tip of his finger in water and cool my tongue, for I am tormented in this flame (Luke 16:22-24).

While the words "eyes" and "tongue" and "flame" are mentioned and the torment of thirst for water is implied, these words clearly have another meaning than that which is attached to them in this life. The physical bodies of both the rich man and Lazarus were corrupting in the grave. Therefore the eyes, tongue, finger, and flame referred to could not be physical. If the "flame" that tormented the rich man in hell was not physical, then we have reason to believe that the flame in the lake of fire is not physical either.

Furthermore, we are clearly told that the lake of fire was "prepared for the devil and his angels" (Matthew 25:41). Physical fire has no effect upon spirit beings. Whatever fire this is must be a special kind of fire for spirits, no doubt far more horrible than physical fire. Indeed, if the damned are in physical bodies and the flames are physical, then it would necessitate a continual, instant-by-instant reconstitution of their burning flesh in order for them to continue to be tormented.

That kind of physical torment hardly seems to be a proper punishment. It makes more sense both logically and biblically for the torment to arise from the burning thirst for God that separation from Him would create, together with the exquisite pain of remorse. The physical torment of incredibly hot fire burning continually reconstituted flesh would be so terrible that it would allow for no contemplation of past wrongs, for no remorse, for no regret for having rejected the salvation God offered. There would be no moral dimension to such torment; it would be simply physical and so overwhelming as to allow for no thought or regret. That hardly seems to fit the crime of rebellion and rejection.

## WHY ETERNAL TORMENT?

*Question:* If there really is such a place as hell or the lake of fire, why can't those people ever be rescued from that fate? It seems so unjust that they should suffer eternally. Wouldn't those in hell be the best candidates for salvation? If all of this is true, surely they would know that truth and would want to repent and believe in Christ.

*Response:* On the contrary, hell is the one place where it would be impossible to repent and from which, therefore, there could be no escape. From the few biblical references we have it seems obvious that the lake of fire is a place of terrible torment. We are told, for example, that immediately after he died the rich man was "in torments" (Luke 16:23) and that the devil "shall be tormented day and night for ever and ever" (Revelation 20:10). Concerning the humans who are consigned there it says that "the smoke of their torment ascendeth up for ever and ever" (Revelation 14:11).

Suffering such great torment (and spiritual torment would be even more excruciating than physical) would make repentance impossible, as already noted. Those in the lake of fire would be so very desperate to escape that they could think of nothing else. Certainly they would be incapable of repenting for the right reasons. No doubt one of the worst torments haunting the damned is the realization that there is no hope.

As for their fate being eternal, it could not be otherwise. Death is not the cessation of existence but the continuation of the eternal being with which God lovingly endowed man—but now in painful separation from God and all else in utter darkness and loneliness. As spiritual beings the damned will continue to exist eternally in a conscious death, for endless existence is the very nature of man's soul and spirit as Adam and Eve were originally made.

## Is God Ignorant Or Impotent?

*Question:* To me, the greatest proof that God does not exist is the suffering caused by evil in the world. The millions of Jews tortured and burned in Hitler's ovens, as well as the millions of babies and children continually dying of starvation or disease, are only a drop in the bucket of pain and evil throughout history! If God could prevent the suffering of mankind and doesn't, then He is the devil and not God. And if He cannot, then He is impotent and not worthy of being looked to as God. Is there any solution to this dilemma?

*Response:* Once again, the answer to this objection is so obvious that one can only question the sincerity of the skeptics who continue to raise it, along with related questions. If man has freedom of choice, then evil is not God's fault. Yet the critics continue to parade this illogical and unfair grievance against God. As one further example, consider the following from Ingersoll:

---

There is no recorded instance where the up-lifted hand of murder has been paralyzed—no truthful account in all the literature of the world of the innocent child being shielded by God. Thousands of crimes are being committed every day—men are at this moment lying in wait for their human prey—wives are whipped and crushed, driven to insanity and death—little children begging for mercy, lifting imploring, tear-filled eyes to the brutal faces of fathers and mothers—sweet girls are deceived, lured and outraged, but God has no time to prevent these things—no time to defend the good and protect the pure. He is too busy numbering hairs and watching sparrows.

---

Such sarcasm flies in the face of logic and fairness and betrays the prejudice of the atheist, a prejudice so vindictive that it will not be moved by reason. Ingersoll wants God to stop the hand of the murderer but is not willing to allow God to stop his own hand from doing that which his puny mind thinks is legitimate but which may not be according to God's will. He wants God to do what he wants Him to do, and so long as God refuses to be bound by Ingersoll's limitations he rejects Him.

In contrast to the impersonal Star Wars Force or Cosmic Energy Source or other impersonal Energy ruling the universe that was the "God" of Einstein and others, the

God of the Bible is personally concerned with mankind's suffering. In contrast to the impersonal "law of karma" which brings suffering and cares not, the God of the Bible cares so much that He came to this earth as a man and suffered the demands of His own justice in payment for every sin ever committed or that will ever be committed by any person, no matter how evil. If Christ Himself, in order to redeem us, could not be delivered from the suffering of the cross and was willing to "suffer for sins, [He] the just [One] for [us] the unjust, that he might bring us to God" (1 Peter 3:18), then one must think more deeply before condemning God for the suffering which plagues mankind.

### SUFFERING, CHOICE, AND SALVATION

If the millions of martyrs were not delivered by God, martyrs who were the victims of unspeakably cruel deaths because of their faithfulness to God and to Christ and whom God surely loves, then there must be good reason for suffering. That fact is reinforced by Christ's prayer in the Garden of Gethsamene that He be delivered from the cross if it were possible. That He had to endure the cross in spite of that prayer ought to be proof enough that there is no easy way for man to be delivered from sin and suffering. Indeed, it gives us confidence in God's love. As Paul wrote, "He that spared not his own Son, but delivered him up for us all, how shall he not with him freely give us all things?" (Romans 8:32).

Moreover, suffering has a maturing and purifying effect upon those who are willing to accept it for that purpose. Marcus Aurelius noted, "Ill fortune well borne is good fortune" because of its salutary moral effect upon those who endure it. The reward for such suffering goes beyond even this life, into eternity. Jesus said, "Blessed are ye when men shall revile you and persecute you, and shall say all manner of evil against you falsely for my sake. Rejoice and be exceeding glad, for great is your reward in heaven" (Matthew 5:11,12). Linton put it like this:

Just as a high and heroic character resulting from adversity and endured hardship is by the consensus of all men ample compensation for all that must be endured to produce it, so the enrichment of eternity by the existence of the glorified beings who "through much tribulation enter into the kingdom of God" will a thousandfold compensate for the travail of man and God that was involved.[6]

Evil and the suffering which it brings upon us all are the consequences of mankind's exercise of the power of choice. Thus evil and suffering could be eliminated by preventing free choice. For God to do so, however, as we have already noted, would destroy mankind totally. God has a better solution—one that provides salvation while preserving free choice and thus the love which such choice alone makes possible.

And here we must honestly confront strict Calvinism's claim that Christ did not die for all, that He did not pay for the sins of all, and that man can choose only evil and is unable to repent and trust Christ without God extending irresistible grace to him. If that is the case, then even though evil may not be attributed to God, it is God who prevents His salvation from reaching all. Those in hell are there, according to strict Calvinism, not because they rejected Christ, for that is all they could do. They are there because God did not love them enough to extend the irresistible grace that would cause them to choose Christ. I can agree with the atheist that such a God is not loving and good. Nor is this the God of the Bible, but the invention of man.

## SALVATION IS FOR SINNERS—BY GRACE

---

*Question:* Let's assume that evil is not God's fault. I can buy that as far as this earthly existence is concerned. What concerns me is that God's punishment of evil seems itself evil. Instead of punishing evil in this life, when it might do some good (even the Bible admits that evil men prosper on earth), why does God choose to

punish people in an eternal hell, when it is too late to rescue them for any good in this life?

*Response:* You are correct in saying that once a person
is in hell it is too late for repentance. One obvious reason
is, as we have already noted, that the suffering is so great
that hell's inhabitants would be compelled to repent not
out of genuine remorse, but because the desire to escape
that horrible place would be so overwhelming.

---

Your proposal, however, about limiting punishment
to this life assumes that you know better how to win
people to Christ than God does. The idea of punishing
evildoers in this life as a means of correcting their
behavior and thereby turning them to Christ is flawed
for many reasons which we have already noted. The
battle is for man's heart, and therefore man cannot be
won by coercion. Love cannot be forced.

Nor is the issue to make man behave. That is the reason for parental or civil punishment and correction, but
behavior has nothing to do with salvation. In fact, one of
the major delusions that keeps man from "repentance toward God and faith toward our Lord Jesus Christ" (Acts
20:21) is his imagined good behavior. The issue is initially
not *behavior* but man's *relationship with God*; and for that
to be made right, man must see his sin and repent, not
clothe himself in self-righteousness.

This very error is promoted and compounded by
many Christians who, with good intent, expend their
time and energy trying to make the world a better place
in which to live. God's design is not to clean up this
world; it is, in fact, destined for destruction. God's plan
is to call His own out of this world to become citizens
of heaven.

And how is that to be done? Can this goal be
achieved by punishment in this life? On the contrary, we
are told that "the goodness of God leadeth thee to repentance" (Romans 2:4) and that it is "the grace of God that
bringeth salvation" (Titus 2:11). Goodness and grace are
appreciated and embraced only by those who know that

these gifts from God are their only hope to escape the just judgment for their sins.

## UNJUSTLY BLAMING GOD

*Question:* I think one needs no further proof that gods do not exist than the evil that has been done in their names. Some of the most devastating wars, the cruelest tortures, and the most hurtful prejudices have been in the name of religion. As for the Christian god, no doubt more innocent people have been tortured and killed in his name than in the name of any other god—and simply because they had a different religious belief from that of their torturers. How can you explain away this obvious evil in god's name?

*Response:* This is an old and sincere argument. I appreciate the problem which it poses, a problem, however, which is based largely upon a misunderstanding that is easily removed by a little thought. It is not reasonable to blame Jesus Christ for whatever anyone who claims to be a Christian happens to do unless Jesus Himself taught and practiced the same. It is equally irrational to blame God for everything those who claim to represent Him do in His name.

Though he did not believe in the God of the Bible but in some "spirit of the universe," the great English poet and radical Percy Bysshe Shelley (1792-1822) pointed out more than 180 years ago the inconsistency of evil done in the name of God:

Persecution for opinion is unjust. With what consistency, then, can the worshipers of a Deity whose benevolence they boast embitter the existence of their fellow being because his ideas of that Deity are different from those which they entertain?
Alas! there is no consistency in those persecutors who worship a benevolent Deity; those who worship a demon would alone act consonantly to their principles by imprisoning and torturing in his name.[7]

No one can argue with this reasoning, which is perfectly biblical. A true Christian is to love even his enemies and never to persecute, torture, or kill others. Tragically, the Roman Catholic Church (to whom Shelley obviously referred) and other religious groups have engaged in deadly crusades against those who would not agree with them.

Sadly, Roman Catholicism is the only "Christianity" that most people in the world have ever known. Few are aware that there have always been millions of true followers of Christ who were not part of the Roman Catholic Church, or that these Christians by the millions suffered at the hands of Rome. See our documentation in *A Woman Rides the Beast.*

One is reminded of the native who was given the choice of dying in the flames or converting to "Christianity" and going to heaven. He asked whether heaven was inhabited by people like those who were threatening him. When told that such persons were the only ones who could get to heaven, he declared that he would rather die than go there!

## Is The God Of The Old Testament Unchristian?

*Question:* I read recently a reprint from an old book which gave a story that I think ought to shatter the "faith" of any Christian: "A mother was talking to her little child of the murder of the Amalekites. She explained that in those days enemies were murdered, but revelation was progressive, and Jesus told us that we are to love our enemies and do good to them that despitefully use us. Said the little girl, 'Now I understand: that day was before God became a Christian!'" It seems to me that the Bible presents two Gods: the vengeful, warring God of the Old Testament, and the compassionate, forgiving and loving heavenly Father of the New, who was introduced by Christ. How can you reconcile the two "Gods"?

*Response:* Again we have an old objection which is based upon a serious misunderstanding of the Bible. The God of the Old Testament is every bit as merciful as the God of the New Testament. Obviously, they are one and the same. The Old Testament prophets made it clear that God took no pleasure in meting out judgment upon sinners. The

Psalms are filled with praise to God for His mercy, kindness, grace, and love. In every one of the 26 verses of Psalm 136 it is said of God that "his mercy endureth forever." Consider these further few examples of many more that could be given:

---

I have trusted in thy mercy; my heart shall rejoice in thy salvation (Psalm 13:5).

Surely goodness and mercy shall follow me all the days of my life, and I will dwell in the house of the LORD forever (Psalm 23:6).

All the paths of the LORD are mercy and truth unto such as keep his covenant and his testimonies (Psalm 25:10).

I trust in the mercy of God forever and ever (Psalm 52:8).

Thou, Lord, art good, and ready to forgive, and plenteous in mercy unto all them that call upon thee. . . .
Thou, O Lord, art a God full of compassion and gracious, longsuffering and plenteous in mercy and truth (Psalm 86:5,15).

The LORD is good; his mercy is everlasting, and his truth endureth to all generations (Psalm 100:5).

The LORD is merciful and gracious, slow to anger, and plenteous in mercy (Psalm 103:8).

It is instructive to go to Mount Sinai, where God revealed Himself to His people Israel and intimately to Moses. It was there that God spoke the law to His people from the midst of fire and smoke on the top of the mount that quaked at His presence. It was a terrifying scene where God also executed severe punishment at the base of the mount upon those who turned to idolatry and immorality even while Moses was on Sinai speaking with Him.

Yet in the midst of this frightening revelation of His power and majesty and justice, God revealed Himself as merciful and longsuffering. Having asked God to reveal Himself to him, Moses journeyed back up onto the mount to meet Him. Here is how God revealed Himself to Moses on that occasion:

> And the LORD descended in the cloud, and stood with him there and proclaimed the name of the LORD. And the LORD passed by before him and proclaimed, The LORD, The LORD God, merciful and gracious, longsuffering, and abundant in goodness and truth, keeping mercy for thousands, forgiving iniquity and transgression and sin, and that will by no means clear the guilty . . . (Exodus 34:5-7).

As for Christ presenting God as a loving Father, He could not make God's love and mercy more clear than it had already been presented in the Old Testament. Furthermore, almost half of the 54 times hell is mentioned in the entire Bible are contained in the New Testament. In the Gospels, Christ Himself warned of hell 17 times and of coming judgment repeatedly.

## WHAT ABOUT THE DESTRUCTION OF ENTIRE NATIONS?

*Question:* God told Israel to wipe out cities completely, to "save alive nothing that breatheth" (Deuteronomy 20:16,17). What justification can there possibly be for such indiscriminate slaughter?!

*Response:* This is a difficult question—not so much as it pertains to the adults, but to children. Such was also the case with Sodom and Gomorrah (Genesis 13:13). When those cities were destroyed by fire (the evidence of which can still be seen in that part of Israel today), the babies and children were destroyed also.

However, that God did not wish to destroy these people is clear from His statement to Abraham when promising him the land of Canaan: "The iniquity of the Amorites is not yet full" (Genesis 15:16). This tells us that God did not at that time consider the wickedness of these people great enough to warrant their extermination. With that understanding, perhaps we can trust God that when He did destroy them, including even their children, it was the only way to cleanse that horribly defiled land.

Let us not forget that God was longsuffering for more than 400 years as the wickedness of these people grew ever greater. At last He had to destroy them for the good of the remainder of the human race. We may be certain that this was done reluctantly. God assures us:

> As I live, saith the Lord God, I have no pleasure in the death of the wicked, but that the wicked turn from his way and live; turn ye, turn ye from your evil ways, for why will ye die, O house of Israel? (Ezekiel 33:11).

We also know that God was not arbitrary; He dealt with an even hand. The judgment upon these nations was to have been an example to Israel, but they did not heed it. Eventually God had to execute similar judgment upon even His chosen people.

We may not fully understand the apparent harshness of this judgment, especially upon infants who are not morally responsible, but it is highly likely that these infants, because of the moral sinfulness of the society in which they were conceived, were all infected with deadly diseases. We may not know all the details, but we can leave to God what we cannot fully understand, and with Abraham rest in this confidence: "Shall not the Judge of all the earth do right?" (Genesis 18:25).

We dare not question God's right to visit judgment as He sees fit. Inasmuch as those who die before they are old enough to have knowingly rejected God are saved, we know that this mercy was extended to the Canaanite infants as well.

## Happy In Destroying Babies?

*Question:* A verse in the Old Testament that I have never been able to reconcile with my belief in God and which therefore has troubled me for years is this: "Happy shall he be that taketh and dasheth thy little ones against the stones" (Psalm 137:9). God is telling Israel to be happy in destroying innocent babies? One preacher tried to say that these heathen were so thoroughly demon-possessed that even the babies had to be killed. Surely God could deliver babies from demons rather than kill them!

*Response:* On the contrary, God is not telling Israel to smash the heads of infants against rocks. He is not speaking to Israel at all. He is pronouncing judgment upon Babylon for its great sin in showing no mercy when it destroyed Jerusalem and led the Jews captive. Here is what God says:

O daughter of Babylon, who art to be destroyed, happy shall he be that rewardeth thee as thou has served us.
Happy shall he be that taketh and dasheth thy little ones against the stones (Psalm 137:8,9).

This is a prophecy in which God is warning Babylon that she will be dealt with in the same manner in which she treated Israel, that she will be destroyed as viciously as she destroyed other nations. The day is coming when an enemy (other than Israel) will rejoice in its triumph over Babylon, an enemy that will be happy in the slaughter. It was not Israel that destroyed Babylon.

## Why Doesn't God Simply Abolish Sickness And Death?

*Question:* Even apart from skepticism as to whether miracles occur, I have problems with the healings which Christ supposedly effected while upon earth. Some accounts seem so straightforward, while others raise questions. For example, the "healing" didn't seem to work for one man and had to be done again (Mark 8:22-25). That hardly sounds as though Christ were God in the flesh. Furthermore, if He could really heal, why didn't He heal everyone? Better still, if God really loves all mankind, why not do away with sickness and suffering completely?

*Response:* You refer to the man who, after Jesus touched his eyes and asked him what he saw, replied, "I see men as trees walking." Jesus then touched him again, "and he saw every man clearly" (Mark 8:22-25). The expression "men as trees walking" seems to reveal the reason for a second touch: The blind man's *sight* was restored, but he didn't *understand* what he saw. Having been blind from birth, he had never seen either a man or a tree and was therefore confused. At the second touch Christ apparently healed his mind so that he understood what he saw. Whatever the explanation, this incident could hardly cast doubt upon Christ's power to heal, in light of the thousands of other cases where a touch or word was sufficient not only to heal but to raise the dead.

---

As for why Christ has not done away with sickness entirely, the answer is quite clear both logically and biblically. There are two basic reasons. First of all, sickness, suffering, and death are the result of sin. So long as mankind continues to live in sinful rebellion against God, so long sickness will prevail. Those whom Christ healed became ill again, and so it would be today.

Furthermore, if God acted so unwisely as to continually heal sinners, He would have removed all incentive for them to repent. Indeed, He would seem to be rewarding their wickedness. Would you have wanted God to keep Hitler alive, immune from judgment, so he could continue his evil? I think not. Then where are we to draw the line between those whom God would always heal and those whom He would not heal? There is no such line, for, as the Bible says and we all know, "*All* have sinned and come short of the glory of God" (Romans 3:23).

Moreover, those whom Christ raised from the dead, such as Lazarus, died again. God has decreed in His righteousness that "the wages of sin is death" (Romans 6:23), and so long as sin continues on this earth people will continue to die. For God to prevent death would be to unrighteously remove the penalty demanded by His justice. Moreover, it would perpetuate mankind's existence in these corruptible bodies and in this evil world. God has something far better in mind: the resurrection of the body into immortality and eternal bliss in a new universe that He will create where sin will never enter.

Only those who have by faith in Christ become a new creation in Christ Jesus (2 Corinthians 5:17) will be allowed to dwell eternally in that new universe of bliss. God's eternal salvation is offered and available to all. To receive it is a choice that each person must make.

*The Lord himself shall descend from heaven with a shout*
*. . . and the dead in Christ shall rise first; then we which*
*are alive and remain shall be caught up together with*
*them . . . to meet the Lord in the air; and so shall we ever*
*be with the Lord.*

—1 Thessalonians 4:16,17

*Then shall that Wicked [Antichrist] be revealed,*
*whom the Lord shall . . . destroy with the brightness*
*of his coming.*

—2 Thessalonians 2:8

*I saw heaven opened, and behold a white horse; and he*
*that sat upon him was called Faithful and True. . . . And*
*I saw the beast [Antichrist], and the kings of the earth*
*and their armies, gathered together to make war against*
*him that sat on the horse. . . . And the beast was taken,*
*and with him the false prophet . . . [and] both were cast*
*alive into a lake of fire burning with brimstone.*

—Revelation 19:11,19,20

# 10

# A "Rapture" and a "Second Coming"?

## DOESN'T THE CHURCH FACE ANTICHRIST?

*Question:* How could it be more clear that the church must face the Antichrist? Paul said, "That day shall not come except there come a falling away first [apostasy], and that man of sin be revealed [Antichrist]" (2 Thessalonians 2:3). I would be interested in how you could argue this point.

*Response:* Paul specifically states that the *apostasy* comes first, but he does not say that the *appearance of Antichrist* comes first. He is actually telling us that the Antichrist will be revealed after that day arrives—in fact, *in* that day. Let me illustrate with a simple example: "Sunday will not come except Saturday comes first, and we have a big dinner. Now you know what prevents the dinner from being held, and it will not be held until that hindrance is removed."

It is specified that Saturday will come first but not that the dinner comes first. One might be confused over whether the big dinner will be on Saturday or Sunday, because that is not made completely clear. However, when one learns what the hindrance to the dinner is and that it cannot be removed until midnight Saturday, then one knows that the dinner will be on Sunday.

Paul goes on to state unequivocally that someone is hindering the revealing of the Antichrist and that he cannot be revealed until "he who now letteth [hinders] . . . be taken out of the way" (2 Thessalonians 2:7). This one who hinders is eternal because He has been preventing Antichrist's takeover for the past 2000 years. Only God is eternal, and only God is powerful enough to prevent Satan from installing his man as world ruler. The Holy Spirit, however, cannot be "taken out of the way," because He is omnipresent. Then what did Paul mean?

## The Unique And Hindering Presence

There is an indwelling presence of the Holy Spirit which has been upon earth since Pentecost. Old Testament saints had the Holy Spirit *with* them and as an anointing *upon* them. That presence, however, could be taken away. The Holy Spirit did not indwell believers prior to Pentecost as an abiding presence that would never leave them. This indwelling is unique to the church, a fact which is clear from many Scriptures. This new presence, which was unknown before Pentecost, can only be removed by removing the church—those in whom the Holy Spirit dwells.

David prayed, "Take not thy Holy Spirit from me" (Psalm 51:11), a prayer that would be meaningless today and would reflect inexcusable unbelief. Christ said to His disciples, referring to the Holy Spirit, "He dwelleth with you, and shall be in you" (John 14:17). John tells us that when Christ was still here upon earth, "the Holy Ghost was not yet given, because . . . Jesus was not yet glorified" (John 7:39). After Jesus was glorified, He sent the Holy Spirit "from the father" (John 15:26) to be with His church in a new way that had been unknown up to that time.

It is this unique presence of the Holy Spirit in the church which will be removed at the rapture, allowing the Antichrist to be revealed and to have free rein to rule the world. Of course, the Holy Spirit, being omnipresent, will remain here to convict sinners of the truth of the gospel and to win multitudes to Christ during the tribulation period. These are the tribulation saints who will be martyred for their faith.

## AN UNBIBLICAL "ESCAPE THEORY"?

*Question:* To imagine that the church will be taken to heaven before the Antichrist appears and takes power and the prophesied seven-year tribulation period begins is a delusion, in my opinion. Christ said we would suffer for His sake. The pre-trib rapture teaching seems to offer an unbiblical escape from that suffering. Why should a certain segment of the church be allowed to escape its allotted suffering?

*Response:* Where does it say that the tribulation under Antichrist is allotted to that fraction of the church which happens to be alive when Antichrist takes power? And why should a certain segment of the church be required to endure suffering at the hands of the Antichrist which no other Christians experienced?

Of course, it *could* be so. Depending upon their time and place in history, different segments of the church have suffered trials and persecutions varying in both kind and intensity. Believers here in the United States, for example, have never (at least until now) been called upon to endure the horrors faced by those who for centuries were tortured and killed in the Inquisitions. Nor did those who were burned at the stake endure the years of imprisonment and slow death by hard labor and starvation which befell millions under Stalin, Hitler, or Mao. But what does the Bible say concerning the church and Antichrist?

There are several clear statements in Scripture which tell us plainly that the church will not be on earth when Antichrist takes power. First of all, the early church was undoubtedly living in expectancy of Christ's imminent appearing: "from whence [heaven] we *look* for the Saviour" (Philippians 3:20); "ye turned to God . . . to *wait* for his Son from heaven" (1 Thessalonians 1:9,10); "*Looking* for . . . the glorious appearing of . . . our Saviour Jesus Christ" (Titus 2:13); "unto them that *look* for him shall he appear" (Hebrews 9:28); etc. If the Antichrist had to come first, it would make no sense to be waiting and looking for Christ.

This expectancy of His imminent return was first taught by Christ Himself, who also associated any thought of a delay in His coming with evil:

> Let your loins be girded about, and your lights burning, and ye yourselves like unto men that wait for their lord . . . that when he cometh and knocketh, they may open unto him immediately . . . . be ye therefore ready also, for the Son of man cometh at an hour when ye think not (Luke 12:35,36,40).

> But and if that evil servant shall say in his heart, My lord delayeth his coming . . . (Matthew 24:48).

If Christ were not going to rapture His saints to heaven before the tribulation period, then He couldn't be expected until the end thereof. In that case, there would be no hope of Christ's coming or appearing until after Antichrist had liquidated the church and the seven-year tribulation period had run its course and Jerusalem was surrounded by the armies of the world and Christ had to intervene to stop the slaughter. Only then could Christ return. Therefore no one would be watching and waiting for His appearing even now, much less in the first century. Such expectant language would not be used in the New Testament at all. It would make no sense.

It is also clear that the church is already in heaven before Christ's second coming at Armageddon. In Revelation 19:7,8 we read, "The marriage of the Lamb is come, and his wife hath made herself ready. And to her was granted that she should be arrayed in fine linen, clean and white. . . ." This marriage between Christ and the Church is taking place in heaven *while the Antichrist is in charge on the earth beneath.* Surely the church can't be in two places at once: being killed by Antichrist on earth and simultaneously present at her marriage to the Lamb in heaven.

## THE "SAINTS" COME FROM HEAVEN TO EXECUTE JUDGMENT

At the end of Revelation 19, the second coming of Christ in power and glory to destroy Antichrist (as in 2 Thessalonians 2:8) is described, and we are told that "the armies which were in heaven followed him . . . clothed in fine linen, white and clean" (verse 14). This is the clothing of Christ's bride, the church. So it must be she who accompanies Him in keeping with the promise that once we are caught up "to meet the Lord in the air . . . *so shall we ever be with the Lord*" (1 Thessalonians 4:17). That conclusion is confirmed by Paul's declaration that "the saints shall judge the world" (1 Corinthians 6:2) and David's statement that the saints will "execute vengeance upon the heathen, and punishments upon the people" (Psalm 149:7).

We have confirmation in other Scriptures of the saints coming with Christ from heaven to execute judgment. For example, "Enoch also, the seventh from Adam, prophesied of these, saying, Behold, the Lord cometh with ten thousands of his saints, to execute judgment upon all [the ungodly]" (Jude 14,15). The expression "ten thousands" simply means an innumerable multitude. In Daniel, too, we are told that "the saints of the most High shall take the kingdom" from Antichrist, who made war with the saints, "and judgment was given to the saints" (7:18,22).

So we know that those clothed in fine linen, white and clean, and who accompany Christ, are "saints." Here we have further evidence that the "armies from heaven" must be the church. Those in the church are consistently addressed as "saints" throughout the New Testament:

"thy saints at Jerusalem" (Acts 9:13); "the saints which dwelt at Lydda" (Acts 9:32); "to all that be in Rome, beloved of God, called saints" (Romans 1:7); "the church of God . . . at Corinth . . . sanctified in Christ Jesus, called to be saints" (1 Corinthians 1:2); "the saints which are at Ephesus" (Ephesians 1:1); and so forth.

Those who truly know God are called saints in the Old Testament as well: "the saints that are in the earth" (Psalm 16:3); "Gather my saints together unto me, those that have made a covenant with me by sacrifice" (Psalm 50:5); "Precious in the sight of the Lord is the death of his saints" (Psalm 116:15); "O God, the heathen . . . have laid Jerusalem on heaps. The dead bodies of thy servants have they given to be meat unto the fowls of the heaven, the flesh of thy saints unto the beasts of the earth" (Psalm 79:1,2). Thus we are persuaded that they too will be in the army which accompanies Christ from heaven.

Indeed, Zechariah tells us that when Christ returns to earth to rescue Israel in the midst of Armageddon, "his feet shall stand in that day upon the mount of Olives" and He will bring *all* the saints" from heaven with Him (14:4,5). Of course, the souls and spirits of the saints who have died were instantly taken to heaven at the time of their deaths to await the resurrection of their bodies. Surely the armies of heaven are not disembodied spirits but whole persons in immortal bodies of glory, indicating that the resurrection must have taken place prior to this event.

The rapture, therefore, must have already occurred, for two reasons. First of all, Paul assures us that the rapture takes place *simultaneously with the resurrection*. Secondly, for *all* saints to accompany Christ when He comes from heaven to execute judgment, the living saints must have been caught up to heaven in transformed bodies also. So here we have further evidence that the rapture is a separate event prior to the second coming and another strong indication of the pre-trib rapture of the church.

## WHO ARE THE "SAINTS" WHOM ANTICHRIST KILLS?

*Question:* Revelation 13:7 says that Antichrist is given authority (and it could only come from God) "to make war with the saints and to overcome them. . . . " Doesn't this prove that the church faces Antichrist and goes through the tribulation? If not, who are the saints whom Antichrist kills?

*Response:* Christ promised that the "gates of hell shall not prevail against" the church (Matthew 16:18). Surely hell would have prevailed if the Antichrist, who is backed and empowered by Satan (Revelation 13:2,4), could "make war with the saints and overcome them." Furthermore, this fact would mean that a post-trib rapture would be practically a non-event because there would be almost no Christians left alive to rapture. Yet one is given the impression that multitudes are "alive and remain" to be "caught up together" with the dead who have been raised (1 Thessalonians 4:17).

Here then is another reason for concluding that during the tribulation the church is already in heaven in resurrected and/or glorified bodies like Christ's own body. The gospel, however, is still being preached on earth by the two witnesses in the streets of Jerusalem for 3 1/2 years (Revelation 11:3) (seen no doubt on worldwide news broadcasts every evening) and by the 144,000 Jewish evangelists (Revelation 7:3,4) as well as by many others. Souls are being saved through the preaching of the gospel.

Those who have heard the gospel and rejected it prior to the rapture have no chance to be saved. Instead, they are given a "strong delusion, that they should believe a lie, that they all might be damned who believed not the truth" (2 Thessalonians 2:11,12). Multitudes, however, who never heard and rejected the gospel are being saved and are paying for their faith with their lives. The Antichrist kills all who do not bow down and worship him as God: "He had power to . . . cause that as many as would not worship the image of the beast should be killed" (Revelation 13:15).

## What About A Resurrection And Rapture For Tribulation Saints?

---

*Question:* What about the tribulation saints? How do they get to heaven? Do they have their own rapture?

*Response:* If not all, then nearly all tribulation saints are killed by the Antichrist and his henchmen. We see in heaven "under the altar the souls of them that were slain for the word of God, and for the testimony which they held; and they cried with a loud voice, saying, How long, O Lord, holy and true, dost thou not judge and avenge our blood?" (Revelation 6:9,10).

---

The martyrs' disembodied spirits are told they must wait "until their fellowservants also and their brethren, that should be killed as they were, should be fulfilled" (verse 11). Clearly, Antichrist will continue to kill those who refuse to worship him right up to the very end of Armageddon. Equally clear is the fact that none of them will be resurrected individually as they are martyred, but all together at the end of the tribulation period.

Therefore the tribulation martyrs who "were beheaded for the witness of Jesus, and for the word of God, and which had not worshiped the beast, neither his image, neither had received his mark upon their foreheads, or in their hands" are resurrected as a group. They will reign with Christ the moment Antichrist is defeated and Christ takes the throne of David to begin His earthly rule from Jerusalem (Revelation 20:4).

## Isn't The Resurrection On "The Last Day"?

---

*Question:* When speaking of the resurrection of those who believe on Him, Christ said that He would "raise [them] up *at the last day*" John (6:40,44,54). Doesn't Revelation 20:4,5 teach that the "first resurrection" takes place after the Battle of Armageddon, and couldn't this be what Christ meant by "the last day"? Certainly a pre-trib resurrection couldn't be on "the last day"! In view of such Scriptures, how can one reconcile a resurrection (and its accompanying rapture) at the beginning of the great tribulation?

*Response:* Nor could a post-trib rapture be on "the last day" if that expression refers to a 24-hour period, for an entire millennium of subsequent days follow. Beware of teaching built on one isolated verse. What do "first resurrection" and "last day" actually mean? The answer can only be found in the context of all Scripture. In John 5:28,29 Jesus spoke of two resurrections: "The hour is coming in which all that are in the graves shall hear his voice and shall come forth: they that have done good unto the resurrection of life, and they that have done evil unto the resurrection of damnation." That this does not all occur in the same "hour" is clear, for the resurrection of the wicked doesn't take place until the end of the millennium.

---

Yes, it says of the resurrection after Armageddon of those martyred by Antichrist, "This is the *first* resurrection" (Revelation 20:5). Obviously, however, this can't be the *entire* "first resurrection," or Wesley, Spurgeon, and even Paul (who, though martyred, was not slain by Antichrist) will never be resurrected, because the only resurrection that remains is of the wicked in verses 12-15. As we shall see below, those resurrected at that time are judged and sent to the lake of fire. Then what about Abraham, Moses, Daniel, and the millions of other saints, both from Old Testament and New Testament times, who lived and died before Antichrist came on the scene? One can only conclude that the statement "This is the first resurrection" must mean that this event is *part of and concludes the resurrection which occurred at the rapture.* Consequently, these martyrs are also part of the church.

That the rapture and resurrection described in 1 Corinthians 15:50-52 and 1 Thessalonians 4:13-17 take place previous to the resurrection of the tribulation martyrs is clear from the fact that in Revelation 19:7 we have the church in heaven as Christ's bride at the "*marriage* of the

Lamb" (not the marriage *supper*, verse 9, which takes place later on earth, when Christ introduces His bride to those who enter the millennium). Christ's bride, composed of the saints of all ages to that time (as we have seen), has already been resurrected, is in heaven with Christ, and accompanies Him at Armageddon, as Zechariah 14:5 and Jude 14 declare.

## The "Second" Resurrection Is To Damnation

Inasmuch as those martyred during the tribulation are resurrected after Antichrist is "taken . . . [and] cast alive into [the] lake of fire" (Revelation 19:20) and Christ is reigning on earth, they will not be raptured to heaven but gathered by angels (along with the living remnant of Jews not already in Israel) into His presence on earth: "Immediately after the tribulation . . . shall appear the sign of the Son of man in heaven . . . they shall see the Son of man coming in the clouds of heaven with power and great glory. And he shall send his angels . . . and they shall gather together [to Jerusalem] his elect from the four winds" (Matthew 24:29-31).

The only resurrection after Revelation 20:4,5 takes place 1000 years later and must be what Christ called "the resurrection of damnation." Those who are raised then are still described as "*dead* in trespasses and in sins" (Ephesians 2:1; cf. Colossians 2:13): "I saw the *dead*, small and great, stand before God; and the books were opened . . . and the *dead* were judged out of those things which were written in the books" (Revelation 20:12). This is the Great White Throne judgment of the lost. As for Christians, they have already appeared before the judgment seat of Christ (Romans 14:10; 2 Corinthians 5:10) immediately after the rapture.

If the resurrection of believers who lived and died prior to the tribulation took place seven years previously, why is the resurrection in Revelation 20 of those slain by Antichrist called "the first resurrection"? Clearly, it is thereby intended to indicate that these martyrs are part of the church, which has already been resurrected. It specifically says that they "reign with him [Christ] a thousand years" (Revelation 20:6), and so do the saints of all ages: "Have thou authority over ten cities" (Luke 19:17); "I appoint unto you a kingdom" (Luke 22:29); "we shall also reign with him" (2 Timothy 2:12).

## WHAT DOES "LAST DAY" MEAN?

What about Christ raising all believers "at the last day"? This "last day" cannot be the 24-hour period during which these martyrs are raised, for at least 1000 years of days follow during the millennium. That expression refers to what is elsewhere called the "last days" or "latter day," expressions found throughout the Bible to designate the "end times." For example, Job testifies, "My redeemer . . . shall stand at the *latter day* upon the earth . . . whom I shall see for myself, and mine eyes shall behold" (Job 19:25,27). Job makes it clear that he will be resurrected: "Though after my skin worms destroy this body, yet in my flesh shall I see God" (verse 26).

Surely Job, who will have been in the grave several thousand years before Antichrist comes, cannot be one of those martyred by Antichrist and who will be resurrected after Armageddon. Yet he anticipates his resurrection in "the latter day." That term includes a period of years at the end of this present state of affairs leading to Christ's second coming and undoubtedly includes the pre-trib resurrection and rapture of the saints as well as the millennium.

In fact, the "last day" is a reference to what is called "the day of the Lord [God]" (Isaiah 2:12; Jeremiah 46:10; Ezekiel 30:3; Joel 1:15; etc.) or the day of Christ (1 Corinthians 1:8; Philippians 1:10; 2 Thessalonians 2:2). It comes "as a thief in the night," when men are saying "peace and safety" (1 Thessalonians 5:2,3) and, instead of expecting Christ to return or God's judgment to fall, boasting that "all things continue as they were from the beginning" (2 Peter 3:4). It must also last until the end of the millennium and the destruction of the old universe and the creation of the new, for Peter says: "The day of the Lord will come as a thief in the night, in the which the heavens shall pass away ... the day of God, wherein the heavens ... shall be dissolved ... we ... look for new heavens and a new earth" (2 Peter 3:10-13). Thus both the pre-trib resurrection at the rapture and the post-Armageddon "first resurrection" of those martyred by Antichrist occur during what is called "the last day."

## What About Mohammed's Ascension To Heaven?

*Question:* Christians claim that Christ ascended to heaven from the Mount of Olives and will return to that location in a "second coming." The Muslims similarly claim that Mohammed ascended to heaven from Jerusalem. How can Christians be so sure that Christ ascended to heaven from Jerusalem (and will return there) and deny that the same thing could have happened to Mohammed? There are more than a billion Muslims who believe in Mohammed's ascension. Isn't that enough?

*Response:* Whether a proposition is true or false depends upon the evidence, not upon how many people, out of loyalty to a particular religion, confess it as an article of their faith. And when faith, instead of being based upon evidence, is imposed under fear of death, as is the case with the religion of Islam, then the belief itself is all the more suspect.

From its very beginning, Islam was spread by the sword. The choice was conversion to Islam or death. Obviously, any "faith" which one must adopt in order to escape execution is not genuine. Tragically, Islam continues to maintain itself under similar threats. Such vicious barbarism is more difficult to enforce in today's world, with the media and various human rights agencies on the watch. Yet it still occurs under Islamic regimes in various places such as Nigeria and the Sudan, where thousands of "infidels" (i.e. non-Muslims) have been slaughtered by Muslims in recent years. Here is what the Koran prescribes and which a devout Muslim is bound to obey whenever possible:

> Slay the idolaters [those who do not worship Allah] wherever ye find them, and take them (captive), and besiege them, and prepare for them each ambush. But if they repent and establish worship [i.e. convert to Islam] and pay the poor-due [tax], then leave their way free. Lo! Allah is Forgiving, Merciful [to those who convert to Islam] (Surah 9:5).

Consistent with forcing conversion under threat of death, the Koran also requires that Islam be maintained in the same manner: "If they turn back (to enmity) [from Islam] then take them and kill them wherever ye find them…" (Surah 4:89). In obedience to the Koran, it is the death penalty in Saudi Arabia today for a Muslim to convert to any other religion. That very fear of death as the consequence of leaving Islam invalidates the testimony of all Muslims. One might swear to anything under such a threat.

Even in countries which profess some freedom of religion and conscience, such as Turkey or Egypt, and where death is not the civil penalty for conversion, a convert to Christianity may still be threatened with execution by family or friends. And that threat is sometimes carried out even today.

## NO EVIDENCE FOR MOHAMMED'S ALLEGED ASCENSION

There is neither Koranic nor historic basis for the belief that Mohammed journeyed to heaven from the rock over which the Dome of the Rock was built. Islam claims no eyewitnesses to this alleged event, nor is it supported at all in the Koran. There is only one verse in the Koran upon which this article of faith rests, but that verse is far from clear:

> Glorified be He Who carried His servant by night from the Inviolable Place of Worship to the

> Far Distant Place [al-Aqsa] of Worship the neigh-
> borhood whereof We have blessed, that We might
> show him of Our tokens! Lo! He, and only He, is the
> Hearer, the Seer (Surah 17:1).

There is nothing about a magical horse nor about as-
cent into heaven. The "Inviolable Place of Worship" is obviously Mecca, but Jerusalem cannot possibly be the "Far
Distant Place of Worship," as is now claimed. It was never
a place of worship for Muslims nor considered to be of any
religious significance until the idea was invented very recently in order to justify the desired takeover of Jerusalem
by the Arabs. In fact, Jerusalem is *not once mentioned* in the
entire Koran. How then can a city which is not mentioned
at all in the Koran and which was never recommended for
worship by Mohammed nor used even once as a place of
worship in his day be identified as the "Far Distant Place
of Worship" to which Mohammed allegedly journeyed?
Obviously it cannot. To maintain that fiction does violence
to the Koran, to Islam, and to history.

Furthermore, Surah 17:1 is conspicuous by its absence among the verses from the Koran inscribed in Arabic inside this majestic Dome. That fact is proof enough
that the idea of Jerusalem being *al-Aqsa* had not even
been imagined when the Dome of the Rock was built in
A.D. 691. Why then should we believe a story which has
no factual basis? There were no witnesses to this alleged
event. It is not supported by the Koran nor is it consistent
with history. In fact, Mohammed's alleged ascension into
heaven from Jerusalem is not essential to Islam at all; that
religion stands without it.

### THE EVIDENCE FOR CHRIST'S ASCENSION

In vivid contrast, there were at least eleven eyewitnesses to the ascension of Christ into heaven, and probably
many more (Acts 1:9-11). Christ foretold His ascension
(John 6:62; 20:17). Furthermore, that event and what the angels declared at the time agreed with the Old Testament
prophecies concerning the Messiah returning to the Mount

of Olives with all His saints to execute judgment on this earth and to establish His kingdom (Zechariah 14:4,5; Jude 14). Moreover, Christ's ascension in a resurrected, glorified body into heaven is an integral and essential part of the Bible, and without it Christianity crumbles.

True Christianity is neither imposed nor maintained by force; there is no coercion to become or to remain a Christian. What one believes as a Christian is based upon the evidence, not the least of which is the consistent historical account presented in the Bible. There is much reason for believing that Christ did indeed ascend into heaven from the Mount of Olives exactly as the eyewitnesses declare, and that He will return to that point at His second coming.

There is, however, no reason for believing that Mohammed ascended to heaven from the rock on Temple Mount. There are in fact many reasons for disputing this allegation. Nor did Mohammed promise to return, nor could he, for his decayed remains are in the grave at Medina, which is visited by devout Muslims to this day. Christ's grave, however, is empty because He rose on the third day.

## THE RAPTURE AND SECOND COMING ARE TWO EVENTS?

---

*Question:* You distinguish between the rapture and the second coming as though they are two separate events. How can there still remain two comings of Christ? Where does it specifically say so in the New Testament?

*Response:* Where does it specifically say in the Old Testament that there would be *two* comings of the Messiah? In fact it doesn't. Yet every premillennial Christian (whether espousing pre-, mid-, or post-trib views) admits that Christ came once and will come again, as He promised: "I will come again" (John 14:3). How then could His disciples or the rabbis or John the Baptist have known that there were to be two comings of the Messiah? That they did not know is clear.

---

The failure to realize there would be two comings was the cause of great misunderstanding. Had the rabbis understood John the Baptist's testimony that Christ had come as "the Lamb of God, which taketh away the sin of the world" (John 1:29) and that He must be crucified, as the prophets had foretold, they would not have mocked Christ when He was on the cross. Nor would the fact of His crucifixion have caused the disciples to lose their faith. What hopeless disillusionment is reflected in these words: "[We] *trusted* [but now know we were mistaken] that it had been he which should have redeemed Israel ... [but] today is the third day since these things were done [i.e. He was crucified]" (Luke 24:21). The disciples were so certain that Christ had come to establish His kingdom on David's throne that His crucifixion devastated them.

## Two Comings Of The Messiah Clearly Implied

Though the Old Testament didn't state it in so many words, that the Messiah would come twice was clearly implied. One could not include in one time frame or in one event all that the prophets said about the coming of the Messiah. Isaiah 53 expresses a seeming contradiction that could be reconciled in no other way than by two comings. We read: "He made his grave with the wicked ... he shall prolong his days ... I will divide him a portion with the great, and he shall divide the spoil with the strong, because he hath poured out his soul unto death" (verses 9-12). One cannot die and prolong one's days at the same time. Nor can one share in the spoils of victory if slain in achieving that victory—unless there is a resurrection and a second coming to earth.

Isaiah declared that there would be "no end" to the Messiah's "government and peace" and that He would rule "upon the throne of David ... even for ever" (9:7). On the other hand, Isaiah plainly stated that the Messiah would be "cut off out of the land of the living" (53:8). Surely one could not simultaneously be killed and yet reign forever. There *had* to be two comings. Yet that fact was never stated explicitly, but only implied.

## SO IT IS IN THE NEW TESTAMENT

One event and one time frame cannot contain all that the New Testament says about the return of Christ. Apparent contradictions abound which can be reconciled in no other way than by recognizing that the return of Christ involves two separate events, one called the rapture and the other the second coming. For example, Christ declared that when the time for His coming had arrived, everyone would know it because every sign would have been fulfilled: "When ye shall see all these things [signs], know that it [my coming] is near, even at the doors" (Matthew 24:33). Yet a few moments later He said just the opposite: "For in such an hour as ye think not, the Son of man cometh" (verse 44). The conditions upon earth cannot be such that everyone would know He is about to return to earth, yet at the same time the conditions be such that no one would even suspect He is about to return. Such contrary conditions cannot occur simultaneously. They indicate two separate events at two different times.

One obvious reason why no one could be taken by surprise at the time of the second coming is that it occurs in the midst of the greatest war in history, when the armies of the Antichrist have surrounded and are about to destroy Jerusalem and Israel. No one could miss that sign! Yet Christ said that His coming would be at a time of peace and prosperity, of ease and business as usual:

> As it was in the days of Noe, so shall it be also in the days of the Son of man. They did eat, they drank, they married wives, they were given in marriage, until the day that Noe entered into the ark....
> Likewise also as it was in the days of Lot: they did eat, they drank, they bought, they sold, they planted, they builded ... (Luke 17:26-28).

At the time of the second coming at the end of the great tribulation, the earth is in great distress. Already in

Revelation 6:8 one-fourth of earth's population has been killed and incredible disasters have taken place in both earth and sky, including earthquakes so great that "every mountain and island were moved out of their places" (verse 14). There have been unprecedented famines and plagues, and an international banking collapse such as the world has never experienced—and now the most destructive war in history threatens to wipe mankind from the globe so that "except those days should be shortened, there should no flesh be saved [alive]" (Matthew 24:22).

## Contradictions Which Demand Two Events, Two Time Frames

The conditions just described at the time of Armageddon are precisely the opposite of the peace and prosperity that prevailed in the days of Noah and Lot, as Jesus describes them. Nor can the parable of the ten virgins who *"all* slumbered and slept . . . while the bridegroom tarried" (Matthew 25:5) be reconciled with conditions at Armageddon. Such complacency could only occur during a time of ease and comfort and plenty.

Christ will come at a time of war, yet at a time of peace. He will come at a time when the world has already suffered unprecedented devastation and is on the brink of total destruction, yet He will come at a time of ease and business as usual and great prosperity. He will come at a time when everyone will know that His coming is at the door, yet at a time when only those who are in touch with Him would even suspect such an event. Surely the seeming contradictions are so great that they demand two events.

At the rapture, Christ comes *for His bride, the church,* to take her to heaven to stand before Him at the "judgment seat of Christ" (Romans 14:10; 2 Corinthians 5:10), there to be cleansed and clothed in white robes and to be married to Him for eternity. At the second coming, Christ comes *with* His church *for Israel,* to rescue the latter at Armageddon and to set up His kingdom on David's throne. These two purposes do not fit together into one event and one time frame. Consequently, by the same implications that should have alerted Old Testament saints to the fact of two comings, so the New Testament implies two different "comings" of Christ yet ahead.

## WHY ARMAGEDDON?

*Question:* I have been taught (and it seems to be biblical) that we Christians will return with Christ at Armageddon and destroy those who are attacking Israel. As a Christian, to kill anyone is repugnant to me. Why is this slaughter necessary?

*Response:* Such destruction is not God's desire. He assures us, "I have no pleasure in the death of the wicked, but that the wicked turn from his way and live" (Ezekiel 33:11). Sadly, at that time there will be no way to stop the destruction of Israel—and, indeed, of all flesh upon earth—except to destroy the armies which are attacking her.

For thousands of years, God has patiently endured the rebellion of mankind. At various times throughout history, however, God has had to destroy wicked people and even whole cities because their sin had become too great to tolerate any longer. That will be the case at Armageddon, when God will be forced by His own righteousness to bring judgment upon intransigent rebels.

As for Christians personally confronting and doing battle with anyone at Armageddon, that will not be necessary. When Christ comes back to destroy Antichrist there will be no battle, no struggle. With one word from Christ those armies will be destroyed. We Christians will simply rest in the victory which Christ will have accomplished in an instant:

To you who are troubled, rest with us, when the Lord Jesus shall be revealed from heaven with his mighty angels, in flaming fire taking vengeance on them that know not God, and that obey not the gospel of our Lord Jesus Christ, who shall be punished with everlasting destruction from the presence of the Lord, and from the glory of his power, when he shall come to be glorified in his saints, and to be admired in all them that believe ... (2 Thessalonians 1:7-10).

## Last Days' Revival—Or Apostasy?

*Question:* I hear so much these days about the last decade of this century (leading up to the year 2000) being a time of unprecedented revival. Is this biblical? What do you think?

*Response:* The Bible, of course, has nothing specific to say about the last decade of this century. However, if these are indeed the last days, then we can expect the very opposite of revival. The Bible spells it out for us: false prophets, apostasy, and unprecedented deception through lying "signs and wonders" so convincing that "if it were possible, they shall deceive the very elect" (Matthew 24:24), plus a "great delusion" (2 Thessalonians 2:11,12) from God to help the world believe the very satanic lie it wants to believe. Regrettably, many Christian leaders are promoting an optimism which actually contradicts Scripture and furthers the very delusion which the Bible foretells.

Consider, for example, "Washington for Jesus '88." The Chairman of the Washington D.C. host committee declared that the march of tens of thousands of Christians in the nation's capital "put Satan on notice that his day is over." [1] If so, one can only wonder why, in the following eight years, there has been no evidence of Satan's demise. Instead, evil only increases, as the Bible declared: "In the last days ... evil men and seducers shall wax worse and worse, deceiving and being deceived" (2 Timothy 3:1,13).

## Promoting A Dangerous Delusion

One must wonder also what Christ meant when He raised the question "When the Son of man cometh, shall he find [the] faith on the earth?" (Luke 18:8). It hardly sounds as though He was referring to a great revival in the last days! From His own warnings about religious deception it seems clear that Christ was referring to the profusion of a false "Christianity" which, like the weeds in His parable of the sower, will have overgrown and choked out true faith. We are lacking the very warnings about deception which we most urgently need.

The last thing the church needs are the false promises about the defeat of Satan. Satan's kingdom is growing throughout the earth, and he will yet rule the world through Antichrist. His day will not be over until Christ returns to destroy him and his evil kingdom, and locks him in the bottomless pit (2 Thessalonians 2:8; Revelation 20:1-3). To suggest that a Christian march or our efforts in any other way will end Satan's day is to deny the clear teaching of the Bible and to promote dangerous delusion.

One cannot fault the enthusiastic zeal, but at the same time one wonders whether the year 2000 hasn't become almost a magical symbol which furthers the deception. Why should so much suddenly be accomplished in the last few years of this decade that was never achieved before? Even more troubling is the silence concerning the rapture. Has that hope been forgotten by those who promote the various marches for Jesus and the climactic celebration planned for the year 2000?

Instead of the hope of being taken to heaven to be with our Lord, there is much talk about entering the third millennium. In all of the planning there seems to be no question that the church will be here indefinitely, and that it is up to us to save the world from the very judgment which God intends to bring upon her.

## Is The Rapture In The Olivet Discourse?

*Question:* I was always taught that the rapture is not found in the Olivet Discourse. Christ's words "two shall be grinding at the mill; one shall be taken, the other left, etc." can only refer to Christ at His second coming taking the wicked from the earth and leaving the tribulation saints. Yet you teach this occurs at the rapture before the tribulation. Can you explain that for me?

*Response:* There are several reasons why Christ cannot be referring to the wicked being taken away to judgment, but to the saints being taken to heaven. The wicked are judged at the second coming, which occurs in the midst of Armageddon in Revelation 19. As already noted, even before Armageddon the earth is in utter devastation. Already in Revelation 6, one-fourth of the world's population has been killed. There have been famine, pestilence, and earthquakes that move mountains and islands out of their places so that the earth has been practically destroyed. And by the time of Armageddon, Christ must intervene (through His second coming) to stop the destruction or no flesh would survive (Matthew 24:22).

---

Yet Christ says that when "one shall be taken and the other left" the conditions on the earth will be as in the days of Noah, with people "eating and drinking, marrying and giving in marriage" (Matthew 24:38), and as in the days of Lot, when "they did eat, they drank, they bought, they sold, they planted, they builded" (Luke 17:28). That description doesn't fit the midst of Armageddon, when Christ comes with His bride to execute judgment upon Antichrist and his followers. It can only refer to a time before the great tribulation, and that is when the rapture must occur.

## MUST THE CHURCH BE PURIFIED TO BE RAPTURED?

---

*Question:* There seems to be a growing teaching that only those Christians who are living holy, victorious lives at the time of the rapture will be taken by Christ to heaven. The rest will have to face the Antichrist and be purified by martyrdom. Could that be what Christ meant by the parable of the ten virgins—the five "wise" are raptured and the five "foolish" are left to face Antichrist?

*Response:* I agree with urging Christians to live holy lives of submission to Christ and to His Word and to the leading of the Holy Spirit. A failure to live fully for Christ, however, was not the problem with the five foolish virgins. They were not saved. There was no oil (symbolic of the Holy Spirit) in their lamps and thus in their hearts and lives.

---

I also agree that we need more emphasis upon holiness and separation from the world. However, the Bible does not teach that genuine Christians who are not fully living for Christ at the time of the rapture will be left behind. If so, then what about Christians who died before the rapture and who, at the time of their death, were not living fully for Christ? They can't be "left behind." Their souls and spirits, no longer having a living body to inhabit, must go *somewhere*.

If those souls don't go to heaven upon the death of the body, then where do they go? We would have to propose some kind of evangelical purgatory! That is not biblical. We are assured that all Christians, on the basis of their saving faith in Christ, go to heaven upon death. To be "absent from the body" is to be "present with the Lord" (2 Corinthians 5:8). Heaven is not attained by good works but by faith in Christ.

Why then would not all Christians be raptured? Moreover, if those left behind at the rapture are purified by facing Antichrist, how will those who have previously died be purified? In fact, we will all be purified *in heaven* the same way: "We must *all* appear before the judgment seat of Christ" (2 Corinthians 5:10).

It is the souls and spirits of those who died trusting in Him whom Christ brings with Him (1 Thessalonians 4:14) to rejoin their bodies at the resurrection. Notice that "the dead in Christ shall rise first; then we which are alive and remain shall be caught up together with them ... to meet the Lord in the air" (verses 16,17). Surely "the dead in Christ" must mean *all* who died with faith in Christ. Therefore, "we who are alive and remain" must also mean *all* of the living whose trust is in Christ. It would seem an affront to God's justice to teach that Christians alive at the time of the rapture must be living better lives than many who have already died, in order to join them in heaven.

## What About "Soul Sleep"?

---

*Question:* Isn't it true that when the body dies, the soul goes to sleep, only to awaken at the resurrection of the body? Isn't this what is meant by the expressions "them which are asleep" and "which sleep in Jesus" (1 Thessalonians 4:13-15)?

*Response:* On the contrary, from what the Bible says, the fact that the souls which have been separated from their bodies by death are conscious is quite clear. We have, for example, the rich man who after his death carries on a conversation with Abraham, who is also dead. (Luke 16:19-31). We also have the "souls of them that were slain for the word of God" crying with loud voices to God for revenge upon those who killed them (Revelation 6:9-11). Paul is "caught up to the third heaven," where he "heard unspeakable words" (2 Corinthians 12:2,4), and he says he doesn't know whether he was "in the body" or "out of the body" (2 Corinthians 12:2,3).

---

The word "asleep" or "sleepeth" is used in the Bible as a synonym for death (Matthew 9:24; John 11:11; 1 Corinthians 15:6) and refers to the body, not to the soul and spirit. In heaven the redeemed are in conscious bliss in God's presence, awaiting the resurrection of their entombed bodies, which "sleep in Jesus" (1 Thessalonians 4:14). It is the conscious souls and spirits of "the dead in Christ" which God will "bring with him" when he comes to earth to resurrect their bodies (1 Thessalonians 4:14). Paul's desire was to "depart [from this life] and to be with Christ, which is far better" (Philippians 1:23), though he was willing, for the sake of those who needed his ministry, to continue "in the flesh," serving them and Christ here on earth (verse 24).

Paul would not have wanted to leave this life of service to Christ and the church simply to fall into a soul sleep. Neither would he have called being with Christ "far better" had it meant to slip into an unconscious state of "soul sleep," as some erroneously teach.

## MUST THE CHURCH BE UNITED BEFORE THE RAPTURE?

**Question:** Many are teaching that the church must be united and purified before Christ can return. Is that biblical?

*Response:* It is neither biblical nor logical that the small fraction of the church which is alive on earth at the time of the rapture must have attained to a status unknown by Christians who have already died, in order to join them at that heavenly marriage to our Lord. Yes, the bride is made ready and robed in white linen (Revelation 19:7,8), but the bride is the *entire* church. If this purification is a prerequisite for being taken to heaven, then what about those who died before the rapture? Clearly they must be "made ready" after they get to heaven. Then why wouldn't this also apply to those Christians who are raptured? Why wouldn't they be "made ready" in the same manner?

Surely this final cleansing can only take place at the judgment seat of Christ (2 Corinthians 5:10), when we give account to our Lord and our works are tried in fire (1 Corinthians 3:11-15). It is then that we are rewarded or suffer loss of reward, though not of salvation. There is no biblical basis for a "last-days revival" that will make Christians worthy to be raptured to heaven. We are worthy of heaven through Christ's finished work and on that basis alone.

Moreover, the Bible speaks of the last-days church as apostate (2 Thessalonians 2:3). Christ even questions whether He will find the faith on the earth when He returns (Luke 18:8). Even the wise fall asleep while the bridegroom tarries (Matthew 25:5). This is hardly the "last-days revived church" we are being told about! Let us therefore watch and be ready for our Lord's return at any moment.

## Didn't Christ Predict Fulfillment Of All Within His Generation?

*Question:* According to Matthew 24:34 Christ declared, "This generation shall not pass till all these things [which he had prophesied] be fulfilled." No one can deny that the "gospel of the kingdom" was *not* preached "unto all nations" (verse 14); that "all the tribes of the earth" did *not* see Christ "coming in the clouds of heaven with power and great glory" (verse 30); or that angels did not "gather together his elect from the four winds" (verse 31) before the generation to whom Christ spoke had passed away. That this is an obviously false prophecy can't be denied. What do *you* make of it?

*Response:* The Greek word *genea*, translated "generation," is open to more than one interpretation. There have been two major theories among Christians concerning what Jesus meant by "this generation." Those known as "preterists" believe, like the critics, that He meant the generation to whom He was speaking. Unlike the skeptics, however, those believers insist that everything Christ prophesied, including even the entire book of Revelation through the middle of chapter 20, came true within that generation, with the destruction of Jerusalem and the scattering of the Jews. By this theory Nero was the Antichrist.

Obviously, however, the generation alive at the time was not in danger of destroying all flesh from the earth with the use of bows and arrows and spears (Matthew 24:22), as our generation can now do with its modern weapons. And we now know, in retrospect, that much of what Christ foretold (as already noted) did not occur in A.D. 70. Therefore the generation alive in Christ's day could not possibly have been the generation to which He referred.

### Two Equally Untenable Theories

The more popular theory (until recently) is held by those Christians known as "futurists." They believe that "this generation" referred to the generation that would be alive at the time when Israel would be brought back into her land in the "last days," as the prophets so clearly foretold. This belief was strengthened by the obvious fact that many of the prophecies throughout the Bible could not be fulfilled until Israel was indeed back in her land.

For that reason there was great expectancy that the pre-trib rapture would occur in 1981, a date calculated by adding 40 years (estimated length of a generation) to 1948, when Israel was restored, then subtracting seven years for the tribulation. When 1981 came and passed without the rapture occurring, many Christians were disillusioned and felt obliged to opt for a post-trib rapture. Some even abandoned belief in the rapture ever taking place.

That neither of these first two interpretations is tenable is quite clear on moral grounds. It would not have been just for the judgment of all of Israel's past sins to "come upon this generation" (Matthew 23:36) or for the "blood of all the prophets, which was shed from the foundation of the world," to be "required of this generation" (Luke 11:50,51) that was alive in Christ's day. Nor would it be any more just for such judgment to come upon the generation alive when Israel was restored to her land. Surely, then, Christ must have been using "generation" to refer to all wicked and unbelieving and evil people throughout all time.

### THE ONLY EXPLANATION OF WHAT CHRIST MEANT

Indeed, here is the only way to understand what Christ meant by "this generation." He specified on many occasions the generation to which He referred as a "generation of vipers" (Matthew 3:7), an "evil and adulterous generation" (12:39), a "wicked generation" (12:45), a "wicked and adulterous generation" (16:4), a "faithless and perverse generation" (17:17; Luke 9:41), an "adulterous and sinful generation" (Mark 8:38), a "faithless generation" (9:19), and an "evil generation" (Luke 11:29).

These are not pleasant terms and obviously describe sinful mankind in all its generations. We can only conclude, therefore, that Christ is indicating (contrary to the expectation of a last-days great revival or of a Christian takeover of the world) that the human race as a whole (except for the few who believe) will remain in unbelief and rebellion against God until the very end.

There is another variation of this interpretation that agrees with Scripture. Inasmuch as Christ was speaking to Israel, we can also conclude that His words had a special application to the Jews. He was saying that, although some Jews would believe in Him and thus be part of the church, Israel as a whole would remain in unbelief and rebellion until all was fulfilled. Thus Zechariah prophesied that Israel as a whole would remain a "faithless generation" (Mark 9:19) and not believe until Christ appeared in the midst of Armageddon to rescue them:

> I will pour out upon the house of David, and upon the inhabitants of Jerusalem, the spirit of grace and of supplications; and they shall look upon me whom they have pierced, and they shall mourn for him, as one mourneth for his only son. . . .
>
> In that day there shall be a fountain opened to the house of David and to the inhabitants of Jerusalem for sin and for uncleanness. . . .
>
> And I will bring the third part [of Israel] through the fire, and will refine them as silver is refined, and will try them as gold is tried; they shall call on my name, and I will hear them; I will say, It is my people, and they shall say, The Lord is my God (Zechariah 12:10; 13:1,9).

## Must We Establish The Kingdom For Christ To Reign?

*Question:* I've been coming into contact more frequently with Christians who seem to love the Lord and believe that we have to take over the world and set up the kingdom before Christ can return. They are convinced that Christ will return to earth to rule here, not to take us to heaven, and that He cannot do so until we have set up the kingdom for Him. They say that those who believe in the rapture will be so shocked to face the Antichrist, when they didn't expect to, that they will be deceived and think he is Christ. Doesn't this make good sense?

*Response:* The real Lord Jesus Christ, as the Bible says, will raise the dead and catch us up to meet Him in the air (1 Thessalonians 4:13-18). Consequently, those whose "Christ" meets them on earth and has arrived to rule over the kingdom they have established in his name have been serving Antichrist. It is that simple when one accepts what the Bible teaches about the rapture.

---

As for being deceived into believing that Antichrist is Christ, the belief in the rapture, once again, protects us from that. Though Antichrist will be able to do great signs and wonders by the power of Satan (2 Thessalonians 2:9,10), there is one thing he cannot do: He cannot simultaneously raise the dead and catch up the living believers to heaven. Those who are watching for the Christ who raptures us to heaven cannot be deceived by a counterfeit who can only rule on earth.

*The religion of Jesus Christ aims at nothing less than the utter overthrow of all other systems of religion of the world, denouncing them as inadequate to the wants of man, false in their foundations and dangerous in their tendency. . . . These are no ordinary claims; and it seems hardly possible for a rational being to...treat them with mere indifference or contempt.*

—Professor Simon Greenleaf [1]

*Jesus said unto her, I am the resurrection and the life; he that believeth in me, though he were dead, yet shall he live; and whosoever liveth and believeth in me shall never die.*

—John 11:25,26

*Jesus saith unto him, I am the way, the truth, and the life; no man cometh unto the Father but by me.*

—John 14:6

# 11
# The Gospel That Saves

## Do All Roads Go To The Same Place?

*Question:* I find it very naive and objectionable that Christians claim that Christianity is the only true religion. Aren't we all taking different roads to get to the same place?

*Response:* Like most people, you apparently consider the popular notion that "we're all taking different roads to get to the same place" to be commendably broad-minded. On the contrary, it is extremely dogmatic and narrow-minded—more so than anything Christianity teaches. Yes, it allows everyone to take the road of his choice, but insists that no matter which *road* is taken we must all end up at the *same place*. I reject such dogmatism and reserve the right to choose my own eternal destiny.

Christianity teaches that there are *two destinations* and that each person has the freedom to choose one of the two: heaven or hell. That Jesus Christ is the only way to heaven can be easily proved. Nor can that fact justify any complaint, since Christ offers Himself freely by grace as the Savior of all who will believe in Him. What folly to insist upon taking your own way to heaven, a place where you have never been and which you don't even know how to reach! Obviously, God alone is entitled to decide whom He will allow to enter there, and upon what terms.

We all know that we have violated God's laws and that keeping the law perfectly in the future (even if that were possible) cannot make up for having broken it in the past. None of the world's religions (Christianity is not a religion but a relationship with God through Christ) offers a righteous basis for God to forgive sins and to welcome the sinner into His presence. Neither Buddha, Confucius, Zoroaster, Mohammed, nor any other founder of a religion even claimed to pay the penalty for the sins of the world. They couldn't even pay for their own sins and are thus still in their graves.

Only Christ (who is God and man in one Person) was able to pay the infinite penalty which His own justice demanded. His resurrection and ascension to heaven proved that fact. On that basis alone can sinners be forgiven. The choice is yours—either to believe this good news that the penalty has been paid and to receive the Lord Jesus Christ as your Savior, or to reject Him. Which will it be? If the latter, remember that you can never blame God for your fate. You have chosen it yourself.

## NARROW-MINDED AND DOGMATIC?

*Question:* There are thousands of religions in the world, each one answering the needs of a particular culture or individual. To insist that only one (as Christians do) is right and all others wrong is, in my opinion, so narrow-minded and dogmatic as to be unbelievable. Religious exclusivism does violence to man's right to freely choose his belief system. What kind of God would reject a sincerely held religious belief?

*Response:* I'm afraid you presuppose a god of your own making and a theology to fit your god. Suppose I said that mathematics is narrow-minded and dogmatic and that we ought to be more broad-minded about the sums of numbers and allow any answer on a math test so long as the student is sincere. Such a suggestion would be preposterous. Why? Because "narrow-minded and dog-matic" is an accusation that is absolutely senseless to make against mathematics.

---

The very nature of reality demands that there be un-changeable absolutes. Without definite and predictable physical laws, this universe could not function. Is it not reasonable that spiritual reality should be just as defi-nitely defined?

Suppose you go to the examining physician for his diagnosis, and he replies: "I wouldn't be so narrow-minded and dogmatic as to come up with a *definite* diag-nosis. What would you like? Open-heart surgery has been very popular lately; or I could transplant a kidney. I think everyone is entitled to the operation of his choice." Would you trust yourself to such a physician? Of course not! Then how can you trust yourself to the equally fool-ish idea that anything goes with God, that He has no def-inite diagnosis of sin and no definite remedy?

Imagine this announcement coming from the cockpit of a passenger jet: "I'm not narrow-minded and dog-matic. I'll just punch some buttons and see where it takes us. All directions lead to the same destination." Would you want to fly with that fool? Wouldn't you prefer a nar-row-minded, dogmatic, fundamentalist pilot who knows where he is going and follows the rules to get there?

Your theory about religion would bring utter chaos and destruction if it were put into practice in ordinary life. Then why should it be acceptable when it comes to that which is most important in life—one's eternal destiny? Is God less concerned about order in heaven than He is about order here on earth? Less concerned about things of the eternal spirit than of the temporal body? Hardly.

Everyone knows that to fly an airplane or practice medicine or even bake a cake one must follow specific procedures. One can't even play a game without rules. Then why attempt to avoid the rules which God has set in the realm of the spirit? Why not accept the good news of the gospel? That good news is explained in these verses, which are usually the first ones that every Sunday school child learns by heart:

> For God so loved the world that he gave his only begotten Son, that whosoever believeth in him should not perish but have everlasting life.
> For God sent not his Son into the world to condemn the world, but that the world through him might be saved.
> He that believeth on him is not condemned, but he that believeth not is condemned already, because he hath not believed in the name of the only begotten Son of God (John 3:16-18).

Sincerity won't get astronauts to the moon, nor will it prevent arsenic from killing the person who ingested it by mistake. Yoga won't even pay a traffic ticket. Nor will church attendance or charitable deeds pay for past sins. It makes no sense to set out from Los Angeles to New York without a map. What folly it would be to refuse to follow a map because maps are so restrictive, and to insist that any road in any direction will do! How much greater is the folly of insisting that any road sincerely followed will take one to heaven!

## What About Those Who Never Heard Of Christ?

---

*Question:* The best argument I know of to discredit Jesus is His statement "I am the way ... no man comes to the Father but by me." There are billions of people alive now and who have lived in the past who never even heard of Christ and Christianity. And they're all damned?

*Response:* There are also hundreds of millions, if not billions, who have heard the gospel of Christ and have rejected it. How do we know that those who haven't heard would believe if they did hear? God knows who would and who would not believe, and we may be certain that He will somehow get the gospel to everyone who would embrace it.

---

Jesus said, "Abraham rejoiced to see my day, and he saw it and was glad" (John 8:56). Yet Abraham grew up in paganism, out of which God called him. If God could do that for Abraham, He can do it for anyone.

Romans 1:18-32 states that every person knows from the universe around him that a God of infinite power is man's Creator, and yet the vast majority of people have rejected that revelation and indulged in idol worship and gross immorality and "are without excuse." Romans 2:14,15 adds that every person knows in his conscience that he has violated God's laws and is under God's judgment. All those who, under conviction of conscience by the Holy Spirit, cry out to God in repentance for His salvation will, in one way or another, be given the gospel.

## WAS A VIRGIN BIRTH ESSENTIAL?

---

*Question:* The virgin birth of Jesus is presented as one of the cornerstones of Christianity for both Catholics and Christians. I don't see why this is essential. My pastor says the Bible doesn't even teach it. The Hebrew word *alma*, translated *virgin* in most Christian Bibles really means "young woman." Is he right?

*Response:* Yes, it is true that *alma* means "young woman." It is never used in the Old Testament, however, except to signify a young woman who is a *virgin*. In Israel a young unmarried woman had to be a virgin. If not, she was stoned. *Alma* never refers to a married woman.

---

Only the rankest critic would argue that *alma* in Isaiah 7:14 ("Therefore the Lord himself shall give you a sign: Behold, a virgin shall conceive and bear a son") could mean anything but virgin. It would hardly be a sign for a nonvirgin to conceive and bear a son. Furthermore, the quotation of this verse in the New Testament (Matthew 1:23) uses a Greek word which, without question, means "virgin."

If Jesus Christ was not born of a virgin, then He was an ordinary man who would have had to die for his own sins and could not have died for the sins of the world. To be our Savior and pay the infinite penalty demanded by

God's justice, Jesus had to be God come to earth as a man. Being God, the body He took ("a body hast thou prepared me"—Hebrews 10:5) when He became a man could not have been created through normal sexual intercourse but only by the creative power of God within the womb of a virgin. If Jesus was not virgin born, there is no salvation and Christianity is a hoax.

## What Does It Mean To Be Saved?

*Question:* I'm not clear on the term "saved." It's certainly not in vogue in many seminaries and churches. However, I find it in the Bible, especially in the New Testament. Just what does it mean?

*Response:* In the physical realm one would have no trouble understanding what it means to be saved, whether from drowning or from bankruptcy or from some other disaster by the act of someone who effected the rescue and would rightly be called one's savior. To suggest that such salvation could ever become old-fashioned and meaningless would be ludicrous. It would be criminal to persuade a drowning man or someone who needed to be rescued from a burning building to reject the emergency help offered because "being saved is no longer in vogue." How much greater the crime to persuade anyone that there is no need for eternal salvation!

One either needs to be saved or he doesn't need to be saved. That necessity is not a matter of fancy but of fact. Christ said that He came to earth "that the world through him might be saved" (John 3:17), thus indicating that *everyone* needs to be saved. Confirming this, Peter declared of Christ: "Neither is there salvation in any other, for there is none other name under heaven given among men whereby we must be saved" (Acts 4:12). Paul put it like this:

This is a faithful saying, and worthy of all acceptation, that Christ Jesus came into the world to save sinners, of whom I am chief (1 Timothy 1:15).

Our own consciences confirm what the Bible declares: Sinners (which we all are) need salvation from the judgment which God has decreed against sin. Old-fashioned idea? Out of vogue? Hardly! And those who make this claim deny the very basic elements of God's existence, our moral accountability to Him and breach of His laws, and our obvious necessity to accept the salvation He lovingly offers us as a free gift of His grace.

## WHAT MUST I DO TO BE SAVED?

---

*Question:* I'm confused about how one gets saved. As a Catholic, my favorite catechism stated: *"What is necessary to be saved?* You have to be baptized, belong to the Church established by Jesus Christ, obey the Ten Commandments, receive the Sacraments, pray, do good works and die with Sanctifying Grace in your soul."[2] That seemed to impose a hopeless burden. If I missed Mass and died with that mortal sin upon me before I could get to confession, I would be lost forever. Since leaving Catholicism I've only become more confused by the contradictory teachings among Protestant denominational churches. Some say baptism is essential for salvation, others that it isn't. Some say that holiness or speaking in tongues are necessary, others say no. How can I know the truth?

*Response:* Your very question "What must I do to be saved?" was asked of the apostle Paul. His concise answer is the truth you seek: "Believe on the Lord Jesus Christ, and thou shalt be saved" (Acts 16:30,31).

---

Note that Paul said nothing about baptism, church membership, penance, Mass, Mary or other saints, good works, or anything else. *Salvation comes through faith in Christ and nothing else.* To suggest that more is needed is to deny the Bible's clear teaching that Christ is the *only* Savior of sinners. Never does the Bible suggest (and common sense also rejects the idea) that Christ can only partially save us, and it is up to us or some other pseudo-Savior to make up for what Christ couldn't do. If Christ was not able to complete our salvation, then it would do no good to look elsewhere for supplemental help.

Of course, to believe on Christ one must know who He is, how He accomplished our salvation, and why we need to be saved. God's infinite justice requires an infinite penalty for our violation of His holy law. As finite beings we could never pay that infinite penalty, but would be separated from God for eternity. God, being infinite, could in one sense pay the penalty His justice demands, but that wouldn't be right because He isn't one of us.

Consequently, because of His great love, God became a man through the virgin birth. He never ceased to be God (an impossibility) and will never cease to be man. In love, He took our sins upon Himself and paid the infinite penalty we deserved. On that basis He offers complete pardon and eternal life in heaven for all who will repent of their sin against God and receive the forgiveness which God offers in Christ.

The following true account, as I remember Billy Graham telling it, illustrates the point very well. When driving through a small town in southeastern United States, he was pulled over by a motorcycle officer who gave him a speeding ticket and brought him immediately before the local judge to pay the fine. It happened that the judge was a barber, and Billy had to wait until he finished a customer.

Having taken off his barber's apron and put on his black robe, the judge pulled a gavel out of the court's drawer and called the court to order. "What is the charge?" he asked the officer.

"Your honor," the officer replied, "this man was doing 35 in a 25-mile zone."

"How does the defendant plead?" asked the judge, turning to Billy.

"Your honor," said Billy, "I wasn't looking at the speedometer, so I'll have to take his word for it."

"That will be $10," said the judge, pounding with his gavel. "One dollar for every mile over the limit." (This was obviously long, long ago!)

Billy took out his wallet, opened it, and began to count out some bills when the judge interrupted him. "Haven't I seen you somewhere?" he asked. Then looking closer, and before his famous defendant could respond, he exclaimed, "Of course! You're Billy Graham! What an honor! I've seen you on TV...."

A friendly conversation followed. In fact, it became so friendly that Billy put his wallet back into his pocket. The conversation seemed to come to an end, and Billy turned to leave.

"That will be $10!" said the judge firmly, pounding with his gavel. "I may just be a barber most of the time, but I try to run an honest court. The ticket has been written out and has to be paid."

Again Billy pulled out his wallet and started searching for the proper amount, but the judge was quicker. Reaching into the barbershop drawer, he pulled out a $10 bill and put it in the court's drawer. Then he wrote out a receipt and gave it to Billy Graham, now a free man.

That's exactly what Christ did for us. The "ticket has been written out" in heaven on all of us: "For all have sinned and come short of the glory of God" (Romans 3:23) and *it must be paid* because God runs an honest court. Billy Graham could easily have paid the $10 in his case, but we cannot pay the infinite penalty assessed against each of us. So God Himself, becoming a man to die in our place, paid the penalty and gives us the paid-in-full receipt the moment we receive the Lord Jesus Christ as our Savior.

## IS THE TRUE GOSPEL IN THE STARS?

*Question:* I recently read two books, *Witness of the Stars* by E.W. Bullinger, and *The Gospel in the Stars,* by Joseph A. Seiss. They were interesting, but something about them troubled me. Is it true that the gospel is really in the stars and that ancient man even before the flood had this witness and knew what it meant?

*Response:* No. While the Bible frequently states that the heavens are given for "signs," it never even implies that these "signs" present the *gospel.* The Bible says, "The heavens declare the glory of God" (Psalm 19:1) and that every person, no matter what his language, understands that message (Psalm 19:3). Indeed, all of creation reveals God's *glory and power*, which are "clearly seen, being understood by the things that are made" (Romans 1:20). *Never* are we told, however, that the heavens or any other part of creation declare the *gospel*. That is presented *only* by God's Word.

---

Those who promote this view admit that the gospel can't be seen in the stars without considerable imaginative interpretation. Seiss confesses that "the starry worlds . . . do not and cannot declare or show forth Christ as Redeemer. . . ."[3] But without Christ as Redeemer there is no gospel! D. James Kennedy, who promotes Seiss' thesis, admits in his sermon *The Gospel in the Stars*: "You can look at the stars in Virgo until you are green in the face and they would never look like a woman!" But Paul says that what the heavens declare is "clearly seen" by anyone who looks at them. Obviously, Paul is talking about something other than what these men promote.

## No Picture Can Present The Gospel

If God had intended the stars to present the gospel, He would have had to arrange them in such a way that they would clearly form the images He wanted man to see in them. Obviously, He didn't do so. Furthermore, there is no way that mere visual images, no matter how clearly the stars had been positioned, could present the gospel. The clearest image the stars offer is the Southern Cross. Yet who would know by merely looking at such a configuration in the sky that Christ would in the future die, or had already died, upon a cross for our sins and that He was the perfect, sinless Son of God who was paying the penalty demanded by His own infinite justice? No visual image could explain those facts!

In fact, the "images" imaginatively associated with certain constellations are open to almost limitless interpretations, and thus do not carry within themselves any safeguard of their alleged message—a message which Seiss acknowledges has been badly corrupted into astrology and occultism. A major purpose of Seiss's work, then, is to tell us what these alleged "signs" *really* meant in ages past. He claims to have recovered this true meaning through much research—a meaning which again he admits has not been ordinarily assigned to them for many centuries. So these marvelous signs have actually failed to accomplish their purpose because it is in fact impossible for them to do so in and of themselves.

Without the Bible, and with only the stars themselves to observe, we could not possibly understand the gospel. That obvious fact undermines this entire thesis. The word "gospel" is used 101 times in 95 verses in the Bible (all New Testament), and it is *never* associated with the stars or the witness of creation. The gospel is *always* preached by *people* and must be perfectly clear and understood for it to be of any effect. The alleged "gospel in the stars" fails to meet these criteria. Moreover, Matthew 24:14, Mark 13:10, etc. indicate that the gospel must yet be preached to all nations. Thus it clearly had not been preached in the stars—certainly not in "all its length and breadth," as Seiss enthusiastically declares.

The Bible states that the gospel *began* to be preached with the advent of Christ (Mark 1:1; Philippians 4:15; 2 Timothy 1:10) and indicates that it had previously been a mystery until then *"kept secret since the world began"* (Romans 16:25). This is hardly consistent with the theory that the gospel had been proclaimed in the stars for thousands of years before Christ. Yet Seiss ardently declares that "all the great doctrines of the Christian faith were known, believed, cherished, and recorded [in the stars] from the earliest generations of our race, proving that God has spoken to man, and verily given him a revelation of truths and hopes precisely as written in our Scriptures, and so fondly cherished by all Christian believers."[4] The Bible never once even hints at such a presentation.

## BEWARE THE HUCKSTER'S GOSPEL!

---

*Question:* Something troubles me about some evangelistic crusades and church services I have attended. It seems to me that the appeal to "come to Christ" is linked to deliverance from sickness, from financial problems, from unhappiness, etc. At other times, even when the true gospel has been preached, it has seemed that the appeal has been based more on emotion than on truth. Isn't something wrong, or am I just too picky?

*Response:* Your concern is well-founded. Our generation is obsessed with numbers and a false view of success that reflects the values of this world rather than of the world to come. It is assumed that anyone can be persuaded to buy any product if the advertising hype and sales pitch are right. Large corporations spend billions on research and advertising in order to peddle their products to the widest possible market. Unfortunately, that mentality has entered the church as well.

---

For many evangelists and churches, Jesus Christ has become a "product" to be packaged and marketed using the same techniques that have proved successful in the world. There is indeed much that we could call deceptive in today's evangelical sales pitch. Christ is preached as a panacea rather than the only remedy for sin and deliverance from judgment. Instead of truth, we are being offered music and entertainment to get us "in the mood," and the gospel is often watered down to make it as palatable as possible. As Joyce Main Hanks of the University of Costa Rica declares in the preface of her translation of Jacques Ellul's *The Humiliation of the Word*:

> Public officials are "electable" in the United States today only if they project an attractive television image. Reaction to presidential "debates," for example, depends almost entirely on image, not substance, truth or coherent rational argument.
>
> Similarly, the Church indulges our desire to "feel good" instead of responding to our need to be spiritually challenged and fed through solid exposition of the Scriptures. The electronic Church in particular panders to our appetite for entertainment rather than authentic discipleship and maturity.[5]

When Christ was approached by those who offered to follow Him, He didn't say to His disciples: "Sign him up quick, Peter! Get him in the choir, John! Make him a deacon, James! Hurry before he changes his mind!" Instead, Christ said something like this: "So you want to follow me? Let me tell you where I'm going. I'm heading for a hill outside of Jerusalem called Calvary. There they will nail me to a cross. So if you are really going to follow me, you might as well pick up your cross right now!" Yes, Jesus said, "If any man will come after me, let him deny himself and take up his cross and follow me" (Matthew 16:24).

Christ must be presented not as an inspiring leader who will help us to feel better about ourselves, or will heal our bodies or prosper our marriage or business, but as the Savior of those who know they deserve God's eternal judgment and cannot save themselves. We must call sinners to repentance and to believe the gospel because it is *true*. All who refuse the truth will be given a strong delusion to believe Satan's lie, "that they all might be damned who believed not the truth, but had pleasure in unrighteousness" (2 Thessalonians 2:12). There is a solemnity about the gospel that must be recovered if we are to see genuine salvation in the place of the plethora of false professions.

## WHO IS REALLY SAVED?

*Question:* If a Roman Catholic believes wholeheartedly in the Lord Jesus Christ and is committed to serving Him as his Lord, and if he believes that the only way his sins can be forgiven is through Christ's death as atonement for those sins, and the believer's repentance, isn't he saved? Suppose a person has salvation by faith alone; does he lose that salvation by believing in infant baptism? Does he lose his salvation by believing that communion is really the body and blood of Christ, as the Lord said it was? Does he lose his salvation if he believes in purgatory?

*Response:* Anyone who believes the gospel, which is "the power of God unto salvation to everyone that believeth" (Romans 1:16), is saved, whether he be called

Catholic, Baptist, Methodist, or whatever. If, however, a Roman Catholic "believes wholeheartedly in the Lord Jesus Christ," as you suggest, then he would find himself in irreconcilable conflict with the doctrines and practices of his Church. It is logically impossible for a Roman Catholic to truly believe the gospel that saves and to believe the tenets of Catholicism at the same time, because they are diametrically opposed.

---

For example, how can a person believe that Christ's sacrifice on the cross for our sins is an accomplished fact of history and that He is now at the Father's right hand in heaven in a resurrected, glorified body and at the same time believe that He exists bodily on Catholic altars as a wafer, perpetually suffering the agonies of the cross (as Vatican II says) "in the sacrifice of the Mass"?[6]

Quite clearly, both of these contradictory beliefs cannot be maintained at one time. How do we know which one is *truly* believed by Catholics who profess both? To remain in the Roman Catholic Church and to continue to participate in the "sacrifice of the Mass" would surely indicate faith in the Roman Catholic Church and its dogma rather than in the true biblical gospel.

## Catholicism's Gospel

How can anyone believe that Christ through His sacrifice on the cross "obtained eternal redemption for us" (Hebrews 9:12) and at the same time believe that "the work of our redemption" is still in the process of being accomplished through the Eucharist (as Vatican II says)?[7] How can a person believe that Christ's redemptive work on the cross is "finished," as He Himself said (John 19:30), and at the same time believe that the Mass is a perpetuation of Christ's sacrifice? No thinking person could believe both at once.

Vatican II states that in the Mass "Christ perpetuates in an unbloody manner the sacrifice offered on the cross. . . ."[8] How can one "perpetuate" an event that was completed in the past? It is logically impossible.

One may *remember* or *memorialize* a past event, but one cannot perpetuate it in the present. How can anyone believe that through Christ's death and resurrection more than 1900 years ago the debt of our sin has been paid in full and at the same time engage in the Mass, which purports to be additional payments on that debt?

*The Code of Canon Law* declares that "the work of redemption is continually accomplished in the mystery of the Eucharistic Sacrifice...."[9] Vatican II says that the Mass is "a sacrifice in which the sacrifice of the cross is perpetuated" and in which "our Lord is immolated ... offering himself to the Father for the world's salvation through the ministry of priests."[10] Here is a brief summary of official Catholic teaching about the Mass from a Catholic dictionary:

> The Mass is a truly propitiatory sacrifice, which means that by this oblation "the Lord is appeased, He grants grace and the gift of repentance, and He pardons wrongdoings and sins, even grave ones. For it is one and the same victim. He who now makes the offering through the ministry of priests and he who then offered himself on the cross" (Denzinger 1743).[11]

The Bible, however, clearly teaches that Christ's sacrifice is not continually being offered in the present but was completed once for all time on the cross:

> *Once* ... hath he appeared to put away sin by the sacrifice of himself... Christ was *once* offered to bear the sins of many (Hebrews 9:26,28); this man [Christ], after he had offered *one sacrifice* for sins forever, sat down on the right hand of God... for by *one offering* he hath perfected forever them that are sanctified ... there is *no more offering for sin* (Hebrews 10:12-18).

## A CHOICE TO MAKE

Christ said, "Come unto me and *I* will give you rest. *I* give my sheep eternal life and they will never perish."

One cannot believe in Christ while looking to a church, Catholic or other, for salvation. The many prayers to Mary to "obtain for us forgiveness of sin and eternal life" are in themselves proof that the Catholic has not trusted Christ for his salvation. If I offered to pay in full a debt you owed, would not your continual petitioning of someone else to pay it be sufficient evidence that you neither believed nor accepted my offer?

One cannot believe in Christ alone and at the same time believe in Christ plus baptism and the sacraments and good graces of the Roman Catholic Church. Paul wrote:

> Though we or an angel from heaven preach any other gospel unto you than that which we have preached unto you, let him be accursed [anathema].
> As we said before, so say I now again [for emphasis], If any man preach any other gospel unto you ... let him be accursed [anathema] (Galatians 1:8,9).

Paul was referring to and cursing those known as Judaizers because they taught that in addition to faith in Christ's finished work one also had to keep the Jewish law. That small addition destroyed the gospel. Yet the Catholic Church has had 1500 years to add far more to the gospel than the Judaizers ever imagined. That false gospel cannot save, and merits Paul's anathema.

Yes, Catholics believe the basics of the gospel: that Christ is God, who came to this earth through the virgin birth, lived a perfect, sinless life, died on the cross for our sins, rose from the grave the third day, and is coming again. But that is not all Catholics must believe. To the true gospel Roman Catholicism has added the Mass (as a propitiatory sacrifice by which sins are pardoned), purgatory, indulgences, intercession of Mary, and the necessity of baptism and being in the Church and participating in the "sacraments of the New Law," which Trent and Vatican II say are *essential for salvation*.

One must believe in one or the other of the conflicting gospels: the biblical gospel or the Roman Catholic gospel. One cannot sincerely believe two contradictory propositions at the same time. Anyone who trusts in Christ alone is saved. Sadly, it is at the same time possible to give lip service to the false teachings of one's church, or not to fully understand its false teachings. God alone can judge such hearts.

## HAS GOD PREDESTINED SOME TO HEAVEN AND SOME TO HELL?

*Question:* I have a friend who turned his back on God after his third year in a conservative evangelical seminary. He was taught that God has already decided who will be saved and who will spend eternity in hell, who will have good things happen to him in life, and who will have bad. Can you help me to help him?

*Response:* There is no doubt that God is sovereign and could have predestined some to heaven and some to hell. Or He could send us all to hell because that is what we deserve. The question is not God's *sovereignty*, however, but His *love*. And that God wants all mankind to be saved and to be in heaven is clear:

For God so loved the *world* . . . that the *world* through him might be saved (John 3:16,17). The father sent the Son to be the Saviour of the *world* (1 John 4:14).

The Lord is . . . not willing that *any* should perish, but that *all* should come to repentance (2 Peter 3:9). Who will have *all men* to be saved, and to come unto the knowledge of the truth (1 Timothy 2:4).

Who gave himself a ransom *for all* (1 Timothy 2:6). And he is the propitiation for our sins, and not for ours only, but also for the sins of *the whole world* (1 John 2:2).

No one will be in hell because God wanted him there or didn't do all He could to persuade him to believe the gospel He has so fully and freely provided for *all*. Those who perish do so because they reject the salvation which

God offers with such loving persuasion. To suggest that God doesn't desire all mankind to be saved is a libel upon His character and a contradiction of the Bible! How could it be that the God who tells us to love our enemies doesn't love all of His? It is inconceivable that God would willingly send anyone He truly loves to hell. That many people nevertheless go there can only be because they rejected the salvation God provided and lovingly offered by His grace.

## Foreknowledge Determines Predestination

If we are to believe that God has predestined certain ones to go to hell, then we must also believe that He predestined that Adam and Eve should sin, and thus predestined all of the evil that followed. That is preposterous. The strict Calvinist says we are so utterly depraved that we cannot choose to receive Christ. But that argument cannot apply to Adam and Eve because they were created in innocence. If they, like us today, could choose only evil, then God's warnings to them not to eat of the forbidden fruit (and His appeals to us to come to Christ) are a farce.

The rebellion in the Garden of Eden by creatures who were until then innocent and living in a perfect environment could only have been the result of *their will* acting *against God's will*. And if it was not a genuine choice, then sin could hardly have *entered* the world by that act, since they must have already been sinners.

Yes, God *foreknew* that Adam and Eve would rebel, and He knew all of the evil that would follow. Therefore He made a provision for *all* sin and *all* sinners to be forgiven through Christ even before He created the world (Revelation 13:8). But He did not *predestine* the evil that began in Eden and pervades this world! If He did, then all of the rape, murder, hatred, jealousy, etc. that has occurred in history and continues to this day is because God *predestined* it. Again, that is totally inconsistent with God's character as revealed in His Word.

Romans 8:29-30 declares, "Whom he did foreknow, he also did predestinate ... called ... justified ... glorified." Clearly, God made certain to get the gospel to all

He knew would believe it. Thus, foreknowledge is the key to predestination.

Strict Calvinists object that to make a choice is a "work," and salvation is "not of works." However, that a man chooses to accept the pardon which God offers in Christ does not constitute any work on his part. If a drowning man, helpless to save himself, accepted an offer of rescue, would he thereby have done *anything* to save himself? Could he say that he had been saved by his own works? Could he be proud (as some suggest of those who receive Christ by an act of their will) that his rescue from drowning was because he was "smart enough, loving enough, wise enough, righteous enough, or anything else enough . . ."? Of course not!

Salvation is all of God and all by grace. Those who accept it have done nothing to earn it. In fact, to be saved a sinner must confess his total unworthiness and inability to merit or earn salvation. He must simply receive it as a free gift of God's grace.

A gift embodies two essential elements: 1) the giving of it, and 2) the receiving of it. One cannot give a gift to anyone unless that person is willing to receive it. God does not force Himself and His grace upon anyone. We must knowingly and willingly receive the gift of salvation. That is why the gospel is preached and must be believed for a person to be saved.

## IS SATAN OUR CO-REDEEMER?

*Question:* I'm not a follower of the so-called "faith teachers" as far as their "health-and-wealth gospel" goes. However, it seems to me that they make a lot of sense when they teach that Christ had to sink into hell to be tortured by Satan. How else could He pay the full penalty for our sins?

*Response:* The penalty for sin is decreed by God's perfect law and exacted by His infinite justice. Satan is not the enforcer of God's righteousness. He does not exact the penalty from Christ. We are told that God "laid on him [Christ] the iniquity of us all" and that "it pleased the LORD [Jahweh] to bruise him . . . [to] make his soul an offering for sin" (Isaiah 53:6,10). There is not a word about Satan having any part in this process of redemption.

---

In contrast to what the Bible so clearly states, here is what one of the leaders in the Positive Confession movement teaches:

> He allowed the devil to drag Him into the depths of hell as if He were the most wicked sinner who ever lived.... every demon in hell came down on Him to annihilate Him ... they tortured Him beyond anything that anybody has ever conceived....
>
> In a thunder of spiritual force, the voice of God spoke to the death-whipped, broken, punished spirit of Jesus ... [in] the pit of destruction and charged the spirit of Jesus with resurrection power! Suddenly His twisted, death-wracked spirit began to fill out and come back to life ... He was literally being reborn before the devil's very eyes. He began to flex His spiritual muscles ... Jesus Christ dragged Satan up and down the halls of hell ... Jesus ... was raised up a born-again man.... The day I realized that a born-again man had defeated Satan, hell, and death, I got so excited ... ![12]

It is both fanciful nonsense and heresy to teach that our redemption comes through Satan torturing Jesus in hell. That would make Satan our co-redeemer. If he didn't torture Jesus enough we wouldn't be saved—and if he did, should we thank him? How do we know he tortured Christ enough to save us?

Satan isn't the proprietor of hell. He hasn't even been there yet. Nor will Satan torture the damned, but he himself will be tormented with "everlasting fire, prepared for the devil and his angels" (Matthew 25:41) when death and hell have been "cast into the lake of fire" (Revelation 20:14).

Before He died Jesus cried in triumph, "It is finished!" (John 19:30), indicating that our redemption had been accomplished *on the cross*. Christ told the thief on the cross who believed in Him, *"Today* shalt thou be with me in *paradise"* (Luke 23:43), *not in hell!* He said, "Father, into thy hands I commend my spirit" (Luke 23:46). He didn't end up, instead, in the hands of Satan!

## ARE WE SAVED BY BAPTISM?

---

*Question:* Mark 16:16 says, "He that believeth and is baptized shall be saved." In his Pentecost sermon Peter urged his listeners to be baptized to wash away their sins. I am confused. Is baptism essential for salvation or is it not?

*Response:* There is not one verse in all the Bible which says that failure to be baptized damns the soul, but scores of verses declare that those who do not believe the gospel are lost. Nor is baptism any part of the gospel. As Paul said, "Christ sent me *not to baptize* but *to preach the gospel"* (1 Corinthians 1:17; cf. 15:1-4). In Paul's clear declaration of "the gospel ... by which ... ye are saved" (1 Corinthians 15:1-4) there is no mention of baptism.

---

It is upon believing the gospel that one is to be baptized ("What doth hinder me to be baptized? ... If thou believest with all thine heart, thou mayest"—Acts 8:36,37). Christ, after His resurrection, sent His disciples forth to preach the gospel worldwide. Of their converts He said, *"baptizing* them in the name of the Father and of the Son and of the Holy Ghost" (Matthew 28:19). That all who believe (and they alone) are to be baptized could not be clearer.

Baptism symbolizes the believer's identification with Christ in His death, burial, and resurrection: "We are buried with him by baptism into death, that like as Christ was raised up from the dead ... we also should walk in newness of life" (Romans 6:4). Therefore baptism in the early church was by immersion: "They went down both into the water ... when they were come up out of the water" (Acts 8:38,39; etc.). Death could only be symbolized in this type of baptism.

## Corrupt Innovations

Unfortunately, various innovations (sprinkling instead of immersion) and even heresies were gradually introduced regarding baptism: that one must be baptized to be saved—indeed, that baptism itself saves the soul even when administered to infants. Catholics even practice an intrauterine baptism of the fetus when there is doubt that it will be born alive.[13] Such heresies became known as the doctrine of baptismal regeneration. Most Protestants holding similar beliefs today are not aware that they originated in the Roman Catholic Church in the Middle Ages.

The Council of Trent (1545-63) stated that while Christ "merited for us justification by His most holy passion . . . the instrumental cause [of justification/regeneration] is the sacrament of baptism. . . . If anyone says that baptism is . . . not necessary for salvation, let him be anathema."[14] Vatican II (1962-5) reconfirms all of Trent[15] and reiterates the necessity of baptism for salvation,[16] as does the universal *Catechism of the Catholic Church* released by the Vatican in 1993: "Baptism is necessary for salvation . . . the Church does not know of any [other] means . . . that assures entry into eternal beatitude. . . . "[17]

Trent anathematizes all who deny that "the merit of Jesus Christ is applied . . . to infants by the sacrament of baptism" or who deny that by baptism "the guilt of original sin is remitted. . . . "[18] Today's *Code of Canon Law* (Canon 849) declares that those baptized are thereby "freed from their sins, are reborn as children of God and . . . incorporated in the Church." Canon 204 states: "The Christian faithful are those who . . . have been incorporated in Christ through baptism" and are thereby members of the one, true Catholic Church.[19]

## What About Infant Baptism?

For centuries before the Reformation, baptismal regeneration was rejected by non-Catholic believers, who taught from Scripture that baptism was only for those who had believed the gospel. Infant baptism was rejected because infants have neither understood the gospel nor believed in Christ. Those who practiced infant baptism justified it by citing alleged biblical precedent where entire families were baptized, presuming that there were infants among them.

That this was not the case can easily be proved. Consider Cornelius' household: They heard the gospel, believed it, and were baptized. That no infants were involved is clear, for they had all gathered "to hear all things that are commanded thee of God" (Acts 10:33), things which an infant could not understand. "The Holy Ghost fell on all them which heard [and, obviously, understood and believed] the word" (verse 44); and they spoke with tongues (verse 46).

That they had "received the Holy Ghost" (verse 47) proved that they were *saved*. Therefore Peter baptized them (verse 48). Here is proof both that one is saved *without baptism* and that only those already saved are to be baptized.

Neither can infant baptism be supported from the case of the Philippian jailer, who "was baptized, he and all his [household]" (Acts 16:33). Again there were obviously no infants present because Paul and Silas preached the gospel "to all that were in his house" (verse 32), and "all his house" believed (verse 34) and were then baptized. The gospel is not preached to infants, not even by those who baptize them.

## ERRORS INHERITED FROM ROMAN CATHOLICISM

The early Reformers such as Martin Luther were one-time Catholics who, unfortunately, retained certain Catholic dogmas, among them baptismal regeneration and infant baptism. These errors are held by some Protestant denominations even today. The issue is a serious one: If baptism is essential for salvation, then to reject that gospel is to be damned; but if salvation is through faith in Christ alone, then to add baptism as a condition for salvation is to reject the true gospel and thus to be eternally lost.

The Bible declares that it is wrong to teach salvation by faith in Christ *plus anything else*, such as keeping the Jewish law (Acts 15:24). Paul cursed (anathematized) those who taught this false gospel that damns the soul (Galatians 1:8,9). A gospel of salvation through Christ *plus baptism* is equally false.

Paul couldn't remember whom among the Corinthian believers he had baptized and he was thankful that it had been very few (1 Corinthians 1:14-16)—a strange attitude if baptism were essential to salvation! Without baptizing them, Paul declared that he was their father in the faith: "In Christ Jesus I have begotten you *through the gospel*" (1 Corinthians 4:15). So they were saved through Paul's preaching and without being baptized.

## Baptismal Regeneration Proof Texts

Then what about Mark 16:16: "He that believeth and is baptized shall be saved"? All who believe the gospel are saved, so of course all who believe and are baptized are saved. That does not, however, say that baptism saves or that it is essential for salvation. Scores of verses declare that salvation comes by believing the gospel, with no mention of baptism: "It pleased God by the foolishness of *preaching* to save them that *believe*" (1 Corinthians 1:21). See also John 3:16,18,36; 5:24; Acts 10:43; 13:38; 16:31; Romans 1:16; 3:28; 4:24; 5:1; 1 Corinthians 15:1-4; Ephesians 2:8; etc. *Not one verse* says that baptism saves.

Surely the Bible would make it clear that believing in Christ without being baptized cannot save, if that were the case, yet *not one verse says so!* Instead, we have examples of those who believed and were saved without being baptized, such as the thief on the cross and the Old Testament saints (Enoch, Abraham, Joseph, Daniel, et al), to whom Christian baptism was unknown.

Yes, Peter said, "The like *figure* whereunto even baptism doth also now save us ... by the resurrection of Jesus Christ" (1 Peter 3:21). That statement is similar to Paul's declaration that we are buried with Christ in baptism and thereby dead to sin—yet we aren't *literally* dead to sin. Peter is no more saying that the physical act of baptism literally saves us than Paul is saying that it literally makes us dead to sin. Water baptism has no such power. It is a *"figure"* or symbolization of a spiritual baptism into Christ effected by the Holy Spirit and which is settled forever in heaven and lived out by faith while we are here upon earth.

Significantly, Christ never baptized anyone (John 4:2) —very odd if baptism saves. The Savior of the world must have deliberately avoided baptizing to make it clear that baptism has no part in salvation. Yes, Christ said we must be "born [again] of *water* and of the Spirit" to be saved (John 3:5), but it is unwarranted to assume that this is a literal "water" and means baptism.

## WATER AND THE WORD

Jesus was speaking to Nicodemus, a rabbi, to whom "water" would not mean *baptism* (unknown in Jewish law), but the ceremonial cleansing of a leper or someone who had been defiled (Exodus 30; 40; Leviticus 13; 15; etc.). And that is what Christ meant. His death would make it possible to "sanctify and cleanse [His church] with the washing of water by the word [of the gospel] (Ephesians 5:25). Christ said, "Now ye are *clean through the word* which I have spoken" (John 15:3).

Like Christ, Paul put water and the Spirit together, referring to the "washing of regeneration" and linking it with the "renewing of the Holy Ghost" (Titus 3:5). We are born again by the Holy Spirit and by the Word, or gospel, of God, which is sometimes called "water" because of its cleansing power. As Peter said, we are "born again . . . by the word of God" (1 Peter 1:23).

It was obviously this figure of Old Testament ceremonial cleansing which Peter invoked for his Jewish audience in his Pentecost sermon: "Repent, and be baptized every one of you in the name of Jesus Christ for the remission of sins" (Acts 2:38). It is clear from the many other Scriptures we have given that Peter wasn't saying that baptism saves but that it offered a ceremonial cleansing uniquely applicable to his Jewish hearers. To be baptized was to be identified before the fanatical Jews of Jerusalem with this hated Jesus Christ. Baptism cost family and friends and endangered one's life, as it still does in Israel and Muslim countries. Those who are afraid to take this public stand in such cultures are even today not considered to be true believers. Thus for a Jew to be publicly baptized at that time and in that culture was, in a sense, to "wash away [his] sins" (Acts 22:16), as Ananias told Saul.

The "gospel of Christ" is "the power of God unto salvation" to everyone who believes it (Romans 1:16). That gospel, as Paul preached it, required faith in Christ's blood poured out in death for one's sins on the cross. It said nothing about baptism. To preach baptismal regeneration is to preach a false gospel, and Paul cursed those who did so. The difference between these two gospels has eternal consequences.

Then baptism doesn't matter? Indeed, it does. It is an act of obedience to Christ, who gave this ordinance to the church. And it is a powerful public testimony to one's faith in Christ and one's desire to allow Christ's resurrection life to be made manifest in him.

*Sustain us, O Virgin Mary, on our journey of faith and obtain for us the grace of eternal salvation.*

—Pope John Paul II, from "The Holy Father's
Prayer for the Marian Year"[1]

*Church teaching is that I don't know, at any given moment, what my eternal future will be. I can hope, pray, do my very best—but I still don't know. Pope John Paul II doesn't know absolutely that he will go to heaven, nor does Mother Teresa of Calcutta. . . .*

—New York's John Cardinal O'Connor
in *The New York Times* [2]

*I have said to Jesus that if I don't go to heaven for anything else, I will be going to heaven for all the traveling with all the publicity, because it has purified me and sacrificed me and made me really ready to go to heaven.*

—Mother Teresa of Calcutta at Washington D.C.'s
National Prayer Breakfast, February 3, 1994

*These things have I written unto you that believe on the name of the Son of God, that ye may know that ye have eternal life.*

—1 John 5:13

# 12
# Assurance of Salvation

## How Do We Combat Doubts About Our Salvation?

---

*Question:* I'm a born-again Christian who received
Christ as my Savior more than 20 years ago. At that
time I literally *felt* Christ come into my heart and
change my life. Yet there are times when I have to fight
doubts because I just don't *feel* right with the Lord. I
know all the gospel verses and believe them, but it
seems to me there must be something I'm missing. Can
you help me?

*Response:* There could be many reasons for not *feeling* right. A child who is secretly doing something of
which his parents would not approve doesn't *feel* right
about it. It doesn't mean he is no longer their child, but he
knows that if they knew what he was doing they would
be upset with him. Of course, God knows all about us.

---

Are you living a carnal life, consuming that brief
span of time allotted to you on this earth in pursuing the
world's vain ambitions and pleasures, forgetting that
time is very short and that eternity is forever? In your
heart you know whether disobedience and neglect are
the problem. Beyond those considerations, one's faith
can wane with the neglect of God's Word and prayer and
failure to fellowship regularly with other believers.

Our confidence in God and in our relationship with Him begins with His Word, feeding upon it and resting in its promises. You could even be doing that and yet have doubts because you don't have a solid enough basis for trusting God's Word. One of the best ways to restore your confidence in the Word is through a study of prophecy. The fulfillment of prophecy provides tangible, empirical evidence which proves beyond any doubt that the Bible is inspired of God and that we can count upon all that it says.

The assurance of faith depends upon the truth of the gospel, and nothing makes that so sure as the fulfillment of prophecies concerning the life, death, and resurrection of Jesus. You need to be thoroughly grounded in God's Word in this regard and then tell this good news and share the infallible proofs with others. The best way to strengthen your faith is to tell others why you believe and to be earnestly involved in seeking to win others to Christ.

Prophecy was the primary tool used by the early Christians in preaching the gospel. We need to do the same today. Paul would go into the synagogue, read from the Old Testament prophecies that promised the Messiah, then show that they had all been fulfilled in the life, death, and resurrection of Jesus of Nazareth. The Jews had no choice, if they were to be honest, but to believe that Jesus was their Messiah. Here is how Luke, who accompanied Paul on his travels, recorded a typical incident in one of the many towns they visited:

> They came to Thessalonica, where was a synagogue of the Jews; and Paul, as his manner was, went in unto them, and three sabbath days reasoned with them out of the scriptures, opening and alleging that Christ must needs have suffered and risen again from the dead, and that this Jesus, whom I preach unto you, is Christ (Acts 17:1-3).

## Isn't There An Inward Assurance
## Of The Holy Spirit?

*Question:* Is the certainty of the Christian faith confined to the fulfillment of prophecy as demonstrated in verifiable facts of history, archaeology, and science, or is there a spiritual confirmation as well? What about spiritual experiences? Isn't there an inward assurance of the Holy Spirit?

*Response:* "Faith cometh by hearing . . . the Word of God" (Romans 10:17). On the one hand, the Word of God stands on its own and needs no outside confirmation, for it is "quick [living] and powerful, and sharper than any two-edged sword . . . a discerner of the thoughts and intents of the heart" (Hebrews 4:12). On the other hand, God has given us outside confirmation so that the Word of God proves itself to us in two ways: by the convicting and convincing power of the Holy Spirit who inspires and speaks to our hearts through His Word, and by the confirmation available to us from outside verification through archaeology, history, and science. When all are in full agreement, we have an unshakable basis for complete assurance.

Of course, outside confirmation is not *essential,* for even without it the Holy Spirit speaks powerfully to hearts willing to hear: "The Spirit itself beareth witness with our spirit, that we are the children of God" (Romans 8:16). Subjective convictions, however, can be misleading. Consider the multitudes who have been led astray by what they thought was the "leading of the Holy Spirit," and it turned out to be wishful thinking or some other delusion.

There is no deficiency on the part of the Holy Spirit, but rather on our part. It is therefore helpful to have some independent confirmation. Human frailty leaves us subject to the deceitfulness of our own hearts: "The heart is deceitful above all things, and desperately wicked: who can know it? I the LORD search the heart" (Jeremiah 17:9,10). We need to be on guard and pray as did David:

> Search me, O God, and know my heart; try me, and know my thoughts, and see if there be any wicked way in me, and lead me in the way everlasting (Psalm 139:23,24).

Furthermore, if we had only what we thought was the inward confidence of the Holy Spirit, but the archaeological and historical evidence contradicted what the Bible said, we could be left in confusion. Remember, of course, that human efforts to gather data through archaeological and historical and scientific research are subject to error. We do not cast aside our confidence in God's Word when the critics claim to have contradictory evidence. They have been proven wrong every time they disputed what the Bible says. It is helpful, however, to know the evidence that backs up the Bible. For that reason we have concentrated mainly on such affirmation in this volume.

## A Knowing That Is Beyond Comprehension

There is, nevertheless, a *knowing* that goes beyond the intellect and the capacity for human understanding. Paul prayed for the Ephesian believers that they might "*know* the love of Christ, which *passeth knowledge*, that ye might be filled with all the fullness of God" (Ephesians 3:19). There is a fullness of the Holy Spirit which is available to believers that removes every possible doubt and empowers the believer to pass on the message of God in convincing assurance without any outside support.

The greatest experiences of life are all beyond our finite comprehension. Love cannot be explained or analyzed. Nor can beauty or goodness or joy. One could have a Ph.D. in all the subjects which this world's universities offer and not be able to explain why a sunset is beautiful. Yet the simplest child can exult in the joy and exquisite beauty of God's creation.

So it is with knowing God. The psalmist likened his desire to know God to the thirst for water of a deer pursued by a hunter (Psalm 42:1). Paul cried out, "That I may know him, and the power of his resurrection, and the fellowship of his sufferings, being made conformable unto his death" (Philippians 3:10). This should be the passion of our hearts. Could anything else be more desirable?

Such knowledge of God and assurance of one's salvation goes beyond intellectual understanding and therefore cannot be shaken by intellectual arguments no matter how seemingly convincing. Jesus said, "This is life eternal, that they might *know* thee, the only true God, and Jesus Christ, whom thou has sent" (John 17:3). God has told us that we will find Him (i.e. have that intimate knowledge of Him that goes beyond the intellect and can only be experienced in the heart by the Holy Spirit) when we seek for Him with our whole heart (Jeremiah 29:13). He has promised to reward with the intimate knowledge of Himself those who "diligently seek him" (Hebrews 11:6). Spend time with Him in prayer and in His Word and your *knowing* Him and *love* for Him will grow, and your assurance of His love and guidance will increase accordingly.

## WHAT ABOUT PURGATORY?

---

*Question:* I've recently heard some rather persuasive arguments by Catholics for purgatory. First Corinthians 3:12-15 teaches a purification by fire of believers after death. Hebrews 12:14 declares that without "holiness . . . no man shall see the Lord." Doesn't that say we must be made absolutely pure to enter heaven? The same standard seems to be required by the statement "Blessed are the pure in heart, for they shall see God" (Matthew 5:8). My assurance of salvation has been shaken. What about such Scriptures?

*Response:* Purgatory is an invention of the Roman Catholic Church and reflects the fact that there is no assurance of salvation in Catholicism. If there were, that Church would be out of business. In fact, the Catholic who dares to believe Christ's unequivocal promise of eternal life as a free gift of His grace with nothing left to be done on our part is anathematized. Trent decreed (and Vatican II reproposes):

---

If anyone says that after the reception of the grace of justification the guilt is so remitted and the debt of eternal punishment so blotted out to every repentant sinner, that no debt of temporal punishment remains to be discharged either in this world or in purgatory before the gates of heaven can be opened, let him be anathema.[3]

In contrast, let us consider the teaching of the Bible together with simple common sense. Quite obviously, even if such a place as purgatory existed no literal fire could purify the soul and spirit. Fire is not the means of *moral* purification. Furthermore, it is the believer's *works* (which he has *built* upon the foundation of his faith in Christ), not the believer himself, that will be tested by fire:

Now if any man *build* upon this foundation gold, silver, precious stones, wood, hay, stubble, every man's *work* shall be . . . revealed by fire; and the fire shall try every man's *work* of what sort it is (1 Corinthians 3:12,13).

Nor is Paul speaking of literal fire any more than he is of literal wood and gold. He is obviously speaking metaphorically, calling some works wood, hay, and stubble (which fire consumes) and others gold, silver, and precious stones (which fire purifies). There is nothing here (or elsewhere in Scripture) to support Catholicism's claim that flames in an imagined purgatory purge the individual and thereby expiate his sins. Paul is dealing entirely with the quality of works one has done for Christ and what reward will therefore be received, if any.

## A QUESTION OF REWARDS

In Revelation 22:12 Christ says, "Behold, I come quickly, and my reward is with me, to give every man according as his work shall be." Entrance into heaven is not the question, but the *reward* which the Christian will receive in heaven for works done on earth, the crowns we will cast at the feet of our Lord who redeemed us (Revelation 4:10). Paul explains, "For we must all appear [in heaven] before the judgment seat of Christ, that everyone may receive the things done [i.e. works] in his body, according to that he hath done [worked], whether it be good or bad" (2 Corinthians 5:10).

It is possible to grow cold in one's love for Christ and to live for self instead of for Him and in His service for others. Such carnality causes the loss, not of salvation, but of a crown or crowns previously won: "Hold that fast which thou hast, that no man take thy crown" (Revelation 3:11). Salvation is by grace alone. The reward received, however, is based upon works, which will be tested and their quality revealed at the judgment seat of Christ.

Paul likens the Christian life to running a race for a prize: "They [athletes] do it to obtain a corruptible crown, but we an incorruptible [crown]" (1 Corinthians 9:25). Paul called his converts his crown of rejoicing (Philippians 4:1; 1 Thessalonians 2:19). There are other crowns to be earned as well: "Henceforth there is laid up for me a crown of righteousness" (2 Timothy 4:8); "ye shall receive a crown of glory" (1 Peter 5:4); "be thou faithful unto death and I will give thee a crown of life" (Revelation 2:10).

## PURIFICATION ALONE BY CHRIST'S SHED BLOOD

As for verses such as Matthew 5:8 and Hebrews 12:14, Scripture is clear in stating that we cannot by our own efforts attain to a personal holiness or purity that qualifies us for God's presence. We are purged of sin, not by our own suffering here or in an invented purgatory, but through faith in Christ and His blood that was shed for our redemption: "when he [Christ] had by himself purged our sins" (Hebrews 1:3).

How did He purge us for heaven? By paying the penalty for sin with the shedding of His blood and forgiving us by His grace. There is no other way of purging the believer.

John reminds us that "the blood of Jesus Christ his Son cleanseth [purges] us from all sin" (1 John 1:7). Of the redeemed during the great tribulation period we are told that they had "washed [purged] their robes and made them white in the blood of the Lamb [Christ]" (Revelation 7:14). There is no reference here or elsewhere in the Bible to a purging that had occurred in some place called purgatory or by any other means than the shed blood of Christ.

## Without The Shedding Of Blood Is No Remission

That no purification of sin could take place in purgatory, even if there were such a place, is clear. There is no blood shed in purgatory and thus no purging of sin there. God declares unequivocally: "Without shedding of blood is no remission [purging of sin]" (Hebrews 9:22). Moreover, the blood shed must be that of a perfectly pure and sinless sacrifice, making it impossible for a sinner to cleanse himself by suffering for his own sins in purgatory or anywhere else.

We are assured that Christ was the "Lamb of God" (John 1:29,36) "without blemish and without spot" (1 Peter 1:19; see also Exodus 12:5; Ezekiel 46:13; etc.). It was by the shedding of His blood alone that we could be purged of our sin. Peter declared, "For Christ also hath *once* suffered for sins, [He] the just for [us] the unjust, that he might bring us to God [not to purgatory]" (1 Peter 3:18).

The false doctrine of purgatory keeps Catholics in bondage, dependent upon their Church and her rituals instead of upon Christ for salvation. As a consequence, the Catholic has no assurance of ever reaching heaven because the Roman Catholic Church can never declare how many Masses must be said for the dead in order to release them from purgatory. If the death of Christ was not sufficient, then who can say that even an infinite number of representations thereof in the Mass will ever bring anyone to heaven?

In fact, there is a fatal deficiency in the Mass. It is called "an unbloody" perpetuation of Christ's sacrifice on the cross. That fact alone robs it of any efficacy. Denying the sufficiency of Christ's sacrifice of 1900 years ago as a completed past event, the popular Baltimore Catechism puts it, "In the Mass Christ continues to offer Himself to the Father as He did on the Cross"[4] but in an "unbloody manner under the appearance of bread and wine." [5] Vatican II declares:

> The Eucharist is above all else a sacrifice. It is the sacrifice [by which] man and the world are restored to God ... [and] being a true sacrifice, brings about this restoration to God.[6] Our Lord [in it] is immolated ... [and] Christ perpetuates in an unbloody manner the sacrifice offered on the cross.[7]

Calvary was a very bloody scene. How there could be an unbloody repetition or continuation thereof is not explained. Furthermore, as already noted, the Bible distinctly says that "without shedding of blood there is no remission [of sins]" (Hebrews 9:22). Yet the "unbloody" Mass is Catholicism's means of providing to its members remission of sins—a remission which Christ already accomplished on the cross and therefore is not needed by those who have come to and trust in Him for salvation. The Bible says:

> And he took the cup ... saying ... this is my blood of the new testament, which is shed [on the cross] for many for the remission [purging] of sins (Matthew 26:28).

> To him [Christ] give all the prophets witness, that ... whosoever believeth in him shall receive [as a gift of God's grace] remission [purging] of sins (Acts 10:43).

Quite clearly, the "unbloody" Mass is of no value in cleansing sin. Nor is the Mass needed. Christ's sacrifice on the cross, which was completed at that time, paid the full penalty for our sins. Before giving up His Spirit to His Father, Christ cried in triumph from the cross, "It is finished" (John 19:30)! We are also told that Christ, having made purification, or purgation, for our sins, ascended to heaven where He now is "seated at the right hand of God" (Romans 8:34; Ephesians 1:20; Hebrews 1:13; 12:2) and "dieth no more" (Romans 6:9). Purification of our sins has been accomplished by Christ once and for all.

## A Key Contradiction

Contradicting the Bible, Catholicism says that though Christ endured the *eternal* punishment for sin, we must personally suffer the *temporal* punishment to become pure enough to enter heaven.[8] Not only does the doctrine of purgatory contradict the Bible, but there is an obvious contradiction within the dogma itself. Christ's death, it is said, couldn't purify us because the purification essential for admission to heaven requires us to *personally suffer* for our sins.

Yet it is also taught that after our death, the celebration of Masses, the recitation of rosaries, the good deeds and suffering of the living on our behalf (such as the stigmata of a Padre Pio), and other means in obedience to the Church can reduce or even eliminate purgatorial suffering entirely. Indeed, "Our Lady of Mount Carmel" promises to personally release from purgatory and escort into heaven all those who (having met certain other conditions) died wearing her scapular.

So the faithful Catholic doesn't have to *personally suffer* after all! Here is a contradiction so serious that it undermines the entire doctrine of purgatory. Amazingly, what Christ's redemptive death on the cross couldn't accomplish, the repetition of the Mass or rosary, penance, good works etc. can allegedly accomplish in relieving those in purgatory of the necessity of suffering at all.

In blessed contrast, the Word of God, for those who believe it, gives absolute assurance that the blood of Jesus Christ "cleanses us from *all* sin" (1 John 1:7). No further purification is necessary nor is it possible. Our confidence is in God, in His Word, His promises, but not in any church or religious system no matter how ancient or large.

## DID JESUS DIE SPIRITUALLY?

*Question:* I've heard it taught that Jesus not only died physically but that His Spirit died also. How could that be possible? That sounds like the doctrine of "soul sleep." If man, who is mortal, has an immortal soul and spirit that will be in heaven or hell, how then could Christ's spirit die? If Christ was God, I can see how His human body could die, but how could God, who is spirit, die? Was the trinity separated? If the Spirit of God died, who was in charge of the universe while God was dead? This question shakes my confidence in the Bible and in my salvation.

*Response:* Uncertainty arises because of several misunderstandings. First of all, the above teaching has been confused with the heresy taught by Hagin, Copeland, and other "Word Faith teachers" that our redemption comes through Christ being tortured by Satan in hell. That is not what is meant when solid Bible teachers say that Jesus died "spiritually."

The Bible says that He "taste[d] death for every man" (Hebrews 2:9). All that we deserved He endured, which must have included death to His human body, soul, and spirit. No, God the Father and the Holy Spirit didn't die; *Christ* died for our sins. Was the Trinity, then, separated? No, God is one. Yet Jesus did cry in agony, "My God, my God, why hast thou forsaken me?" (Psalm 22:1; Matthew 27:46; Mark 15:34). What could that mean?

Here we confront a mystery beyond our comprehension. Who can understand the statement that "it pleased the Lord [Jahweh] to bruise him; he hath put him to grief, when thou shalt make his soul an offering for sin" (Isaiah 53:10)? We only know and believe that the full penalty demanded by God's infinite justice against sin was paid by Christ upon the cross, and that Christ was made "to be sin for us, [he] who knew no sin, that we might be made the righteousness of God in him" (2 Corinthians 5:21). Christ was punished by God as though He were sin itself, so that we could be forgiven and have eternal life as a free gift of His grace.

## WHAT DOES IT MEAN TO DIE?

There are two other misconceptions: 1) that to *die* means cessation of conscious existence; and 2) that only the body dies. We are body, soul, and spirit (1 Thessalonians 5:23; Hebrews 4:12). Confusion arises because, contrary to the teaching of "soul sleep," the soul and spirit remain conscious after physical death.

Jesus said to the thief on the cross, "Today shalt thou be with me in paradise" (Luke 23:43)—a meaningless statement if neither of them would be conscious. Jesus said that the rich man was consciously in torment in hell, while in paradise (where the souls and spirits of Jesus and the converted thief went upon death) Abraham and Lazarus the beggar (and by implication everyone else) were consciously in a state of bliss (Luke 16:19-31). Though physically dead with bodies deteriorating in graves, the souls and spirits of those both in hell and paradise were conscious.

The Bible clearly teaches that body, soul, and spirit die. Spiritual death comes first, while we are still in our physical bodies. In fact, we are born spiritually dead, causing a progressive physical death to be at work in our bodies from the moment of birth, a fact which medical science acknowledges but cannot explain. Adam died spiritually (i.e., in his soul and spirit) the very moment he ate of the forbidden tree: "In the day [moment] that thou eatest thereof thou shalt surely die" (Genesis 2:17). His body, however, wasn't dead—yet. He must therefore have been spiritually dead, as are all of his descendants from the moment of birth. Even before our bodies die we are spiritually dead in trespasses and sins (Ephesians 2:1; Colossians 2:13).

## SPIRITUAL DEATH AND NEW LIFE

Christ, however, the "second man" (1 Corinthians 15:47), wasn't spiritually dead prior to the cross. He was the only man on earth, the only one since Adam and Eve, who was spiritually alive; and thus He alone could die. Surely, then, as part of the penalty for sin, He had to taste the spiritual death that sin brings.

These same verses say that when we are born again through faith in Christ we are "made alive." Certainly the condition of our bodies hasn't changed, so we must be made alive spiritually and thereby restored to fellowship with God. Physical death, however, already at work in our bodies, is not yet eliminated or even reversed.

At the death of the body, the Christian's soul and spirit are taken into heaven ("absent from the body...present with the Lord"—2 Corinthians 5:8). At the rapture the body is resurrected and reunited with the soul and spirit, which have been with Christ in heaven and which God will "bring with him" (1 Thessalonians 4:14). The bodies of those who are alive at the resurrection are instantly transformed and caught up to heaven with those who have been raised from the dead:

> Behold, I show you a mystery: We shall not all sleep [die], but we shall all be changed, in a moment, in the twinkling of an eye, at the last trump; for the trumpet shall sound, and the dead shall be raised incorruptible, and we shall be changed.
>
> For this corruptible must put on incorruption, and this mortal must put on immortality. . . . Then shall be brought to pass the saying that is written, Death is swallowed up in victory (1 Corinthians 15:51-54).

## A "SECOND DEATH"

The Bible says, "The soul [Hebrew *nephesh*, used for soul throughout the Old Testament] that sinneth . . .

shall die" (Ezekiel 18:4,20). This tells us that: 1) souls die, and 2) a worse death awaits the sinner than that which has already come upon Adam's race. Although man is dead in his soul and spirit and is dying in his body, the consummation of God's judgment still lies ahead for the lost. It is called both the *second death* and the *lake of fire*, a place that was not made for man but "for the devil and his angels" (Matthew 25:41). Into it shall be cast "whosoever [is] not found written in the book of life" (Revelation 20:15).

As the substitute dying in our place, Christ must have endured the full, infinite penalty that God's judgment demanded for sin, including the second death. Since He is both God and man, He was not separated eternally from God, but, being infinite, He was able to endure the fullness of that penalty in those few hours upon the cross.

How could God die? Death is separation from God, so the question could also be stated, "How could God be separated from and forsaken by God?" Though it is beyond our comprehension, we believe that Christ endured that horrible and eternal separation which we deserved, for He cried out, "My God, my God, why hast thou forsaken me?" (Psalm 22:1; Matthew 27:46).

We cannot explain it, but are assured that He tasted "death for every man" (Hebrews 2:9). This can only mean that He experienced the full horror of eternal separation from God that will imprison Christ rejecters for all eternity. The death Christ died for us, therefore, must have included death (separation from God) to the human spirit. Without that complete payment in full of the entire penalty pronounced against us for sin, we could not be saved.

## Do Some Christians Not Quite Make Heaven?

*Question:* Jesus warned that many who thought they were God's children would be "cast into outer darkness" (Matthew 8:12; 22:13; 25:30). In fact, Matthew 24:50,51 says that "the lord of that [evil] servant . . . shall cut him asunder and appoint him his portion with the hypocrites;

there shall be weeping and gnashing of teeth." Are these "servants" carnal Christians who must be in an outer courtyard of heaven for a time while the more spiritual Christians go directly into God's presence? How can I have assurance of being taken immediately upon death (or the rapture) into God's presence?

*Response:* Assurance of salvation does not depend upon the believer's good works but upon Christ's finished work upon the cross. One is either a Christian or not a Christian, saved or lost. There are not two levels of Christians, the lower of which must spend some time in an intermediary state of weeping and wailing and gnashing of teeth (like the Catholic purgatory) before they are allowed into heaven. Such an idea cannot be found in the Bible. Luke 12:46 uses "unbelievers" in place of the "hypocrites" of Matthew 24:51.

---

It is apparent that Christ's words here have a double meaning that can be applied both to Jews and Gentiles. Abraham's physical descendants are by birth potentially children of the Davidic kingdom and can thus be called "servants" in a way not true for Gentiles. But unless they have the same relationship with God through faith in Christ that Abraham had they will be lost forever.

The weeping and gnashing of teeth Christ warns of is the weeping and agony of the damned. We have an example of this weeping on the part of the rich man in Luke 16 who sees Lazarus afar off with Abraham in bliss while he is in torment. That those who are cast into "outer darkness" are not, and *never were*, true believers (though they may have posed even as Christian leaders) is clear from these words of Christ:

Many will say to me in that day, Lord, Lord, have we not prophesied in thy name? And in thy name have cast out devils? And in thy name done many wonderful works?

And then will I profess unto them, I never knew you, depart from me, ye that work iniquity (Matthew 7:22,23).

## WHAT ABOUT "ETERNAL SECURITY"?

*Question:* The Bible clearly says that "he that en-dureth to the end shall be saved" (Matthew 10:22); and that we are "made partakers of Christ, if we hold the beginning of our confidence steadfast unto the end" (Hebrews 3:14). Our ultimate destiny is therefore dependent upon whether or not we remain true to Christ and maintain our faith in Him to the end. In light of such statements, how can you then teach an "eternal security" which has no such requirements for remaining saved?

*Response:* "He that endures to the end shall be saved" refers to those who have survived the Jew's worst holocaust (which is yet to come under Antichrist) and are alive when Christ returns to rescue Israel in the midst of Armageddon. Paul referred to them with the words "all Israel shall be saved" (Romans 11:26). Surely that couldn't mean all Jews who ever lived, but all those who are alive when Christ visibly returns at His second coming and, seeing Him, believe that He is their Messiah. The subject is not the salvation of those who are in the church, but of Jews alive at the end of the great tribulation.

As for the salvation we receive as a free gift of God's grace through faith in Christ, our Lord said: "I give unto them [my sheep] eternal life, and they shall never perish" (John 10:28). This is a double promise: that He will care for believers as a shepherd for his sheep, and that this secure relationship is eternal. Moreover, we don't become His sheep in eternity but here and now, the moment we put our faith in Christ. And the moment we become His sheep, we receive eternal life as a free gift of God's grace: "The gift of God is eternal life through Jesus Christ our Lord" (Romans 6:23). We are given this assurance repeatedly in Scripture.

"Eternal life" would be a strange description of something that didn't last forever. It could hardly be *eternal* life if one could *have* it and *know* it (1 John 5:13) today and not have it tomorrow. Moreover, if, in spite of Christ's unconditional promise that His own "shall never perish," some of those who were at one time His own lost that status and did indeed perish for any reason whatsoever, we could have no confidence in anything else He would say.

We know, however, that the One who is the truth cannot lie. Therefore we have complete confidence that it is impossible for Christ's sheep ever to perish. Once we belong to Him He keeps us and will never let us be lost.

### IMPOSSIBLE TO GET SAVED MORE THAN ONCE

Hebrews 6:1-9 confirms the fact of eternal security. The first three verses urge the believer to move on from those elementary things of the faith which pertain to the beginnings of the Christian life, such as repentance, faith, baptism, and so forth. Verses 4 through 6 give the reason why we must not engage in what verse one calls "laying again the foundation":

> For it is *impossible* for those who were once enlightened, and have tasted of the heavenly gift, and were made partakers of the Holy Ghost, and have tasted the good word of God and the powers of the world to come, if they shall fall away, to renew them again unto repentance, seeing they crucify to themselves the Son of God afresh, and put him to an open shame.

Clearly those to whom this passage refers are genuine believers. Moreover, it doesn't say *"when* they fall away" but that *"if* they fall away" it would be *"impossible"* for them to get saved again. The reason why it is impossible to get saved again is explained.

First of all, if the death of Christ were not sufficient to *keep* them saved, then for them to get saved again would require that Christ die again...and again, every time they needed to be saved once more. Secondly, if Christ's death is not sufficient to *keep* one saved, then He is held up to ridicule for having done something so foolish as having procured salvation at infinite cost and then given it to creatures to maintain who are not able to effect their own salvation and certainly can't maintain it. This would be like committing a fortune to the safekeeping of an infant who would surely lose it.

That the falling away is hypothetical is indicated again by verse 9, which says, "But beloved, we are persuaded better things of you, and things *that accompany salvation*, though we thus speak." In other words, falling away does not "accompany salvation." Those who are truly saved can never fall away.

## DID JESUS DESCEND INTO HELL?

---

*Question:* I've read your rejection of the teaching that Jesus was tortured in hell by Satan. Yet the Apostles' Creed says that Jesus "descended into hell." Did Jesus descend into hell or not? I've searched and searched the Scriptures and asked several pastors about this and still have no satisfactory answer.

*Response:* First of all, the so-called "Apostles' Creed" is misnamed. There is no record that it was either composed or recited by any of the apostles. Even if it had been, like Catholicism's so-called "apostolic tradition," there would be no way to know for certain by tracing it back to the apostles. There were no tape recorders in that day and it is not part of a known written record as are the epistles. Even Catholic encyclopedias admit that this creed does not come from the apostles but is a forgery that was composed sometime in the fourth century.

---

In the Old Testament the Hebrew word *sheol,* meaning the place of the dead, is sometimes translated "hell" and at other times simply as "grave." The comparable words used in the New Testament are *hades* or *gehenna,* the place of the departed dead. In telling the fate of the rich man ("in hell [*hades*] he lift[ed] up his eyes, being in torments"—Luke 16:23) and of Lazarus the beggar, Jesus taught that before the cross there were two compartments in *sheol* or *hades*: one for the lost (hell) and one for the saved, known as "Abraham's bosom" (Luke 16:22) or "paradise."

It was to the latter that Christ went in death, as did the believing thief crucified with Him, to whom He said, "Today shalt thou be with me in paradise" (Luke 23:43). There He spent "three days and three nights" as prophesied (Jonah 1:17; Matthew 12:40). During that time He undoubtedly proclaimed to the redeemed the good news that His death upon the cross had paid the full penalty for their sins.

Those in the place of the damned could hear what Jesus said (see Luke 16:23-31); and He may even have addressed a few words specifically to them. Thus Peter writes, "He went and preached unto the spirits [of the dead] in prison [hell], which sometime were disobedient ... in the days of Noah" (1 Peter 3:19,20). After His resurrection, Jesus took the souls and spirits of the redeemed to heaven: "When he ascended up on high, he led captivity captive" (Ephesians 4:8; cf. Psalm 68:18).

Since Christ's resurrection, the souls and spirits of the redeemed go immediately upon death to be with Christ: "absent from the body ... present with the Lord" (2 Corinthians 5:6-8). From thence He will bring them to rejoin their resurrected bodies at the rapture of the saints (1 Thessalonians 4:13-18). On this subject, as on every other, the Word of God all fits together beautifully and assures believers of eternal salvation.

## ARE GOOD WORKS ESSENTIAL FOR SALVATION?

*Question:* James says that faith without works is dead (James 2:20,26). Paul wrote, "Work out your own salvation with fear and trembling" (Philippians 2:12). Shouldn't we conclude, therefore, that good works are necessary for salvation? And wouldn't we be in a dangerous position if we failed to recognize that good works are essential for salvation? Christ even says that if we don't forgive others we can't expect God to forgive us. What about that?

*Response:* If good works are essential for salvation, then we must have some standard for those works. The gospel would have to specify how many good works and of what kind. Where does one find such teaching? Nowhere. There is no mention of good works in the "gospel by which we are saved" (1 Corinthians 15:1-4). In fact, Paul argues that "a man is justified by faith without the deeds of the law" (Romans 3:28), and he reminds us that "not by works of righteousness which we have done, but according to his mercy he saved us" (Titus 3:5).

---

Nevertheless, all the world's religions are based upon works. The idea that we must live up to a certain standard of works to be saved is the foundation of paganism. Somehow the gods must be appeased by human effort or sacrifice. The same idea is innate in all people: "If You will get me out of this predicament, God, then I'll do this or that for You!" Clearly that is not what James is teaching under the inspiration of the Holy Spirit.

A works-for-salvation mentality marks every cult. Indeed, even atheists justify their rejection of Christianity on this basis. Famed atheist Robert Ingersoll sarcastically complained against the gospel of God's grace:

> They [Christians] say a certain belief is necessary to salvation. They do not say, if you behave yourself you will get there; they do not say, if you pay your debts and love your wife and love your children, and are good to your friends and your neighbors and your country [like we atheists are], you will get there. That will do you no good; you have got to believe a certain thing.
>
> No matter how bad you are, you can instantly be forgiven; and no matter how good you are, if you fail to believe that which you cannot understand, the moment you get to the day of judgment nothing is left but to damn you, and all the angels will shout "hallelujah."

Christianity alone rejects this universal delusion. We have already seen that keeping the law perfectly in the future could not make up for having broken it in the past. As Paul said, "Therefore by the deeds of the law there shall no flesh be justified in his sight, for by the law is the knowledge of sin" (Romans 3:20). It is therefore clear that we cannot be saved by good works.

## CLARIFYING JAMES' MESSAGE

James is not saying that we are saved by works, but that a professed faith that is not evidenced by works is dead and cannot save: "[if] a man *say* he hath faith" (2:14). James is warning us that a mere profession of faith, from the lips but not from the heart, can be empty, and that if we are not willing to live what we profess, then it is likely that our faith is not genuine.

James is critiquing false faith. He is not suggesting that we are saved by works or else he would be contradicting dozens of other passages in the Bible which unequivocally state the opposite. As mentioned previously, for example, "by the deeds of the law there shall no flesh be justified in his sight" (Romans 3:20).

The issue in James is not *how to be saved*, but the good works which follow and demonstrate that *one is already saved*. James is speaking of works that spring from faith and which demonstrate the reality of one's faith. He is not saying that a man is justified by works without faith. Paul states clearly, however, that a man is justified by faith without the deeds of the law.

James is saying, "Show me thy faith without thy works, and I will show thee my faith by my works" (2:18). It is not the works but the *faith* that saves. The works simply demonstrate that faith. The doing of the works will not justify; it is faith alone that justifies.

Some works advocates complain about adding "alone," but if, as Scripture says, a man is justified by faith without the deeds of the law, then he is justified by faith *alone*.

We have already noted that 1 Corinthians 3:15 says that even if all of a man's works are burned up, he himself is saved. That is justification by faith alone, without any works even to demonstrate it. James is speaking from the human standpoint. We cannot know the heart, so we must go by the works. God, however, knows the heart, and He needs no works to demonstrate anyone's faith.

As for working out one's salvation, please note that it does not say, "Work *for* your salvation." In fact, we are to work *out* in our lives the salvation that we already have in our hearts. Paul is not for a moment saying that we must work *for* our salvation.

All of the above is not to say that a convert may live any way he pleases and yet be assured of God's blessing on his life. Good works come as a result of our salvation, not as a means of obtaining it; and they are motivated by love for our Savior rather than as a means of obtaining our salvation. Paul put works and faith in the proper balance when he wrote:

> For by grace are ye saved, through faith, and that not of yourselves; it is the gift of God, not of works, lest any man should boast. For we are his workmanship, created in Christ Jesus unto good works, which God hath before ordained that we should walk in them (Ephesians 2:8-10).

As for forgiving others, Christ is not setting the criterion for being saved; He is giving us a practical example for testing whether we are genuinely His. He is saying that a person who has truly received the grace of God will be gracious to others. He is challenging us to examine our professed faith. How can I expect God to forgive me if I am not willing to forgive others?

There are those who claim to be Christians, yet they have nursed animosity against others for years because of the wrong that has allegedly been done to them. Christ here and elsewhere says that such a person needs either to repent and allow God's love to work in his heart the same forgiveness that Christ has effected for him, or else admit that he is not saved at all.

# Notes

### Why Believe?

1. *Los Angeles Times*, June 25, 1978, Part IV, pp. 1, 6.
2. *Harpers*, February 1985, pp. 49-50.
3. Douglas Dewar and L.M. Davies, "Science and the BBC," in *The Nineteenth Century and After*, April 1943, p. 167.
4. From an interview by AP correspondent George W. Cornall, quoted from *Times-Advocate*, Escondido, California, December 10, 1982, pp. A10-11.

### Chapter 1—Evidence, Reason, and Faith

1. Cited in Samuel P. Putnam, *400 Years of Free Thought*, (NY: 1894), p. 56.
2. Ibid, p. 120.
3. Cited in Josh McDowell, *Evidence Theat Demands a Verdict*, (Campus Crusade, 1972) p. 136.
4. Paul E. Little, *Know Why You Believe* (Scripture Press, 1967), p.53.
5. Gordon Allport, "The Roots of Religion, "*Pastoral Psychology*, April 1954, p.20.
6. Sir James Jeans, *The Mysterious Universe* (The MacMillan Company, 1929), p. 140.
7. Paul Yonggi Cho, *The Fourth Dimension* (Logos, 1979), p. 44; Paul Yonggi Cho, *The Fourth Dimension, Volume Two* (Bridge Publishing, 1983), pp. 25-28, 68.
8. Sir John Eccles, with Daniel N. Robinson, *The Wonder of Being Human—Our Brain & Our Mind* (New Science Library, 1985), p. 54.
9. Erwin Schroedinger, cited in *Quantum Questions: Mystical Writings of the World's Great Physicists*, ed. Ken Wilbur (New Science Library, 1984), pp. 81-83.
10. S. Maxwell Coder and George F. Howe, *The Bible, Science and Creation* (Moody Press, 1965), p. 39.

### Chapter 2—Who Is God?

1. Carl Sagan, *Cosmos* (Random House, 1980), p. 243.
2. Putnam, *400 Years*, p. 64.
3. See Dave Hunt, *A Woman Rides the Beast* (Harvest House Publishers, 1994), p. 424.
4. *Vatican Council II, The Conciliar and Post Conciliar Documents*, General Editor Austin Flanery, O.P. (Costello Publishing Company, 1988 Revised Edition), p. 367.
5. Will Durant, *The Story of Civilization: The Age of Faith*, Volume IV (Simon and Schuster, 1950), p. 163.
6. Durant, *Civilization*, p. 163.
7. Durant, *Civilization*, p. 163.

8. May Long, "Visions of a New Faith," in *Science Digest*, November 1981, p. 39.
9. Herbert Scholssberg, *Idols for Destruction* (Thomas Nelson, 1983), p. 171.
10. Eccles and Robinson, *Wonder*, p. 61.
11. Samuel P. Putnam, *400 Years of Freethought* (The Truth Seeker Company, New York, 1894), Frontispiece.
12. Putnam, *400 Years*, p. 13.

## Chapter 3—Is The Bible Reliable?

1. John Lea, *The Greatest Book in the World*, as cited in Frank Morison, *Who Moved the Stone?* (London, Faber and Faber, 1958), p. 15.
2. Josh McDowell, *Evidence That Demands A Verdict* (Campus Crusade for Christ, 1972), p.19.
3. Abraham Rabinovich, "In pursuit of history," in *The Jerusalem Post International Edition*, Week ending November 25, 1995, pp. 18-19.
4. Rabinovich, *History*, pp. 18-19.
5. Bernard Ramm, *Protestant Christian Evidences* (Moody Press, 1953), pp. 230-31.
6. F.F. Bruce, *The Books and the Parchments* (Fleming H. Revell, 1963), p. 178.
7. J. Harold Greenlee, *Introduction to New Testament Textual Criticism* (William B. Eerdmans, 1964), p. 15.
8. Irwin H. Linton, *A Lawyer Examines the Bible* (W.A. Wilde Company, 1943), p. 31.
9. Linton, *Lawyer*, pp. 46-47.
10. Sir Arthur Stanley Eddington, *The Nature of the Physical World* (MacMillan, 1929), cited in *Quantum Questions: Mystical Writings of the World's Great Physicists*, ed. Ken Wilbur (New Science Library, 1984), p. 5.
11. Putnam, *400 Years*, p. 101.
12. Wilbur M. Smith, *Therefore Stand: Christian Apologetics* (Baker Book House, 1965), pp. 425,584.
13. Professor Thomas Arnold, *Sermons on the Christian Life* (London, 1859), p. 324.

## Chapter 4—Contradictions in the Bible?

1. Cited in John W. Lea, *The Greatest Book in the World* (Philadelphia), pp. 17-18.
2. *Los Angeles Times*, January 28, 1989.
3. John Elder, *Prophets, Idols and Diggers* (Bobbs-Merrill, 1960), p. 160.
4. Will Durant, *The History of Civilization: Caesar and Christ* (Simon and Schuster, 1944), Volume III, p. 231.
5. Linton, *Lawyer*, p. 89.
6. William Paley, *Horae Paulinae*, as cited in Linton, *Lawyer*, p. 88.

## Chapter 5—Challenges to Faith

1. R.A. Torrey, *Difficulties in the Bible: Alleged Errors and Contradictions* (Moody Press, no date given), pp. 9-10.
2. Larry Whitham, "Book backs theory Jesus visited India before public life," in *Washington Times*, November 27, 1987, p. E6.
3. Torrey, *Difficulties*, pp. 14-16.

## Chapter 6—Evidences of Authenticity and Inspiration

1. *Collier's Encyclopedia* (F.P. Collier & Son Corporation, 1959), Volume 10, p. 155.
2. Mark Hopkins, *Evidences*, cited in Linton, *Lawyer*, pp 165-69.
3. Translated by William Whiston (originally published in 1737), *The Life and Works of Flavius Josephus* (The John C. Winston Company, Philadelphia, 1957), p. 535.
4. Whiston, *Josephus*, p. 598.
5. Thomas Hartwell Horne, *Introduction to the Holy Scriptures*, quoted by Hopkins in *Evidences* and cited by Linton, *Lawyer*, p. 235.
6. Hopkins, *Evidences*, cited in Linton, *Lawyer*, p. 164.
7. Hopkins, *Evidences*, cited in Linton, *Lawyer*, p. 164.
8. Cited in Linton, *Lawyer*, p. 164.
9. Simon Greenleaf, *The Testimony of the Evangelists*, p. 31.
10. Linton, *Lawyer*, p. 231.

## Chapter 7—What About Prayer?

1. A.E.C. Brooks, compiler, *Answers to Prayer from George Muller's Narratives* (Moody Press, undated paperback), p. 10.
2. Brooks, *Answers*, inside title page.
3. Robert Schuller, *Peace of Mind Through Possibility Thinking* (Spire Books, 1977), p. 14.
4. Robert Schuller, "Possibility Thinking: Goals," an Amway Corporation tape.
5. Peter Kreeft, *Bookstore Journal*, February 1992, p. 30.
6. *NRI Trumpet*, October 1993, p. 14.
7. *Catechism of the Catholic Church* (Libreria Editrice Vaticana, 1994), par. 971, p. 253; Austin Flannery, O.P., Ed., *Vatican Council II* (Costello Publishing, 1988, Revised Edition), p. 421.
8. St. Alphonsus de Liguori, *The Glories of Mary* (Redemptorist Fathers, 1931), pp. 82-83, 94, 160, 169-70.
9. Official Edition, *Devotions in Honor of Our Mother of Perpetual Help* (Liguori Publications, undated), pp. 46-47.

## Chapter 8—What About Evil, Satan, and Demons?

1. Charles F. Pfeiffer, *The Dead Sea Scrolls and the Bible* (Weathervane Books, 1969), inside back of jacket.
2. Manly P. Hall, *The Secret Teachings of all Ages: An Encyclopedic outline of Masonic, Hermetic, Qabbalistic and Rosicrucian Symbolical Philosophy* (The Philosophical Research Society, Inc., Los Angeles, CA 90027, 1969), Sixteenth Edition, p. CXVIII.
3. C.S. Lewis, *The Screwtape Letters* (Fleming H. Revell, 1976), Preface.
4. Eccles and Robinson, *Wonder*, p. 54.
5. Eddington, *Nature*, p. 345.
6. C.S. Lewis, *They Asked for a Paper* (London, 1962), pp. 164-65.
7. Quoted in Herbert Benson, M.D., with William Proctor, *Your Maximum Mind* (Random House, 1987), p. 46.
8. "GeoConversation," an interview with Dr. Robert Jastrow, in *Geo*, February 1982, p. 14.
9. C.G. Jung, *Memories, Dreams, Reflections* (Pantheon Books, 1963), p. 183.

10. Carl Jung, *Collected Letters, Vol. 1* (Princeton University Press, 1973), p. 43.
11. Quoted in Harold Sherman, *Your Mysterious Powers of ESP* (New York, 1969), p. 120.
12. M. Scott Peck, *People of the Lie* (Simon & Schuster, 1983), pp. 184, 188.
13. Peck, *People*, p. 196.
14. Eddington, *Nature*, pp. 258-59.
15. Hall, *Secret Teachings*, pp. LXXXVII-LXXXVIII.
16. R.A. Torrey, *Difficulties in the Bible* (Moody Press, undated), p. 53.

### Chapter 9—What About Suffering and Hell?

1. Putnam, *400 Years*, pp. 389-90.
2. Ellul, op. cit., p. 60.
3. Ibid.
4. Linton, *Lawyer*, p. 122.
5. Putnam, *400 Years*, pp. 389-390.
6. Linton, *Lawyer*, p. 122.
7. Percy Bysshe Shelley, from a letter written at the age of about 20 to Lord Ellenborough in behalf of a D.J. Eaton imprisoned for publishing Paine's *Age of Reason*, quoted in Putnam, *400 Years*, p. 341.

### Chapter 10—A "Rapture" and a "Second Coming"?

1. *Chalcedon Report*, July 1988, p. 1.

### Chapter 11—The Gospel That Saves

1. Simon Greenleaf, *Testimony of the Evangelists* (Baker Book House), Introduction.
2. Fr. William J. Cogan, *A BRIEF CATECHISM FOR ADULTS: A Complete Handbook on How to be a Good Catholic*, p. 49.
3. Joseph A. Seiss, *The Gospel in the Stars*, p. 13.
4. Seiss, *Gospel*, p. 15.
5. Ellul, *Humiliation*, p. vii.
6. *Vatican Council II, Documents*, Vol. 1, pp. 102-03.
7. *Vatican Council II, Documents*, Vol. 1, p. 1.
8. *Vatican Council II, Documents*, Vol. 1, p. 103.
9. Coriden, Green, Heintschel, Eds., *Code of Canon Law*, p. 646.
10. *Vatican Council II, Documents*, Vol. 1, p. 103.
11. John A. Hardon, S.J., *Pocket Catholic Dictionary* (Image Books, Double-day, 1985), p. 248.
12. Kenneth Copeland, *Believer's Voice of Victory*, September 1991.
13. *Handbook of Medical Ethics for Nurses, Physicians, and Priests* (The Catholic Truth Society, Montreal, 1943) pp. 224-29.
14. Schroeder, *Canons and Decrees*, pp. 33, 53.
15. *Vatican Council II*, Vol. 1, *Documents*, p. 412.
16. *Vatican Council II*, Vol. 1, *Documents*, p. 365.
17. *Catechism of the Catholic Church*, pp. 224, 320.
18. *Trent*, op. cit., pp. 22, 23, 54.
19. *Coriden, Green, Heintschel,Code of Canon Law*, pp. 122, 614.

### Chapter 12—Assurance of Salvation

1. This is the next to last sentence from Pope John Paul II's official prayer for the Marian year, 1988. The entire prayer was addressed *to* Mary

and asked her to do what she would have to be God to accomplish. For example: "To you, Mother of the human family and of nations, we confidently entrust the whole of humanity with its hopes and fears. Do not let it lack the light of true wisdom. Guide its steps in the way of peace. Enable all to meet Christ...."

2. *The New York Times*, February 1, 1990, pp. A1, B4.

3. Schroeder, *Canons*, op. cit., Can. 30, p. 46.

4. *The New Saint Joseph Baltimore Catechism*, No. 2 (New York: Catholic Book Publishing Co., 1969), p. 171. See also the new universal *Catechism of the Catholic Church*, pp. 284-304.

5. *Baltimore Catechism*, p. 168, see also Vatican II and the new universal *Catechism*.

6. *Vatican Council II, Documents*, Vol. 2, p. 75.

7. *Vatican Council II, Documents*, Vol. 1, pp. 102-3.

8. *Vatican Council II, Documents*, Vol. 1, p. 63; the new catechism, etc.

# Index